Female Alliances

Female Alliances

Gender, Identity, and Friendship in Early Modern Britain

Amanda E. Herbert

Yale

UNIVERSITY PRESS

NEW HAVEN AND LONDON

Published with assistance from the Annie Burr Lewis Fund.

Yale University Press books may be purchased in quantity for educational, business, or promotional use. For information, please e-mail sales.press@yale.edu (U.S. office) or sales@yaleup.co.uk (U.K. office).

Set in Fournier type by IDS Infotech Ltd., Chandigarh, India.
Printed in the United States of America.

Library of Congress Cataloging-in-Publication Data
Herbert, Amanda E.
Female alliances : gender, identity, and friendship in early modern Britain / Amanda E. Herbert.
pages   cm
Includes bibliographical references and index.
ISBN 978–0–300–17740–4 (hardback)
1. Female friendship—Great Britain.   2. Women—Great Britain—Social conditions.   I. Title.
BF575.F66H47 2014
302.34082'0941—dc23
2013024192

A catalogue record for this book is available from the British Library.

This paper meets the requirements of ANSI/NISO Z39.48-1992 (Permanence of Paper).

10 9 8 7 6 5 4 3 2 1

For my brother

Contents

Acknowledgments

This book was completed with the help and generosity of many people and institutions. I began working on this project at The Johns Hopkins University, where fellowships, awards, and teaching stipends from the Department of History, the Program for the Study of Women, Gender and Sexuality, the Expository Writing Program, and the School of Arts and Sciences enabled me to live and work in Baltimore. My research was made possible by generous financial support from the American Antiquarian Society, the Folger Shakespeare Library, the Haverford College Library, the Huntington Library, the Virginia Historical Society's Sydney and Frances Lewis Fund for Gender and Women's Studies, the University of Warwick, and the Yale Center for British Art; the Andrew Mellon Foundation provided funding for several of these grants. The administration at Christopher Newport University has been invested in the success of this project since I began work there in 2009 and has offered grants and subventions for travel, publication, and research, including a fellowship at Harris Manchester College, Oxford.

I would like to express my sincere appreciation for the hardworking and knowledgeable archivists, curators, librarians, and staff at the American Antiquarian Society, the Bath Guildhall Archives and Central Library, the Beinecke Library at Yale University, the British Library, the British Museum, the Bodleian Library at Oxford University, the Chester and Cheshire Archives and Local Studies, Dr. Williams's Library, the Folger Shakespeare Library, the Harris Manchester College Library at Oxford University, the Haverford College Library, the Huntington Library, the Magdalen College Archive at Oxford University, the National Archives of Scotland, the Cecil H. Green Library at Stanford University, the Victoria and Albert Museum, the Virginia Historical Society, the Wellcome Library, and the Yale Center for British Art, all of whom helped me to find the materials that went into this book. Particular thanks go to Paul Erickson, Susan Killoran, Diana Franzusoff Peterson, Marinella Vinci, Owen Williams, and David Wykes.

Drafts and pieces of this work have been circulated at numerous conferences in the United States and the United Kingdom, but I owe my thanks to Oxford University Press for permission to reproduce material from "Gender and the Spa: Space, Sociability and Self at British Health Spas, 1640–1714," *Journal of Social History* 43, no. 2 (Winter 2009), 361–82; and to the University of Pennsylvania Press for permission to reproduce material from "Companions in Preaching and Suffering: Itinerant Female Quakers in the Seventeenth- and Eighteenth-Century British Atlantic World," *Early American Studies* 9, no. 1 (Winter 2011), 73–113. Thanks as well to the Beinecke Library, the British Library, the British Museum, the Folger Shakespeare Library, the Huntington Library, the Library of the University of Illinois at Urbana-Champaign, and the Wellcome Library for allowing me to reproduce images from rare books, manuscripts, and works of art held in their collections.

It has been a pleasure to work with Yale University Press on this project. I am grateful to Nancy Moore Hulnick, Lawrence Kenney, Ash Lago, Jeffrey Schier, and Christina Tucker as well as to the press's designers and publicists for their time, attention, and labor on the book's behalf and for their patience and good humor. My special thanks go to Laura Davulis, whose guidance, vision, and good conversation made the book possible—she has been a wonderful editor and advocate. I would also like to express my appreciation for the anonymous readers who offered their helpful comments as well as their great enthusiasm and support for *Female Alliances*.

I have been both happy and lucky to incur debts to insightful colleagues, mentors, students, and friends on both sides of the Atlantic, and I thank them all for their help. For their work in reading, critiquing, editing, and helping to provide material for this book, I offer particular thanks to Julia Abramson, David Bell, Jessica Clark, Toby Ditz, Jonathan Eacott, Mary Fissell, Laurel Flinn, Amy Froide, Lou Galambos, Jamie Gianoutsos, Laura Gowing, Katherine Jorgensen Gray, Mark Hanna, Katie Hindmarch-Watson, Jason Hoppe, John Hyland, Rei Kanemura, Seth LeJacq, Elaine Leong, Fritz Levy, Dan Livesay, Catherine Molineux, Kate Moran, Nick Popper, Laura Puaca, Alisha Rankin, James Roberts, Jessica Roney, Kenneth Sheppard, Phil Stern, Nancy Taylor, Fredrika Teute, Judy Walkowitz, Molly Warsh, Olivia Weisser, Karin Wulf, and

Nadine Zimmerli. This book is the better for their help. My colleagues at Christopher Newport University have been enthusiastic, encouraging, and supportive, and they, too, have my appreciation. Thanks are owed as well to the members of the JHU "Geminar" Gender History Workshop and the Omohundro Institute of Early American History and Culture, as both groups have provided me with the best senses of scholarship in community. But my greatest intellectual debts are to John Marshall, for his unfailing support and sound advice, for his patience, his humor, his rigor, and especially for his time. John's dedication to his students is matchless, and my gratitude for his supervision goes beyond what words can convey: thank you so much.

Much love is offered to the members of my family, both new and old, and especially to my partner, David Woodworth, whose kindness and intelligence have shaped the book in so many ways. My parents have also made their marks on it: Annette Herbert has graciously read and edited every piece of writing I've produced since grade school, and she worked tirelessly to produce the notes and the index for this book; Daniel Herbert was the first to encourage me to pursue studies of gender and sexuality, urging me to take "GWSS 200: Introduction to Women Studies" at the University of Washington in the fall of 1997 because he thought it was important, and he thought I would like it. (He was so right.) But the book itself is for my brother David Palmer Herbert, as it was promised to him with love and appreciation on my first day of graduate school.

Female Alliances

Introduction

Writing to her son's tutor in the 1670s, Mary Evelyn summarized the duties that were expected of elite women. These included "the care of children's education, observing a husband's commands, assisting the sick, relieving the poor, and *being serviceable to our friends*."[1] Historians have long recognized the importance of early modern women's responsibilities to their husbands, to their children, and to society's sick and poor through philanthropy. Yet they have seriously neglected Evelyn's fifth topic, the construction and maintenance of early modern women's social networks, and have largely ignored early modern women's relationships with other women. In this period, many women lived in largely "homosocial" worlds, surrounded by female relatives, children, and friends. Seventeenth- and eighteenth-century British women, especially elite women who lived at this place and time, prayed, ate, worked, learned, read, recreated, and slept in the company of other women. Revealing and understanding these same-sex experiences and alliances are critical tasks for scholars of early modern Britain.

Using an extensive range of sources produced both by and for women, this book examines women's social networks in early modern Britain. Female friendships and alliances were expressed in many ways, and the sources explored in this book reflect the variety and complexity of these relationships. Women's alliances were inscribed into letters and literature, and the sources studied here include every genre of early modern women's manuscript writing: correspondence, household accounts and recipe books, autobiographies, spiritual journals, personal diaries, and literary compositions. And material culture informed and expressed women's friendships, for exchanges of objects such as pieces of embroidery, portraits, sugared confections, and homemade medicines referenced feminine skills and methods of personal cultivation while simultaneously conveying emotion and building feelings of friendship. The creation and exchange of these objects, many of which were made by hand, are therefore critical to this story. Female alliances were constructed within specific environments, in spaces that were claimed by or relegated to women: household kitchens and dairies, hot spring spas, crowded ships' cabins, religious meetings, and even prison cells, and so all of these spaces will be considered in this book. Women's gendered spaces ranged from the very small—the inside of bedchambers and household work spaces—to the very large—across the streets and buildings of cities. Alliances were also formed through missionary work and through emigration, as women traversed Britain's first empire. The many methods by which women formed social networks often allowed them the textual or artistic or spatial room in which to further female education and knowledge, celebrate women's skills, and gain financial and social advantage. Female alliances not merely provided solidarity and support but also frequently offered other tangible advantages to many early modern British women.

To study female alliances is to learn about constructions of identity, nationality, and gender. In its examination of women's social networks, *Female Alliances* explores central elements of the origins of modern femininity. Seventeenth- and eighteenth-century prescriptive guidebooks for women helped to structure and inform elite female behavior by articulating the characteristics of an ideal woman. By the later seventeenth century this genre of literature had been reconceived and had expanded rapidly. The genre encouraged female readers to display qualities such as love, care, compassion, and empathy. Reacting to these printed texts, many early modern British women utilized alliances in actions and performances of their feminine concord and love. This is not to say that early modern women's bonds were formed naturally, instinctively, or easily. Although same-sex friendships were considered essential to female life, women often struggled to maintain harmonious relationships with their female companions. This book discusses some evidence of times when alliances broke down, when women expressed rivalries or staged fights, and explores on occasion how women negotiated differences. But, overwhelmingly, the many forms of writing and handicraft observed in this book describe and reflect female alliances as positive, mutually supportive, and friendly. Powerful social norms bound early modern elite women together.

Female Alliances begins to help us to develop a more nuanced account of modern understandings of British identity. It focuses on the late seventeenth century and early eighteenth, a period when traditional systems of British governance were being challenged, and a period marked by heightened maritime communication and commerce across Britain's first empires. This expansion forced Britain's boundaries outward and, as women and men traveled more widely and frequently, scattered Britons themselves abroad. In the face of these changes, social cohesiveness was maintained by cultivating interpersonal ties, emotional friendships, and individual connections. In ways that have not been adequately appreciated or studied, however, women were tightly implicated in the process of forming and maintaining friendships and familial connections abroad as well as at home and thus in building Britain's first empire. This book includes evidence about a range of domestic and urban spaces, and it analyzes sources not merely from England, Scotland, and Wales but also from British colonies in Ireland, America, and the West Indies. It reveals the importance and durability of female friendship in many diverse spaces and geographies of early modern Britain.

The History of Studying Female Alliances

Scholarly study of early modern European women's communities took new directions in the late 1960s, when feminist scholars sought to establish the existence of unified female communities in the past.[2] Historical topics such as the imagined "paradise of women," the *Querelle des Femmes*, and salon culture inspired these feminist historians to seek out and analyze women's cultures, identifying female homosociability in everything from the works of Christine de Pizan and her *Book of the City of Ladies* in the thirteenth century to the literary debates of *salonnières* in the eighteenth.[3] Many of these early works on women's communities sought to show that early modern women lived in supportive, mutually beneficial communities, in which, rather like these feminist scholars themselves, protofeminists bound themselves together in displays of agency and resistance. In the 1980s, in her pathbreaking work *Women, History and Theory*, the Renaissance scholar and feminist historian Joan Kelly tied the modern feminist movement directly to the communal efforts of women in early modern Europe:

> All feminist work emerges out of the spirit and reality of collectivity. Mine has. When women are scattered and cannot work together, a

condition that originated in the early modern state, women suffer a loss in position and in the possibility of feminist expression. When some connection among women exists, even if it is only a literary one (as it was among the participants in the *querelle des femmes*), it creates an impressive tradition of feminist thinking. . . . [I]t is fair to call this long line of pro-women writers that runs from Christine de Pizan to Mary Wollstonecraft by the name we use for their nineteenth- and twentieth-century descendents.[4]

For Kelly and other feminist historians, early modern European women's homosociality provided evidence of a rediscovered, proud, and empowering history of women's collective action.

But an important correction to this cooperative, rosy vision of women's communities began to surface in the 1990s, when a further generation of scholars sought to historicize, dehomogenize, and complicate the idea of early modern women's culture. These authors have shown convincingly that salient disparities in social status, race, nationality, employment, education, and religion divided many early modern women. They have argued that these critical differences influenced many early modern women's relationships; that not all interactions between women were harmonious; and that many female–female interactions were marked by acrimony. These historians have shown that early modern women fought with one another, slandered and censured the behavior of their female associates, and evaluated and criticized the bodies and moral characters of the women who surrounded them.[5] In her book *Common Bodies* (2003) Laura Gowing argues convincingly that early modern Britain "was not a world in which all-female environments were necessarily associated with support and validation."[6] Gowing is unquestionably correct. But, as the letter by Mary Evelyn quoted above illustrates, female alliances were considered by many early modern women themselves to be an essential component of their lives, and these relationships were often described as beneficial, mutually supportive, and positive. How do we reconcile these findings? Kelly and her colleagues certainly offered views of women's communities which were unduly optimistic; but to understate the importance of positive female alliances would be to ignore the very many attempts these early modern women themselves made to forge positive bonds with other women. And it may well be the case that female alliances and friendships were all the more necessary amidst the other forms of acrimony and contestation, including those among women, that were so present in early modern Britain.

It is time to analyze the evidence of early modern European women's friendships and alliances. While men's social networks have been the subject of many studies, too little work has been done in exploring the facets of female sociability in early modern Britain and its colonies.[7] Some historians, among them Amy Froide, Naomi Tadmor, and Karin Wulf, have established the importance of women's communication networks in this period by breaking away from older scholarship that privileged the strictly conjugal or nuclear definition of family, but their valuable studies have not made homosociability a central focus.[8] Others, including Alan Bray, Valerie Traub, and Hariette Andreadis, have attempted to trace women's methods of identity creation through analysis of homoeroticism and homosexuality in Britain and colonial British America. These works, typically in the field of literary criticism, help to establish the presence of vibrant same-sex cultures in the past, and the authors introduce crucial methods of interrogating and listening to sources. But these scholars tend to focus on the eighteenth and nineteenth centuries, when overt expressions of love, sensibility, and emotion were common in both public and private writing, and they concentrate very heavily on literary texts and representations of friendship rather than on the data of historical evidence.[9] There has been some good preliminary work on women's alliances themselves in collections of essays by a diverse group of literary critics, dramatists, historians, and women's studies scholars, but no focused monographic work on female alliances has hitherto been attempted.[10]

These books and articles have helped to clear the ground for the study of female alliances and friendships in early modern Britain, and they represent various essays into the territory itself. But this topic calls for a work that has as its central concern the range and meaning of female alliances in Britain in the early modern period.[11] That is the purpose of my book. *Female Alliances* examines women's social networks in early modern Britain and its colonies. Study of these female communities is critical to our understanding of early modern history. This book seeks to recover historical evidence of women's relationships, especially in the later seventeenth and early eighteenth centuries, and especially (but not exclusively) of elite women. In the chapters that follow I will explore hundreds of examples of the letters, social activities, labors, and gifts and services that bound early modern women together. In so doing, I will inquire into the many ways early modern women thought and wrote about their alliances, and I will show that prescriptive literature helped to shape early modern ideas about gender identity, nationality, sociability, and politeness.

Subjects and Sources

What were the female subjects of this book like? and how did they live? The majority of women featured in this project possessed education, wealth, and privilege. Most could read and write, and many had received training in foreign languages, usually French or Italian, dancing, the playing of musical instruments, and singing. They generally lived in large houses in respectable urban neighborhoods or on prosperous rural estates and were responsible for the maintenance of these buildings and for the hiring and management of the staff who worked in them. They often wore expensive clothing made of silk, linen, and fur, and they wore shoes. They usually ate well; they could afford to either cultivate or purchase exotic fruits and vegetables, and they wrote of enjoying salmon, venison, and partridge, foods which, in the seventeenth century and early eighteenth, generally were reserved for people of high social status. They labored extensively without pay in such employments as the care and education of children, sewing and embroidery, tending the sick and manufacturing medicines, managing household staff, preserving and candying fruits, and cultivating herbs and vegetables. Several of the women whose lives are depicted in the book possessed hereditary titles, and some of them would even have been familiar with the rituals of court required for audience with or attendance on the monarch. But only a very few were of the high rank required for close or constant proximity to queens and kings. As Amanda Vickery has described the subjects of her book on eighteenth-century Georgian women, "As a group they defined themselves as 'polite,' 'civil,' 'genteel,' 'well-bred' and 'polished' . . . their possessions were contrived to have a genteel effect, rather than a dazzling elegance, and their entertainments aimed at generous liberality not sumptuous magnificence . . . while polite manners could be practiced at lower social depths and amplified at greater heights, this label captures the moderate social eminence I wish to convey, combined with an emphasis on outward behaviour, while not prejudging an individual's source of income."[12]

Although the subjects of this book lived one hundred years earlier than Vickery's Georgian women, they too sought to attain "moderate social eminence" through displays of "outward behavior," through acts they imagined to be polite, civil, and genteel. The idea of moderate eminence should not be misleading: these elite women certainly lived far better than a majority of seventeenth- and eighteenth-century Britons, female or male. And therefore I will describe them throughout this study, and as they understood themselves, as elite women. But elite was a flexible, uncertain category. In early modern Britain elite women frequently experienced financial hardship and ruin, declines in family revenue and lifestyle, and even loss of house and home. They often lived on the borders of prosperity, and this sort of financial insecurity made female alliances all the more critical to them.[13]

Elite women left behind them an astonishing array of manuscript sources, and only recently have scholars begun to use these systematically and to full advantage. This book considers every genre of seventeenth- and early eighteenth-century elite female writing: letter collections, diaries and autobiographies, travel logs, recipe books, spiritual journals, literary compositions, and books of household accounts. This wide variety of sources is in some ways a reflection of the rank and education of the women themselves, for as Margaret Hunt has argued of her "middling sort" subjects, these were "women [who] enjoyed a high and growing rate of literacy and tended to associate 'respectability' with reading and writing."[14] Such a variety of sources is itself an advantage. While the documents illustrate the many types of sociable leisure activities women enjoyed with their friends, they simultaneously allow one to explore the functioning of female alliances within many diverse aspects of women's lives, from formal correspondence to daily negotiations with local shopkeepers.

The writings of elite women are not the only sources I explore. Although most of the manuscript collections examined here belonged to such wealthier women, the collections themselves contain many small, fragmentary documents which were composed—either written or dictated—by lower-status women. Letters, work contracts, culinary and medicinal recipes, business receipts, and shopping lists and bills composed by both the laboring and nonlaboring poor (those physically incapacitated or too old to work for pay) are therefore also among the sources I discuss.

Most scholars of early modern British women organize their subjects into three firm categories: women who were low-status, usually urban laborers; women who were middling, bourgeois or newly capitalist; and women who were aristocratic, landed and titled.[15] This division, which orders women according to their source of income, has at its heart considerations of economics and the development of structures such as class; but, these distinctions can be misleading in describing early modern women's lives, and it is artificial to separate entirely the lives of laboring, middling, and aristocratic women. These women not only inhabited many of the same spaces, but also might face real changes in their sources of income and employment over the course of their lifetimes, for servants could become mistresses, and mistresses could become servants. Higher-status women were at times dismissive of and hostile toward servants and poor women, but they were not necessarily estranged from the lower-status individuals who surrounded and served them: agricultural laborers, chambermaids and artisanal craftswomen, women who supplied milk, who were shopkeepers, who did laundry, or who worked in kitchens and sculleries, and even those who sought relief through alms. Elite women's own writings attest to the many cultural, emotional, religious, and financial ties they shared with both the poor and the rich. Despite their differences, these women could work in cooperation and collaboration, could share complex associations, and could be implicated in common goals. Certainly the ties between these women were unequal, and unquestionably partitions of social status dictated a major part of the character of their relationships, but it would be wrong to presuppose distance or hostility between lower- and higher-status women.

Geographically speaking, this book encompasses all of seventeenth- and early eighteenth-century Britain: Scotland, Wales, England, Ireland, the West Indies, and the British colonies in mainland North America. This is a British project for two reasons: first, because many of the women I examine were mobile, and their writings reveal evidence of extensive travel around Britain as well as the construction of national and regional identities. The higher-status women featured here owned property both in London and on rural estates in Scotland, Wales, and England, and they traveled between their homes frequently. Several of the women whose records are analyzed were part of the colonization projects in Ireland. Some of the subjects studied were women who emigrated across the Atlantic Ocean to begin lives either on the British American mainland or in the West Indian island colonies. And the female Quaker missionaries explored in chapter 5 spent years at a time in travel, making repeated transatlantic voyages, walking and riding through the mainland American colonies, and sailing between the islands of the Caribbean.

This book is also a British project because it traces communication across long distances. Sociability, communication, and commerce were influenced by gender in the early modern period, but many of the recent scholarly works on commercial expansion and politics have focused to date mainly on masculinized exchange.[16] While these historians have done excellent work in describing the many connections between seventeenth- and early eighteenth-century Atlantic enterprise and masculinity, they have provided only half of the picture.[17] Women were vital contributors to and participants in the many forms of commerce and exchange featured in the British and British Atlantic world, and *Female Alliances* begins to tell part of this underexplored story. As early modern women traveled across and between all of the spaces of Britain, they worked to maintain contact with the friends and family members they had left behind. Women composed longer and more frequent letters to their far-flung friends, and they sent medicines and treats to homesick family members. They sought advice on immigration from women who had already established themselves in the New World, and they felt obligated to inform distant relatives of central life events like births, deaths, and marriages. Those individuals who stayed in metropolitan Britain used goods and received gifts and news from abroad. The culture of female alliances affected early modern women whether they lived in Belfast, Boston, Bridgetown, or Bristol. This book will show how these women organized the character and scope of their alliances in order to adapt to Britain's rapid expansion in the seventeenth and eighteenth centuries.

Gender Identity and "Modern" Femininity

Female Alliances also traces critical changes in early modern British ideas about identity and selfhood, especially as they relate to gender and to practices of sociability. In the past ten years, several leading scholars of western Europe have explored a key question: what are the origins of our definitions of our selves, our senses of being, our modern identities? Historians, literary critics, and philosophers alike have marked a shift in the late seventeenth century and the eighteenth, arguing that during this period Europeans began to envision themselves in a new way. They have asserted that alleged categories of being, including race and class and gender, supposedly became increasingly fixed across the two centuries as European women and men began to see themselves as embodiments of a concrete, immutable—and, some have even argued, a biologized—type of person.[18] These constructions of identity have been described as recognizably modern as they universalized, systematized, categorized, and enshrined difference.

Even if we accept the argument that identities or selves became modern in late seventeenth- and early eighteenth-century Europe, the definition of identity and selfhood being deployed in this account presents challenges. Looking mainly at the evolution of ideas about selfhood among elite male philosophers in the seventeenth and eighteenth centuries, Jerrold Seigel and Charles Taylor describe the development of an autonomous, individualized sense of self.[19] For Seigel and Taylor, whose works have been extremely influential among scholars of this period in Europe, modern selfhood is bound up in the emergence of theories about natural rights, rational subject-hood, and the masculine pursuit of individuality: it is autonomous, even autarchic, wholly contained within and about individuals. But to define self-hood solely by these categories is to deny that most early modern Britons, female or male, possessed an articulated sense of self, and this limitation is particularly acute when trying to describe early modern women's selves and identities.

Those scholars who have attempted to incorporate evidence about early modern women into this developing vision of the self have done so largely through analysis of gender identity, of early modern constructions of femininity and masculinity. While concepts of self and identity are not necessarily synonymous, Michael McKeon, Anthony Fletcher, and Dror Wahrman have argued that many of the categories, characteristics, and constructions that today we associate with feminine or masculine identity became more salient in the eighteenth century.[20] Constructions of modern feminine identity especially are located by these scholars in prescriptive liter-ature, in which, they maintain, seventeenth- and eighteenth-century readers were encouraged to internalize behavioral dicta, becoming self-critical, self-regulating people. Ingrid Tague asserts that in the eighteenth century a British woman who read prescriptive literature was expected to be "constantly aware of the fact that she was a woman, one who never stopped checking her behavior and thoughts against the standards of ideal womanhood. Once internalized, the rules of a conduct manual would create a completely self-regulating woman."[21] And as Anthony Fletcher posits in his book *Gender, Sex, and Subordination*, "an increasingly rigid and elaborate scheme of gender construction ... [was] laid down between 1660 and 1800 in a burgeoning prescriptive literature directed specifically at men and women, but more especially women."[22]

It is true that many of the characteristics scholars have associated with modern identity, for example, the naturalization of gender and sex difference, *women have particular talent for friendship* the internalization of prescription, the universalizing of female and male, the impulse toward surveillance and criticism of others, are present in early modern prescriptive literature for women, and each will be examined in this book.[23] These texts naturalize gender differences, for instance, as they posit that early modern British women were naturally inclined toward love and sociability: in her edition of 1675 of the *Gentlewomans Companion*, Hannah Woolley described women as not merely culturally but also physiologically disposed to pleasantness and affability. It was "the sweet blood of Females," Woolley declared, that made "the framing and fashioning of a Woman, whose behaviour should be such as to please in all companies."[24] Seventeenth-century authors of prescriptive texts for women may be said to have also universalized their readers, as they projected feminine stereotypes onto higher- and lower-status women alike; Woolley went on to state that her *Gentlewomans Companion* was intended to be "a Compleat Book, that might have a Universal Usefulness," and William Hill's *A New-Years-Gift for Women* (1660) boasted that its own "Epistle Dedicatory" was "directed to the Feminine Gender," a fact which made the book special, distinctive, and new because while "many have dedicated [their works] to one or two vertuous Ladies . . . never any (as this is) to the whole Sex of Women, of what rank or quality soever they be."[25] And many seventeenth-century prescriptive authors did expect female readers to monitor and discipline the behaviors of other women. John Shirley promised the readers of his *Accomplished Ladies Rich Closet* (1691) that once women "ma[d]e an Essay" into good behavior, they would then "becom[e] an Admonisher of others to make the like improvement."[26]

But all of this evidence must be treated with caution. Prescriptive literature did not spring unbidden from the eighteenth-century printing press; it had intellectual genesis in the classical tradition of rhetorical modeling. This literary genre, within which gendered prescriptions had appeared for centuries, had a lasting impact in early modern Britain.[27] This evidence also has stark implications with regard to the study of early modern women. Scholars like Wahrman and Fletcher have seen these processes of modernization as largely negative for seventeenth- and eighteenth-century European women, isolating and limiting them as they were told to internalize masculine prescriptions and to turn on one another in displays of critical surveillance.[28] At best, these authors seem to suggest, early modern women might achieve a few hard-won freedoms in becoming autonomous individuals. Describing French women in the eighteenth century, Dena Goodman writes that "for women in the eighteenth century, choices were always constrained, and autonomy was always an achievement . . . writing letters and engaging in correspondence helped women to achieve moments and degrees of autonomy within the context of human relationships—from family and friendship to social and gender systems, systems that were becoming modern as they were themselves."[29] But the idea that women could achieve autonomy or become modern only as they became increasingly solitary, self-regulating, and critical of others is both depressing and, as we will see throughout this book, not borne out by the experiences of many women in the seventeenth and eighteenth centuries.

It is perhaps necessary to reconsider our definitions and understandings of modern identity and selfhood. In her groundbreaking book *Lesbian Ethics*, the feminist theorist Sarah Lucia Hoagland coins a new term, *autokeonony*, to describe

> a self who is terrified neither of solitude nor of gatherings, a self who is both elemental and related, who has a sense of herself making choices within a context created by community. I mean to invoke a self who is both separate and connected. So I create a word for what I mean: "autokeonony." Which I take from the Greek "auto" ('self') and "koinania" ('community or any group whose members have something in common'). What I mean by "autokeonony" is the "self in community." The self in community involves each of us making choices; it involves each of us having a self-conscious sense of ourselves as moral agents in a community of other self-conscious moral agents. And this is not a matter of us controlling our environment but rather of our acting within it and being a part of it.[30]

Hoagland's autokeonony has been revived recently by scholars associating themselves with the third wave and even the new fourth wave of feminism to express their desires for a feminist movement which is simultaneously positive, inclusive, and activist.[31] But the idea of autokeonony is also useful for thinking about women's identities and alliances in early modern Europe. So are Nancy Chodorow's ideas about a sense of self that is in opposition to a bounded, masculinized conception of identity. In her works on psychoanalysis and feminism, Chodorow advocates a "feminine personalit[y] founded on relation and connection, with flexible rather than rigid ego boundaries."[32] Some historians of early modern Europe have also begun to push back against a definition of selfhood that is predicated on solitary masculinity. In his book on autobiography in early modern England, Michael Mascuch demonstrates that although modern selfhood "has come to be equated with a masculine, middle-class subject . . . the historical agents active in its original production were rather more diverse."[33] And in their book on women's literary efforts in self-writing, the editors Elspeth Graham, Hilary Hinds, Elaine Hobby, and Helen Wilcox assert, "What we say of ourselves must also be understood by someone. . . . we need to construct ourselves in relation to others."[34] The authors claim that, among other things, these constructions arose from women's shared experiences of language, sympathetic emotion, and the physical body. This sense of the relational self stresses that feminine and communal ties, not masculine, individualized ones, were themselves also very meaningful cultural constructions in the later seventeenth and eighteenth centuries.

Certainly in order to understand the development of women's and men's selves, all of these theories—and especially those of scholars like Hoagland and Chodorow, who are not historians—must be placed within an approach which is historically precise, and in any interpretation of the feminine self focused on relation and connection there is a risk of eliding the conflict and antagonism that often erupted among early modern women. Nonetheless, these theoretical approaches allow a break with the idea that a modern self must or should be autonomously autarchic. Seventeenth- and eighteenth-century women were expected to be not autonomous, but "autokeononous"; and their selves-in-relation were part of the late seventeenth- and eighteenth-century developments in gender identity. Throughout this book we will see that feminine gender identities in this period were created through relational acts of sociability: the exchanging of gifts and services, traveling together, providing health care and medicine to others, sharing religious experiences, and even in the collective labor that women performed in domestic work spaces. The ability to relate to others, and especially to other women, was considered to be an essential component of this modern feminine identity. And women of the time used these connections to enrich and empower their lives.

Tied closely to elite women's constructions of early modern gender identity were early modern conceptions of social status. Seventeenth- and eighteenth-century Britons who possessed wealth, power, and privilege placed great emphasis on the cultivation of qualities they termed politeness and civility. Politeness and civility represented behavioral ideals: speech, activities, and gestures practiced and performed in public by elites to signal their status, wealth, power, and education to others.[35] Whether carried out in the coffeehouse, at the spa, or within the spaces of elite homes, these acts of civil, polite speech and gesture created a "cultural discourse" among genteel Britons.[36] And these practices were figured by many men of the era as political tools, requisite for all those who wished to participate in government.[37] While political, masculine understandings of sociability, civility, and politeness were unquestionably vital in early modern Britain, my work highlights the adoption and feminization of polite practices by elite women.

As we shall see, elite women adapted and adopted many identity constructions—of civility and politeness, of gender and femininity—from prescriptive texts. And although prescription does not necessarily indicate historical practice, these works must be taken seriously, for they help one to understand more fully the rules that formed and influenced early modern British women.[38] These claims have been supported by other scholars. Ingrid Tague shows that study of prescriptive books allows historians to understand how texts "systematically sought to create the ideal woman," and she argues convincingly that guidebooks "provide a particularly useful source for the historian seeking to trace ideals of femininity."[39] The literary critic Jonathan Goldberg has written that prescriptive literature "serve[s] to instruct on the socially countenanced modes for a self-production that can never be separated from the fictive simulations that structure the real," and the historian Anne Kugler has shown that "specific prescriptive texts" played an essential role in an elite woman's "selection and fashioning of her own personal reflections."[40] This book will offer many examples of early modern British women's frequent attempts to conform to gender identities as they were articulated in contemporary prescriptive texts, illustrating the prevalence and wide influence of this literature. But even as these women reproduced ideas that were presented in guidebooks, and even as they understood they were expected to be loving and kind, sociable, civil, and friendly, *Female Alliances* demonstrates that British women readers exploited prescriptive dicta in fascinating ways. Appropriating prescriptions in order to structure the letters, material objects, gifts, and services that facilitated their connections with other women, female Britons often worked to secure financial resources and to defend female skills and spaces.

Defining and Understanding Alliances

I want to explain briefly my book's use and understanding of the term *female alliances* in its title and text. The term is designed to encompass the wide variety of women's social activities and broadly positive interactions, and over the course of this book I will explore many dimensions and meanings of female relationships and friendships. The word *alliance* was in use throughout the seventeenth and eighteenth centuries, particularly to describe bonds between families during marriage. When Elizabeth Lindsey Bertie congratulated Lady Danby on her son's marriage in 1674, she hoped not just for the happiness of the newly married couple but also for the success of Danby's newly extended alliance network, wishing her "all the hapynes imagnable, bouth in this, and ever other Aliance you ether have, or shall hear after mack [make] . . . as Good suckes [success] as you dissarve, wich is as much I am shur as can be wished to you, ether by me, or any other of your frinds and ralations."[41] Early modern women also employed the terms *friend* and *friendship* to describe some of their homosocial bonds. Alice Thornton noticed that there had "ever . . . bin a strict league of affection and freindship betwixt" her mother and her aunt.[42] And Mary Sinclair wrote to London from Edinburgh in 1673 to assure Lady Lauderdale that "your noble freindshep . . . is dearer to me then any other earthly filicytie."[43] All of these terms—*friendship, alliance, felicity, affection*—were used to denote positive social relationships between women, and to some degree these terms are used interchangeably throughout this book.

But this book deliberately employs the term *alliance* because its examination of women's social networks includes some study of interactions between higher- and lower-status women. In their collection on early modern women's friendships, Susan Frye and Karen Robertson aptly define female alliances as "range[s] of relationships," naming "not only marriage and kinship, but also defensive and offensive unions, intellectual, educational, and religious connections, friendship, and same-sex love" as integral to early modern female sociability. Following Frye and Robertson's model, I too examine ranges of relationships. Some chapters analyze activities and tasks that both higher- and lower-status women undertook together, such as shared domestic labor. Other chapters discuss the social practices which facilitated moments of alliance between these women, such as exchanges of gifts and services, travel, and the provision of health care. This is a wide-ranging definition of alliances, one which tries not to privilege only a few of the many, varied interactions between British women. Salient divisions of social status, education, religious preference, and geographic or regional identity certainly existed between early modern British women, but my book, rather than seeking to segregate women's friendships, tries throughout to explore the diverse character of female relationships.[44]

An example from one of the sources I use extensively, a diary written by a woman named Sarah Savage, illustrates some of the problems that arise from the attempt to classify and categorize female relationships. Savage shared a relationship with a woman named Mary Bate. Savage and Bate met when Bate was a young woman and was hired to work in Savage's home in the early 1700s. At this time, Bate worked for pay as Savage's maid: serving meals, attending church services, sewing, and cleaning. This relationship lasted for several years, but when one of Savage's daughters married and moved away Bate followed the daughter to her new home. It is unclear whether this new relationship also involved pay for work, but it seems that Bate acted as a companion to Savage's daughter. Their relationship was apparently so close that when Savage's daughter had her first baby in 1719 Bate stood as godmother. By 1723 Savage and Bate were still associates; now married and with children of her own, Bate visited Savage's home several times to socialize with her.[45] Over the course of twenty-plus years, Bate had acted as an employee, a family companion, a godmother, and finally an independent visitor and friend. Her relationship with Savage defies any single label or definition of friendship or alliance. It is therefore impossible (and, I would argue, unhelpful) to classify early modern women's relationships too narrowly. It is certainly necessary to acknowledge the pressures that age, piety, social status, and education exerted on female friendships, but any study of early modern female alliances must take into account that these elements were constantly changing and were negotiated by women in disparate ways throughout their lives.

Methods and Structure

Female Alliances is written as a series of interlocking microhistorical studies, each of which illuminates a distinct component of women's social networks. Historians who study subjects for which there are few surviving primary sources—such as those who study women, gender, and sexuality in early modern Europe—face ongoing, serious methodological challenges. Because literacy rates among early modern British women were lower than they were among their male counterparts and because in many instances they were discouraged from writing, records left by these women tend to be scattered and sparse. It can be difficult to construct historical scholarship from such historical fragments. Scholars of early modern women have responded in various ways to these challenges, but a frequent approach has been to create a microhistory of one prominent elite woman, someone whose papers are unusually rich and detailed.[46] Stand-alone microhistories typically take one of two forms: either they describe an extraordinary or famous event or individual in order to establish the importance of that topic; or they explore an ordinary event or individual thought to be intrinsically illuminating.[47] Such stand-alone studies are often rich and inviting and unearth intimate, fascinating details about the past. As David Bell has contended, the best of these interpretations of the past emerge with an almost "cinematic intensity," capturing the imagination of readers while revealing crucial insights about the past.[48] Much has been gained from these microhistories, but the limitation of any study of this type lies in its attention to a single case in its detail and specificity.

Female Alliances offers an alternate methodological approach: it is structured as a series of interlocking and interrelated microhistories. Each topical or thematic microhistory illustrates elements of female friendship and women's lived experiences: the writing of letters, the exchange of gifts and services, the performance of domestic labor, the provision of health care, and the act of shared travel. By examining separately the various ways by which early modern women formed alliances, it is possible to showcase many short but suggestive excerpts from women's own manuscripts and papers. Through this method, even brief letters, incomplete receipts, or scraps of inventories—each of which on their own might provide historians with scant information about the past—can instead be analyzed and incorporated into a more comprehensive record of female interactions. In this book, each microhistorical chapter provides a nuanced account of one dimension of early modern women's relationships, but, taken together, all of the chapters dovetail in attempting to present a richly elaborated picture of female alliances in early modern Britain. This method is intended to allow readers of *Female Alliances* to gain a better understanding of the complexity of female sociability and to impart a sense of the weight, scope, and importance of women's friendships within the period as a whole.

This technique results in my use of a large, diffuse group of sources. Some of the women whose papers are featured in here are well known to scholars of early modern Europe; many more of these women, however, contributed only a few brief lines to the canonical historical record. A source base of this proportion is at times unwieldy, but throughout this project I have erred on the side of inclusion. As we seek to learn more about women's lives in early modern Britain, I hope this fresh approach to the study of female alliances will generate further work on the topic. Inclusiveness is useful as well given the construction of early modern female alliances themselves. Because women were prohibited from joining many of the fraternal associations populated by men, their friendships and associations were, by their very nature, more informal and scattered. There were no membership rolls, clubhouses, or stated rules of conduct for early modern women's alliances. To trace the formation and characteristics of seventeenth- and early eighteenth-century female friendships, it is therefore necessary to piece together many small fragments of information from many sources, composed by many types of women, and created in many locations.

The arrangement of the chapters allows us to trace women's networks from the local to the global. Early chapters of the book focus on women's interactions in their "closets," homes, and neighborhoods, while the later chapters, reflective of the ties British women formed across larger and larger distances, expand their scope in examining women's travel, first domestic and then foreign. The first facet of female sociability is examined in chapter 1, with analysis of seventeenth- and eighteenth-century literate women's written descriptions of friendship and alliance. The chapter explores some ideas about women's friendship as they were articulated in early modern literature, including neoclassical works, religious texts, pamphlets about vernacular medicine and physiology, epistolary guides, and prescriptive books. Examining the many ways in which women interacted with these texts, I show that some literate early modern British women challenged gendered stereotypes in asserting their capacities for friendship, and others creatively drew on these stereotypes—that women were "naturally" more emotional and passionate—in order to build social networks both at home and abroad.

Chapter 2 moves beyond textual representations of women's friendship to examine female alliances that were built through the exchange of gifts. Elite women frequently made presents by hand and then offered them to female friends and family members in order to create and maintain alliances. The presents themselves were expensive, rare, or "curious" and were often made from goods imported across the Atlantic. Fruit conserves, embroidered and dyed cloth, distilled perfumes, and painted art objects were intended to speak to the gendered tastes, skills, and habits cultivated by privileged women in this period and therefore to create bonds between elites. But in creating and giving these luxury objects, women stressed instead their economy and thrift. This chapter examines the reappropriation of luxury by illustrating the ways in which elite women manipulated expensive ingredients in order to use them in ways that emphasized their supposedly feminine attention to emotion, care, and household economy. Chapter 3 continues this work on household economy by focusing on women's interactions within domestic work spaces. Higher- and lower-status women experienced moments of reciprocal work and cooperation through their mutual involvement in the production of food, drink, and handcraft and through their shared care of children. By examining three distinct but related sources, namely, household inventories, frontispiece images from prescriptive literature, and women's manuscript recipe books, the chapter reveals higher- and lower-status women's close interactions in domestic kitchens, bedchambers, dairies, gardens, breweries, and laundries. It demonstrates how women and their employees labored together within the highly challenging material conditions of these shared work spaces and how they negotiated with one another in navigating these spaces and in some cases registered mutually positive interactions within them.

In chapter 4, my study of female alliances broadens in traveling away from domestic spaces. I describe the bonds formed between early modern British women at hot spring spas. Elite women who traveled to spas to "take the waters" participated in extensive same-sex socializing and bathed in sex-segregated environments. British spa towns were claimed by higher-status women as locations for female homosociability, and they were experienced by lower-status women as places where female labor and entrepreneurship were privileged. By making medicines, caring for children, offering medical advice to friends, tending the sick, and doing business within largely female communities, women at the spa feminized their hot spring experiences. And in chapter 5 the book traces women's social networks at their broadest geographical scope, in the special spiritual partnerships shared between itinerant Quaker women. Female Quaker preachers in the seventeenth and eighteenth centuries undertook extensive, dangerous travels, making recurrent sea voyages across the Atlantic, over the Irish Sea, and between the West Indian islands. These women also traveled overland on foot and horseback across England, Scotland, and Wales and through every mainland British American colony. The wide-ranging travels undertaken by Quaker women were almost always accomplished in the company of a female companion, a spiritual partner who was intended to provide affection, solace, and aid. Female members of the Society of Friends attempted to mitigate hardships through the spiritually and emotionally meaningful relationships they formed with these partners, whom they called their yokemates.

The sixth and final chapter of the book examines closely the life of one woman who rejected many traditional practices of female sociability. Sarah Henry Savage was an early Presbyterian who believed that her faith prevented her from forming friendships with many other women. As a Dissenter, Savage was ostracized by most women in her neighborhood, and, as we will see, her solitude even put her family in danger. Savage's example demonstrates the conventionality, necessity, and centrality of female alliances to the lives and experiences of most women in early modern Britain.

1. "Small Expressions of My Passionate Love and Friendship to Thee": The Idioms and Languages of Female Alliances

Between 1685 and 1691 Anne Dormer composed a series of ardent letters to her most beloved confidant. Addressing the recipient of her letters as "My Deare Soul," Dormer confessed, "I love you dearer then my owne life." She reassured her companion of her constancy, stating that she did "not pass any houre without thinking of yow" and expressed her joy in the relationship, exclaiming, "Ah my deare heart . . . you make me infinitely happy." Commenting explicitly on the messages conveyed in her fervid letters, Dormer then begged her correspondent to "kindly accept those small expressions of my passionate love and friendship to thee." These letters were not written to a husband, nor did they allude to a forbidden relationship; instead, Dormer was writing to her sister Elizabeth Trumbull, and she closed one of the letters with her wish to "tell thee never sister loved more than thy faithfull friend Anne."[1]

The expressions of sororal love and fidelity expressed by Dormer in her letter were not empty conventions, nor were they peculiar to Dormer herself. Dormer's letter instead reflected one dimension of early modern British women's complex and rich understanding of women's alliances. This first chapter examines textual representations of female alliances. The sentiments and statements about female alliance which elite women expressed in their writings were an emotional praxis, drawn in part from the relationships themselves and in part from canonical works that elite women utilized in order to give value and meaning to their homosocial relationships. Through their descriptions of female alliances, literate women worked simultaneously to express their feelings of connectedness and solidarity and to construct and maintain social networks with their family, neighbors, and friends.

In their recent work *Love, Friendship, and Faith in Europe, 1300–1800*, the editors, Laura Gowing, Michael Hunter, and Miri Rubin, argue that the term *friend* had "copious and special meanings to early modern people." Early modern friends were tied together in many ways: economically and philosophically, in business, in family, and in faith. Gowing, Hunter, and Rubin decry the fact that "social and cultural historians have been slow to take up the challenges of taking friendship seriously" and urge future scholars to examine each of the many meanings of early modern friendship carefully, suggesting the need for "historical study of female friendship."[2] Such an exploration of some of the meanings of female friendship is my aim here: to the early modern women examined in this book, *friendship* and *alliance* had overlapping and sometimes mutually reinforcing meanings. I will explore some of the major dimensions of the words that were chosen by women themselves to articulate their friendships and alliances, and I will flesh out some of the central ideas that shaped female sociability. Several key features of female friendship are identified by tracing the impact of five literary forms and traditions that influenced elite women's understandings of sociability, alliance, and friendship: first, writings on idealized, classically inspired friendships, a kind of relationship that early modern men often denied as being possible for women but, as we will see, was explicitly claimed by some women as constitutive of their own alliances; next, spiritual discourses on Christian friendship, which were used by women to explain and justify the ties they shared with other women, often in ways which challenged women's subordination to men; third, vernacular, cheap-print medical pamphlets on such emotions as affection and love, said to be involved in women's friendships; fourth, correspondence and epistolary guides, which helped to structure and inform women's letters to their female friends, relatives, and neighbors; and finally—and critically for this book, because of their impact on constructions of gender identity—works of prescriptive literature about female behavior, which recounted how women were expected to act toward their friends.

Much of the manuscript evidence cited here, especially the evidence in the section on epistolary guides, comes from women's manuscript letters. Early modern women's personal correspondence is an invaluable resource for understanding female alliances.[3] The letters themselves provide concrete evidence of female relationships, as each missive represents an act of communication between two women. But these letters commonly offer insights as well into the languages and ideas with which women spoke about their alliances. In their correspondence, literate women were particularly open and forthcoming in describing their relationships. Study of the idioms and languages that women used to characterize their homosocial friendships provide evidence of an essential dimension of women's social networks. Combined with analysis of the many crucial nonliterary methods by which women forged social connections—for example, women's gift exchanges, practices of health care, activities in domestic labor, and experiences in travel, all of which are explored in subsequent chapters of this book—such a study can begin to afford a basis by which to recognize the complexity and intricacy of female alliances in early modern Britain.[4]

Classical and Neoclassical Texts

Classical and neoclassical descriptions and definitions of friendship were circulated widely in early modern Britain. In their book *Discourses and Representations of Friendship in Early Modern Europe*, Daniel Lochman, Maritere López, and Lorna Hutson identify "the works best known" for discussing friendship in early modern Europe as "Plato's *Lysis, Symposium, and Phaedrus*, Aristotle's two works on ethics (the *Eudemian* and the *Nicomachean*), and Cicero's *De amicitia* and *De officiis*."[5] Many contemporary scholars have provided manuscript evidence that supports this assertion, tracing the extensive use and repetition of Platonic, Aristotelian, and Ciceronian ideas on friendship among literate, early modern British men.[6] These classical male philosophers, theologians, and scholars denied women's capacity to participate in the type of allegedly perfect friendship practiced by men. But some literate women explicitly rejected this supposition, and themselves drew upon classically and philosophically inspired ideas about friendship in articulating their alliances and friendships. Refusing to accept that women were incapable of conducting or appreciating perfect friendships, literate women engaged with philosophically inspired texts in order to justify and strengthen the bonds they shared with others.

One of the central ideas employed in classical texts and in early modern neoclassical discourses on friendship was that perfect unity could be achieved by people who were intellectual and social equals. The Greek term *philia* and the Latin terms *amicitia* and *arête* were used most often to articulate this type of friendship. When two such similar people became friends, it was said that their identities merged, to the supposed benefit of both. These friendships were seen as self-sustaining as well as permanent, in that they were based on the virtues shared by the two friends.[7] This idea of friendship was employed by many educated men in early modern Europe; in 1580 the French philosopher Michel de Montaigne portrayed his bond with his friend Étienne de la Boétie in his essay "On Friendship" as one in which "our souls mingle and blend with each other so completely that they efface the seam that joined them, and cannot find it again."[8] References to female–female friendships in classical texts do exist. David Konstan shows in his *Friendship in the Classical World* that women's relationships were depicted in generally positive terms by authors like Antiphon, Aristophanes, and Josephus, in whose works terms like *philēn* and *philai* were used to delineate female–female friends.[9] But early modern women were often deliberately excluded from understandings and practice of neoclassical styles of friendship. Early modern male philosophers like Montaigne defended sublime friendship as solely the purview of men, arguing that "the ordinary capacity of women is inadequate for that communion and fellowship which is the nurse of this sacred bond . . . nor does [woman's] soul seem firm enough to endure the strain of so tight and durable a knot."[10]

Although most early modern women were discouraged from studying the ideas in Latin and Greek texts, many elite women nonetheless read classical works, and some maintained that they were indeed capable of such deep friendship. Elite and middling women in both Britain and its colonies read Aristotle, Cicero, Homer, Horace, Livy, Ovid, Plato, and Virgil, sometimes in their original languages but most frequently in translation.[11] Although early modern women were imagined to be inferior to early modern men mentally, legally, educationally, and physically, in matters of the soul they were often acknowledged to be equals; following the intellectual traditions of Aquinas and Augustine, John Donne famously said that, like men, women were "in possession of a reasonable and an immortal soul."[12] And some literate women in early modern Britain employed the idea of "shared souls" in articulating their alliances. In her discourse of 1667 on friendship the female philosopher and painter Mary Beale characterized "friendship [as] the nearest union, which distinct Soules are capable of."[13] Beale's ideal centered on the bonds between a husband and wife, but in the autobiographical portion of her *Memoirs of the Life of Colonel Hutchinson*, Lucy Hutchinson drew upon the neoclassical idea of shared souls when portraying the bond between two sisters, her mother and aunt, "who had contracted such an intimate friendship . . . that they seemed to have but one soul."[14] Some women were so confident of their capabilities and understandings of neoclassical friendship that they even bragged to men of their knowledge of these ideas. Dorothy Osborne chastised her lover William Temple in 1653 for his misunderstanding of ideal or perfect friendship, writing, "In my opinion you doe not understande the law's of friendship right; 'tis generaly beleeved it owes it's birth to an agreement & conformity of humours . . . tis wholly Governde by Equality." Osborne then powerfully asserted her right to practice and embody this rarified type of friendship, writing to Temple, "I have always beleeved that there might bee a friendship perfect like that you discribe and mee thinks I finde something like it in my selfe."[15]

Some early modern British women thus explicitly rejected the idea that they were incapable of forming the types of friendship advocated by neoclassicists, and, though their comments were often brief literate women indirectly or directly referenced the idea of shared souls when explaining their female–female alliances. Mary Eliot assured her mother, Johana Barrington, that "I can truelye saye though [you are] absent in the body yet [you are] present in the soul."[16] Constantia Fowler wrote of her friend Katherine Thimelby in the 1630s that "I have reson to love her equall with my soule."[17] Mary Lewis Leke addressed her sister Elizabeth Hastings in a late seventeenth-century letter as "Deare sole" and assured her again later in the missive that "thare is nothing in the world can love you so nearle as [I do] dear sole."[18] And in Anne Dormer's letters to Elizabeth Trumbull in the 1680s (quoted at the beginning of this chapter), Dormer expressed her love for her sister in the same terms, by telling her that, "I love thee as my own soule."[19]

Religious Texts

In addition to drawing upon classical and neoclassical works to depict their relationships, women's descriptions of female alliances derived from their understandings of theology, faith, and religion. Identifying faith as one of the most central themes in early modern friendship, Gowing, Hunter, and

Rubin argue that religion "not only bound people to each other, but also marked those who were outside the circle of amity."[20] Early modern British women often cited ideas about spiritualized friendships and religious alliances in many of their writings and in doing so adapted these ideas to label not merely their marriages but also their homosocial relationships.

Whereas neoclassical friendships were supposed to be built on the mutual and identical esteem that two men held for one another's virtues, early modern Christian fellowship stressed that approbation of friends should be balanced by humility, modesty, and even servility.[21] Early Christian discourses written by Augustine, Jerome, Paulinus of Nola, and John Cassian pronounced true friends as men who were united in their love of Jesus Christ, members of the same brotherhood of Christian followers. Instead of using terms like *philia* and *amicitia* to designate bonds between friends, these authors employed the Greek *agape* and the Latin *caritas*, both of which were intended to explain a universal, brotherly, and communal love.[22] In many cases, the men who articulated these ideas about early Christian brotherhood and spiritually inspired friendship borrowed from familial models. Speaking of early Christian philosophers, Konstan avers that "the preferred metaphors for Christian solidarity were derived from kinship . . . rather than from the domain of *amicitia* or *philia*."[23] Within the family of Christian believers not everyone was equal, but they didn't need to be. By embracing caritas, or charity, followers of Christ were prompted to love one another despite their differences and inequalities and to beneficently and charitably offer succor to all members of the Christian community.

In early modern Britain women were not excluded from agape or caritas as they often were from philia and amicitia. Early modern philosophers and theologians generally considered women to be inferior to men, but, because Christian caritas was predicated on difference, it was held that women could engage in this sort of fellowship by joining a religious organization for women, such as a convent or a priory. By the 1530s, however, Henry VIII's dissolution of the monasteries prevented early modern British women from joining religious communities of the sort envisioned by early Christian and medieval authors, unless they left for convents on the Continent.[24] But early Christian theologians and the early modern philosophers who drew on their works also argued that women could participate in caritas through marriage. In marriage, women were held to be subservient to their husbands but were believed to enjoy a special Christian friendship with them. Constance M. Furey shows in her article "Bound by Likeness: Vives and Erasmus on Marriage and Friendship" that sixteenth-century male philosophers used Augustine's marriage treatise *De bono coniugali*, in which Augustine states that a "true union of friendship [has] one governing and the other obeying," to categorize early modern European marriages as friendships between nonequals. As Augustine writes, "Women should be chaste, obedient, and subservient . . . recognizing that the man is the head of woman just as God is the head of man."[25] In the mid-seventeenth century these ideas were adapted for Protestant British audiences by the highly influential Anglican divine Jeremy Taylor, who wrote a letter to his friend the poetess Katherine Philips on the subject; this tract was later published and widely circulated, appearing in print seven times between 1657 and 1684.[26] Taylor posited that women could participate in what he called "noble friendship": "I differ from the morosity of those cynics, who would not admit your sex into the communities of a noble friendship. I believe some wives have been the best friends in the world . . . [but] I cannot say that women are capable of all those excellencies . . . a female friend in some cases is not so good a counselor as a wise man, and cannot so well defend my honor; nor dispose of reliefs and assistances."[27] According to Taylor, female friends were not to be trusted for the provision of advice, the defense of honor, or the disbursement of charity. They could, however, "love as passionately, and converse as pleasantly, and retain a secret as faithfully" as male friends.[28] For Taylor, women's alliances were marked by love, sociability, and trustworthiness, and women themselves embodied a gendered type of friendship, as "virtuous women are the beauties of society and the prettinesses of friendship."[29] But Taylor believed that women's best and truest friendships were realized only in the marital relationship between husband and wife. Calling marriage "the queen of friendships . . . made sacred by vows and love, by bodies and souls, by interest and custom, by religion and by laws, by common counsels and common fortunes," Taylor privileged the bonds between husband and wife.[30] In this partnership, women were placed under the guidance of their husbands; a reflection of caritas, marital pairs could in theory offer a pure, spiritual—and distinctly unequal—friendship to one another.

But the idea of Christian caritas was complicated, and its exclusive tie to traditional heterosexual marriage and subordination was subverted when some literate women wrote of sharing this type of bond with their female friends rather than with their husbands. That female friends could be "married" to one another was a conceit employed by some elite women in their correspondence. When Mary Stuart (later Mary II) famously referred to her friend Frances Apsley in their correspondence as "dear husband," the allusions had significant political as well as personal connotations.[31] Nonroyal women drew upon the same terminology, using it to emphasize the love, trust, and fidelity shared by female friends. The Scot Isabella Seton, Countess Perth, made reference to a woman as a female spouse when writing to her sister Anna Livingston in 1617 of a mutual friend of theirs, who was accompanying Livingston on a journey. Calling the unnamed woman "my sweet wife," Seton expressed her gratitude that the woman would keep Livingston company: "Sence my ladie our mother gois not wast [west] with yow I am fre [from] my hirte most gleaid that ye ar[e] to have the companie of my sueit wyf [sweet wife] thair."[32] In the mid-seventeenth century William Blundell called his sisters Frances and Winifred husbands; the two sisters were single and lived together.[33] In September 1662 Elizabeth Oxenden asked to be remembered to a woman whom she called her wife when writing to her mother-in-law: "Pray give my service to my wife whom I hope to see ere long." Six months later, in March 1663, Oxenden wrote again on the same topic, asking her mother-in-law to "pray give my humble service to my wife and tell her I have earnestely wished for her."[34]

Elite women also challenged the idea of Christian, marital friendship by reimagining the boundaries of what a married relationship might mean. Katherine Austen, a widow in late seventeenth-century London, wrote of friendship as a unique, open type of marriage. Austen envisioned herself as bound lovingly, usefully, and permanently to multiple friends of both genders, circumstances in which she could "be married in the dearnesses and usefulness and benefits of friendship."[35] Mary Leke wrote of her desire to cohabit with her sister Elizabeth Hastings, explaining that she "shuld beleve my salfe perfettly happey if the house you have at Wabrege was beg enofe for me to be somtimes with you."[36] Although both women were married, had children, and spent most of the year on separate country estates, Leke wrote of her fantasies that the two might live together in the capital but acknowledged simultaneously such cohabitation was socially questionable: "I fancy we may keep house together, thes [idea seems] very resenabell but perhaps thes every body will not like so weall as I do."[37] In August 1636 Constantia Fowler, the Catholic daughter of a gentleman from Staffordshire, envisioned her ideal relationship as a tripartite bond. Fowler shared a passionate relationship with a woman named Katherine Thimelby, who was being courted by Fowler's brother Herbert Aston. Fowler urged Aston to continue the courtship and celebrated the intense emotions she shared with both parties. Fowler wrote in a letter to her brother that "you two are dear partners in my heart, and it is so wholly divided betwixt you." For Fowler, this relationship excluded all others, "for that I have got so much ado to get leave of it to place any other friend of mine there." The ties shared by Fowler, Thimelby, and Aston were imagined by Fowler to have altered Thimelby, for, according to Fowler, Thimelby herself had become "treable harted. For first, her owne hart must needes bee unighted to yours . . . and then [to] mine, which has been the keeper of yours."[38] Fowler thus triangulated, ordered hierarchically, and then reinforced her relationship with both Thimelby and Aston.[39]

Many literate women believed their alliances were not just modeled on the example of God's love for man but were actually mediated and supervised by God. A Catholic woman named Jane Barker, who emigrated from England in order to join a convent in France, characterized the spiritual import of female alliances in a poem she dedicated to her close female friend, a woman she called her "dear friend and play-fellow, Mrs. E.D." Barker believed that God's power united her with Mrs. E.D. and that it made both individuals more spiritual, drawing them onto a higher, holier plane of existence: "Friendship's that mysterious thing alone, that can unite and make two hearts but one. / It sublimates the soul and makes it move, towards perfection and celestial love."[40] Similar ideas about God's mediation of female alliances were expressed by a Protestant woman named Rebecca Sherbrook, who wrote to her granddaughter Dorothea Crisp that although she was "not your naturall mother," she believed that God had made it possible for the two to share a special alliance. Sherbrook wrote that she held "the same efections" for her granddaughter as she would a natural-born child because of the women's shared religiosity. Sherbrook believed that Crisp had been "born again" as her spiritual daughter, for "I travell [travail] in berth again for your immortall soull."[41]

Not all literate women believed that holy friendship could be realized on earth. Some believed, instead, that truly spiritual alliances could be achieved only after death, when religiously minded women would be reunited in company with their creator as well as with each other. In her extreme old age the Anglican Bridget Croft expressed nostalgia for her long-dead female friends and, writing in 1690, expressed her hope that she would eventually join these friends, whom she called "unparalleled Ladies," in heaven: "With the thoughts of all those unpareled Ladys I often entertain my self. . . . [I] trust with the infinite mercys of allmighty God and my saviour Jesus christ I shall pertake of the eternall bliss that they injoy."[42] Similarly, when Elizabeth Masham traveled away from her mother, Johana Barrington, in the seventeenth century, she "confes[sed] it did much afect me to part from you" but assured herself of their eventual reunion in heaven, for "[it] doth revive my spirits . . . to think of living together in heven worlde without end."[43] When women lost close female friends they often comforted themselves with the idea that death carried their companions to a better, happier place. Elizabeth De Grey expressed consolation and comfort to her daughter-in-law after the death of a sister by telling her, "I hope she is happer then the liveing."[44] In a similar vein, in reflecting on the death of a female relative, Elizabeth Fanshawe told her friend Cecilia Tufton about "how much happier my Lady is then she could possiabely have beene heare."[45] Some women imagined heaven even as a place of pleasant female sociability. Writing to her son Theophilus Hastings to tell him of the death of her daughter (and his sister) Elizabeth Langham, Lucy Hastings explained that "[God] was pleased to take to himself and to the heavenly society from our conversation heere upon earth my deare daughter your sweete sister Elizabeth Langham."[46] For Hastings, the "conversation heere upon earth" she had shared with her daughter had been replaced by the postmortem "heavenly society" that Hastings believed Langham was experiencing.

In all of these ways women complicated and expanded the traditional idea of Christian friendship as expressed by theologians like Taylor in portraying their friendships with other women. But one group of early modern women, more than any other, strove to incorporate ideas about spiritual friendship into their female alliances: Quakers, who frequently referred to themselves as members of the Society of Friends. I look at the meaningful relationships shared between Quaker women below (see chapter 5), where I highlight Quaker expressions of compassion, succor, empathy, and the sharing of burdens within friendship. Here I want to point out that, through their actions and their words, Quakers worked to embody a new and different concept of caritas. Quaker devotion was supposed to be solitary, filled with private prayer and intense personal contemplation, but, as Phyllis Mack has convincingly shown, even if Quakers came to their calling as individuals, much of the practice of their religion was interactive. The stereotypical but designating activity of this religious sect, quaking, was often understood as "dissolution of the individual personality," of melting into a collective, group identity.[47] Quakers deliberately modeled their relationships on apostolic examples, focusing on the mutual and bodily sacrifices which friends were called upon by God to make for one another. Even the structure of Quaker worship, with its separate Woman's Meeting by the later seventeenth century, in which female Quakers would gather to pray and attend to community concerns, stressed the import of female society and friendship.[48]

Quakers valued equality between the sexes, and they championed parity in their female alliances. Traveling preachers were partnered with spiritual companions, and these Quaker yokemates, as they were called, were expected to furnish physical, emotional, and spiritual support to one another. In choosing their companions, some female missionaries attempted to dissolve the boundaries of rank and station, deliberately choosing as their supposedly equal companions servant women who had been previously in their employ.[49] Female travelers were taught to pair themselves in age-discrepant partnerships, with an older woman acting as a mother, or mentor, and a younger companion providing youthful energy and stamina. Beginning her missionary work at eighteen, Deborah Bell was paired with "an ancient and worthy woman" named Elizabeth Richardson, whom Bell called "my dear motherly Companion." Age-discrepant partnerships were so valuable to Bell that she urged the practice on other Quaker missionaries: "It hath ever been my Inclination, the little Time I have been concerned to travel on Truth's Account, and hitherto it hath been my Practice, to make Choice of an elderly experienced Friend for a Companion; and the Help and Benefit I have found in it, engages me to recommend it to all young Ministers."[50] For Bell and other Quakers like her, true spiritual companionship was achieved only when friends viewed one another as they imagined God had made them: as equals and equally loved.

Medical and Physiological Texts

While ideas about religious friendships led some early modern women to style their female alliances as spiritual bonds, other texts enabled them to depict friendship as a naturalized, bodily experience. On May 6, 1695, Rebecca Sherbrook (whose close relationship with her granddaughter

Dorothea Crisp was mentioned above) understood female alliances as derived from women's bodies. The Sherbrooks were merchants and lived in London "behind St. Patchers [Peter's] church." Sherbrook wrote to her granddaughter Crisp, whom she called her "Loving Dolle," to offer her consolation: smallpox had struck the Crisp family, and Dorothea had been very ill. The disease had apparently made a "deformite of her prity fase," but Crisp had survived; her infant sister, however, had not been able to fight off the infection and had died "the first of May." Sherbrook was devastated at this news, for, she wrote proudly, "all thos swett and comly grandchildren the Lord had on[c]e bestood upon me [were] 20 in Number," and it was not until the outbreak of smallpox that her descendants had experienced "any blemish or deformety." The emotions Sherbrook felt at this family tragedy were so enormous that she believed they had corrupted her body: "corrupt natur in thos great efections I had disturbs me so . . . it alterd me." But Sherbrook believed her emotions were inescapable because as a woman she was "by natur full of efections and thay produc sorrow."[51]

Sherbrook articulated the emotions that bound her to her family members in physiological terms. This was not accidental. Early modern women's sentimentality was thought to have a physiological basis: the passions that supposedly governed women's and men's bodies were understood to have a greater impact on women.[52] In early modern Britain, treatises on the physical functions of women and men were popularized in cheap-print medical pamphlets, prescriptive guides, and physicians' tracts. Early modern women consumed these works readily, and they relied on this literature in describing the emotions and feelings they believed bound them to their friends, relatives, and neighbors.[53] Although both women and men were thought to possess all four Galenic humors (blood, yellow bile, phlegm, and black bile), early modern physicians and philosophers held that women's bodies contained larger proportions of phlegm and black bile than men's. This supposedly made women's bodies softer, colder, and physically weaker.[54] But humors were thought to affect the brain as well as the body. In men's bodies, higher concentrations of hot, dry humors like blood and yellow bile reputedly afforded men nimble thought and reason. Women's brains, influenced by phlegm and black bile, were imagined instead as being weak, irrational, uncontrollable.[55] Margaret Cavendish, the Duchess of Newcastle, asserted that women's brains were "mixed by nature with the coldest and softest elements."[56] Imagined as lacking the dry, reasoned temperaments attributed to men, women were viewed as affective beings, driven by love and passion, prone to tears and ardor.[57] This patriarchal vision of women's bodies and minds subordinated early modern women, placing them firmly below and ideally under the care and guidance of the men around them. But such an understanding of women's physiologies and of their supposed capacities for love, emotion, desire, and passion simultaneously allowed women to designate themselves as physiologically and mentally attuned to the experience and expression of affection and friendship.

Many early modern authors believed that women could feel love more keenly, sympathize more readily, and express their passions more elaborately than men. Thomas Heywood, in his *Generall History of Women* (1657), positioned women's alliances over men's, writing under the heading "Friendship in Women" that "there is not any vertue for which men have been famous, in which some women or other have not been eminent: namely, for mutual love, amity and friendship."[58] William Hill argued in his *New Years Gift for Women* (1660) that when God "set forth the excellent grace of Love," he built it into women, "who are more apt and prone to abound therein."[59] The anonymous author of the *Whole Duty of a Woman* (1696) affirmed that women's compassion was "Natural to [their] Sex" and situated their superlative emotions in women's hearts and chests, where their "soft Breasts were made to entertain tenderness and pity."[60] And John Pechey, a member of the College of Physicians in London, wrote in his *General Treatise of the Diseases of . . . Women* (1696) that women had a "kind nature" and were "designed . . . to perform the tender offices of love."[61] Women were imagined by male medical practitioners and philosophers as embodying emotion and affection.

Stereotypes of women's excessive and innate passions were, undeniably, negative. Yet in early modern Britain women repeatedly used these expectations about gendered passions to their own ends, playing upon medical and physiological assumptions about natural feminine emotions to explain the strength of their love to women with whom they were allied. Authors of epistolary guidebooks told women to refer to their hearts in securing their alliances. Hannah Woolley told readers of the *Gentlewomans Companion* (1673) to make reference to sincere, heartfelt emotions when writing letters to their female friends by including lines such as "The remembrance of her love shall be deeply engraven in your heart."[62] And in their manuscript letters women did indeed often style their hearts as loving and soft, symbols of their femininity and of the heightened emotional connections that were attributed to their gender. In 1673 Mary Sinclair based her alliance with her Scottish friend Elizabeth Maitland on the "serten knowledg I hav of your goodnes and tender heart."[63] Elite women's letters and the sentiments expressed in them could even win hearts. In the late seventeenth century a woman named Henrietta Borlase wrote that her friend Lady Alltom's "kind letter" had contained so many "affecttionat lines that thay winne all hartes that reede them."[64] In 1672 Priscilla Rolle made reference to the perceived source of her happy emotions, her heart, when writing to Elizabeth Lewis to congratulate her on her marriage. Rolle called her letter itself "the mesenger of a harte full of joye," and she went on to express "harty wishes for all happyness to atinde your nuptiualls."[65] The idea that women's hearts engendered strong emotions of affection was also used in 1661 by an elderly woman named Beatrix Clerke, who pledged her affection to the Hastings family by begging them to "accept of my pore heerte in all the dementiones of it."[66] Clerke's reference to her "pore heerte" was intended to reveal affection as well as invoke pity and compassion. And the gentlewoman Bridget Croft depicted her own devotion to the Hastings family through complex metaphors about her heart and her emotions. In 1671 Croft divulged her affection through the use of a botanical allusion, writing that the "kindeness I have for you has to[o] deepelye rooted in my harte easely to be removed."[67]

A case study from the Hastings papers demonstrates literate women's frequent gendered references to hearts and emotions. The papers reveal that lower-status women wrote of their feminine hearts, and in doing so relayed complex messages about loyalty, obligation, and affection. At Theophilus Hastings's marriage to Elizabeth Lewis in 1672 two female tenants, Sarah Brookes and Dorothy Harvey, who lived in the village near the Hastings's Nottinghamshire estate, each sent letters of congratulation to the couple along with gifts of handmade cheese. Offering these organic products of the estate back to the Hastings family might have been done to showcase the women's talents as well as to remind the new couple of their traditional obligations to their tenants. But both of the letters and even the cheeses referenced Brookes's and Harvey's hearts and emotions. Brookes wrote that she gave "a cheese praying for your health and happinesse with your Honorable Consort all joy and comfort and all humble service."[68] For Brookes, the gift and the letter worked together to signal her happiness, with the cheese presented simultaneously with her congratulation and pledge of "humble service." And when Harvey sent her the cheese and letter, she first pictured (and excused) its presence among the other, more luxurious gifts and elite congratulatory correspondence that she imagined the Hastings family was receiving: "Amongst those many rich and lordly presents which are or will bee exhibited to youre Lordship selfe, I humbly crave that mine may have your gratious acceptation, which I confess it cannot claime as being worthy of it, nor of my selfe such a one." Harvey's congratulations were then communicated through multiple references to her heart. She wrote that, though her gift and letter were not "rich and lordly" they were the result of "the widdowes mite and that it proceeds from a sincere heart." Harvey was so eager to express the sincere congratulatory feelings of her heart that she impressed them, literally, upon her gift: so that "I might the more express your sincerity of the present, I have imprinted or impressed the effigies of a hearte upon the cheeses."[69]

Ideas about women's hearts played a critical role in both the expression of their affections and their ideas about the strength of their emotions in love and friendship. In addition, women often created and maintained their alliances by writing of and also by performing acts of weeping and crying.[70] When Beata Pope's daughter Frances North was ill in the 1670s, Pope wrote to reassure North of the allegiance of her female relatives. Referring to sadness and tears, Pope underscored the strength and seriousness of feeling held by North's female relations: "Your sister Finny was so fearde that you should groue worsh, that shee would not be presuded to leve weeping tell her eies weare very much swelld."[71] In 1638–39 Constantia Fowler recounted her intense love for her brother's fiancée, Katherine Thimelby. Fowler referenced the strength of her affections by explaining that she could not even write of their friendship without weeping: "For I speake [of our friendship] to you with my eyes drownd in tears; I thinke, nay, I am certayne the grefe of [losing] it would kill me."[72] These ideas were also ascribed to lower-status female servants. In letters to her sister Elizabeth Trumbull, Anne Dormer wrote of the deep, intense bond that was shared between her servant Moll and Moll's sister Betty. Dormer wrote that she had, "never heard of two sister[s] more passionately fond of one another." When Betty died unexpectedly, Dormer relayed that "the Death of Betty had very neere killed Mol shee lay three months non[e] knew whether shee would live or die and all that time her griefe was so extream." Dormer noted especially that Moll's "extream" grief was marked by excessive tears, for "nobody dares name Betty before her, for upon hearing her spoke of or seing anything that was hers she weepe three houres together."[73]

Acts of passionate weeping were also called on by lower-status women to express loyalty to their elite employers. Another example from Anne Dormer's correspondence illustrates this point. When Dormer's female servant Frances ("Frank") left Dormer's employ to work in another woman's household, Dormer noted approvingly her former servant's loyalty by commending her tears: "Honest good Frank . . . went last weeke into Shropshier with Mrs. Brook shee wept extreamly to leave me and truely I have had a greate loss of her whose cheerful compeny has helpt me pass of many a mellancholly houre." Dormer, whose sustained emotional and verbal abuse by her husband is documented in her correspondence, clearly missed Frank's "cheerful compeny," but her letters relate that she was soon comforted by her replacement, a servant named Doll, who, Dormer wrote, "has shewed much love and concern for me of late and weepes when her Mr. is cross, she tends me and takes more care of me then ever." Doll's tears at her master's spousal abuse (which Dormer marked with the phrase "when her Mr. is cross") were taken by Dormer as a sign of her support and care. That Dormer made a point of writing of these acts of weeping was also noteworthy; she wrote to her sister that Doll's and Frank's performative tears were signs that the women were "honest" and "very faithfull," concluding that "truely all my maids [are so] and I bless God I have many comforts."[74] Dormer's relationships with her female servants were meaningful to her and made more emotionally rich to Dormer by the performance of mourning and tears.[75]

Notwithstanding the many performances of weeping documented in women's writings, early modern women were discouraged from such displays, which were judged by male physicians and philosophers to be dangerous to female health. J. Hill's *Young Secretarys Guide* (1696) offered advice on demonstrating friendship through correspondence; in the sample letters from which readers could copy, women were urged to check their grief lest their emotions overwhelm them. The "Letter of Consolation to a Mother, upon the loss of her Son" opened with a caution, warning the fictional female recipient of the letter to be "moderate in your Lamentation . . . moderate this mighty stream of Greif, which otherwise, by the weakening Nature, cannot but impair your Health." In this fictional letter feminine emotions were imagined to be uncontrollable and perhaps even dangerous. But Hill's expectations of and instructions to men who wished to disclose their emotions were quite different. Men's entitlement to reason apparently allowed them to express strong feelings without risking a loss of control. The "Letter of Consolation to a [Male] Friend" acknowledged that masculine loss would "truly raise a Tempest of Sorrow, even in the most obdurate Mind." But men were pressured to grieve, "for so great a loss . . . I must have you weep, and sigh, and sit a while in the Shades of Sadness." While this kind of emotional display might harm women, Hill identified "Manly force" as typically enough to mitigate any risk for men, allowing them a "noble" sadness: "I would have you, as much as the Manly force you are endued withal will contribute, to moderate the unruly Passion, that it may not altogether overwhelm your noble Faculties." Hill averred that men could be trusted to balance pain with masculine reason, to grieve slowly, practically, and even "gently" over long periods of time: "By the assistance of Time and Reason, gently, and by degrees, put a period to your Affliction."[76] Gendering uncontrolled grief as "effeminate" and yet also "heartless" in its instructions for men's condolence letters, Jean Puget de la Serre's *Secretary in Fashion* (1668) stated even that a true man would "not suffer himself to be carried away with a fruitless grief . . . as [would] an effeminate and heartless man."[77]

Simultaneously pronounced in patriarchal medical literature to be prone to weeping and condemned for weeping, women's ritualized acts of weeping involved multiple levels of expression of the strength of their emotional attachment to one another. Despite prescriptions that urged them to be obdurate and resigned, women manipulated stereotypes about so-called feminine emotions in expressing their affections for one another. A final example, from two seventeenth-century letters written by a husband and wife, Anne and Gervase Jacques, to Mary Hastings, the daughter of the Earl and Countess of Huntingdon, can help to prove this point. Anne and Gervase Jacques were both literate, but they were not of high status; Anne provided child care for the Hastings family, and Gervase acted as their occasional servant and land agent. Anne and Gervase each wrote a letter to Mary Hastings when they parted from her after a visit in 1669. In her letter Anne told of feelings of overwhelming sadness that were accompanied by weeping: "The greatness of my trouble for parting from your Honor has made mee as uncapabel as I am unworthy, to write to your Honor for I am not able, to this minute so much as to think of your Ladyship with out floods of teares." Anne's expressions and feelings of devotion were apparently so great and so singular that she vowed that "no person breathing can more truly love, honor and desire to serve your Ladyship, (if it were with the sacrefice of my life)."[78] These powerful declarations stood in stark contrast to the succinct letter

Gervase sent at the same time, tucked into the letter packet alongside his wife's florid missive. Gervase explained some business he had conducted on Hastings's behalf, informing her simply that after their visit he had "beene with Mr. Gray of Langley and have given a stopt to the Treaty betwixt him and Mr. Cooke for his leases at Melorne." Gervase was not ignorant of the alternate conventions and gendered languages of women's letters, however; in his postscript he made sure to tell Hastings that "Madam my wife . . . mabe will drowne [her]selfe in teares for the losse of your Ladyship."[79] Expressions of feminine pity, empathy, and mutual suffering were intended to impart depth of feeling among women, and they were understood to be markers of early modern feminine identity.

Seventeenth- and eighteenth-century women's acts of weeping conveyed complex messages. When an early modern woman cried, it was understood to be the result of the cold and wet humors that governed her body and mind. Because these humors were associated so strongly with women, expression or proof of them became an indication of femininity, for women who wept were imagined to be enacting their natural capacities for pity, love, and sympathy. Women were frequently discouraged, by male doctors, philosophers, and writers from performing these passions, which were imagined simultaneously as indulgent and perilous. But elite and lower-status women alike flaunted these prescriptions strategically, employing and writing about their deluges of tears and throbbing hearts in order to express their devotion to friends, relatives, and employers.[80] This is not to suggest that genuine feeling or sorrow were divorced from women's performances of weeping. These emotions were surely as varied as the women and the situations in which they were experienced: some women may have wept because they were truly sad or empathetic, while others may have wept because it was expected. Whatever individual women's motivations for weeping might have been, women themselves strategically ignored medical and scientific prescriptions on controlling women's natural emotions with the aim of creating and maintaining female alliances.

Epistolary Texts

The many examples I have given of women expressing their emotional attachments to other women in letters are not accidental, for letters served as a major mode of communication in the early modern British world, and they were centrally integrated into early modern British culture. Literate women learned practical and moral letter-writing methods from published self-help guides, structuring their missives around examples of letters that were provided for copying. For recreation, literate women read printed books and pamphlets that were constructed as exchanges of fictional female correspondence. Letters and ideas about letters were major cultural and intellectual frameworks within which early modern British women conceived of and wrote their own correspondence. And letters, both fictive and real, helped to structure and shape these women's alliances.

Ideas about women's letters and the roles they were supposed to play in creating and maintaining female alliances were expressed in many widely circulated early modern epistolary guides. Close study of these texts helps one trace the impact of correspondence on female alliances. One of the most widely circulated early modern epistolary guides for women appeared in a book attributed to Hannah Woolley titled *The Gentlewomans Companion*.[81] Woolley regarded correspondence as essential to women's alliances. She told her readers that when "distance of place, will not admit of Union of persons, or converse *Viva voce*; that deplorable defect is supplied by a Letter or Missive." Overcoming this "deplorable" distance between women was "unavoidable" as well as crucial, for "the necessity of conversing with one another as long as we live, layeth an unavoidable cogency of communicating our affairs to each other."[82] Woolley wrote that correspondence was tied closely to constructions of idealized femininity. She persuaded her female readers to "polish [their] Epistolical compositions" and assured them that her own books offered "instructions how you may talk and that elegantly, to the same persons at a distance whether relations, friends or acquaintance, and that is by Letter."[83] Pairing weak writing habits with "impertinency," a quality damaging to amiable relationships, Woolley grumbled, "I met with Letters my self sometimes, that I could even tear them as I read them, they are so full of impertinency, and so tedious."[84]

Epistolary guides like Woolley's and the idealized images of women letter writers they contained left their mark on early modern British women's manuscript letters to their female family members and friends. When women could not communicate in person, they proclaimed that letters could help them maintain their alliances. In 1656 Bridget Croft expressed her pleasure that her relationship with Lucy Hastings remained strong despite the distance that separated them, writing that she was delighted that "hetherto noe absence has in the least degree lessned your . . . affection." Croft professed that she, too, continued to feel intense affection for her friend despite her absence, "for when I am from you my thoughts are often on you."[85]

These expressions were especially common among Welsh, Irish, and Scottish women, whose family commitments required frequent travel to England. Sarah Savage, who lived outside of Chester on the border between England and Wales, remarked in 1688 that "tho' I cannot see Dear Relations often yet it is my comfort that I can hear from them in the compass of the last week I have had a letter from each of my Sisters and my Brother, blessed bee God that yet there is no distance nor strangeness of affection between us."[86] Changes in politics and royal successions could alter the ways in which female alliances were characterized and experienced by elite women. During periods of Stuart rule, elite Scottish families spent more time in London, acting as advisors, servants, and companions to the royal family. This necessitated long absences from their estates in the north, and the practice concerned many elite Scottish women, who wanted to maintain the ties they shared with female friends and relatives. Sometime between 1611 and 1616 Henrietta Stuart, the youngest daughter of Charles I, wrote to her friend the Scot Anna Livingston of her yearning to see Livingston in person and to testify "with [her] own mouth" of the affection the two shared: "Je jouettrois chere cousine davoir quelque bonne occasion de vous voir pour vous temoigner de bouche ma fidella affection mais puis que cella ne peut ester [I hope to enjoy, dear cousin, some good occasion to see you and to testify with my own mouth of my faithful affection, but right now that cannot be]."[87] Stuart's letter served as a proxy mouth, voicing her affections from afar.

Large-scale colonization movements and acts of war also affected female alliances. When Mary Pease heard that her daughter Mrs. Baynes was considering emigrating to Ireland in 1651, she wrote to try to dissuade her from the move. The Baynes family was planning to accompany John Lambert, who had been made lord deputy of Ireland following the death of the previous lord deputy, Oliver Cromwell's son-in-law Henry Ireton. Pease was horrified at this news. She wrote frantically to Baynes, "I hear that General Lambert is to goe into Irleand and that you and your husband doth intend to goe with him which is noe littill grefe to me." Pease warned her daughter that moving to Ireland could cause a break in their communication and worried that this would damage their relationship. Pease had apparently suffered such a loss before: "I had once a brother with his wife and children that went thether and I feared never heard of them more or what became of them." Clinging to her English identity, she advised her daughter to "let nether profitts nor performents draw you out of your owune cuntrey being the lord hath beene pleased to bestowe uppon [you] well and riches sufficient, I desire you that you would be therewith content and live at home." Nearing the end of her letter, Pease tied this advice to the detrimental emotional and physical effects of emigration; she warned her daughter against the international move, "lest you bring my gray haires with mo[u]rning to the grave."[88] Women who emigrated from England to the Irish plantations in the seventeenth century used letters to maintain ties. When Eliza Blennerhassett accompanied her family in the 1650s to their new estate in Trellick, near Galway on the western shore of Ireland, she worked hard to stay connected with other English women. Portraying Ireland as solitary, foreign, and ungodly, Blennerhassett wrote despondently to Eleanor Hastings in October 1656, "Your letters, I assure that your La[dyshi]p are the only suports of my spirits," and begged her friends to continue writing, for "I beseech you not to debare me of [your correspondence] when occasions are offereed."[89]

The strain that elite women faced in maintaining alliances across wide geographic barriers became even more evident when friends, neighbors, and relatives were separated by the Atlantic Ocean. Recent scholarship on the lives and experiences of émigrés to colonial British America has shown that seventeenth- and eighteenth-century colonists labored to keep up ties with friends and relatives in their home countries.[90] In 1649–52 Katheryne Hunlocke sent a series of letters from London to two of her children, a daughter and son, who had immigrated to the colonial British American colony of Virginia as indentured servants. Hunlocke worked to help her children thrive in Virginia by planning their futures and advising them to behave in ways she considered to be loving and familial. Relieved in 1649 to learn that her daughter Margaret had been purchased out of her indenture by a new husband, she laid out her plans for releasing her son from his own indenture contract. Hunlocke promised Margaret that "next year" she would "send you one servant . . . to Release your Brother for." Hoping that her children could eventually cohabit in the colony, Hunlocke explained, "I desire that your Brother maye come to live with your husband." Hunlocke worked to cultivate ties with her distant children by supplying them with goods and commodities. She wrote that she had "sent the[m] goods to neer the value of one hundred pounds," items which included household furniture, clothing, food, medical supplies, personal toiletries such as combs, handkerchiefs, a brush, and a chamber pot, and many sewing supplies. This extensive list hints at the character of colonial life in seventeenth-century Virginia, which was austere, laborious, blighted, and often short-lived, especially for indentured servants.[91] But Hunlocke's letters are evidence that sending these supplies allowed her to transmit her affection and love. Hunlocke wrote of her wish that her children "injoy my labore" in picking out and packing the goods, and she made special mention of "a Grogram gowne of mine" which she had sent to her daughter Margaret "to make you a gowne to weare." Far from being a castoff, the dress was a meaningful and emotional gift. Gifts of personal clothing were valued by early modern British women for their associations with their donors, as they were often handmade and carried a loved one's shape and smell (see chapter 2). When Hunlocke sent Margaret her grogram dress, she shipped an embodiment of herself thousands of miles across the sea. Despite the enormous distance between Virginia and London, Hunlocke valued the ties she shared with her children and prized her ability to correspond with them, writing sadly, "I hope I shall not bee a mother which shalbe forgetful of you."[92]

Another example of women's transatlantic correspondence dates from the early eighteenth century. In August 1711 a woman named Mary Stafford, who had immigrated to the colony of South Carolina, wrote to her female cousin in England. Stafford, her husband, who was either an apothecary or a barber-surgeon, and their children had moved to South Carolina after incurring enormous debts in England, where, Stafford wrote, they faced "a Gaol for my husband, and want to my self and Children." The family had departed in haste, without notifying their families, and Stafford now wanted desperately to regain contact with women back in England. She missed her female friends and relatives, and she believed these feelings were made worse by the distance between South Carolina and England. Stafford complained that her loneliness was "very terrible at this distance. . . . I despaired of it; my greif was so great I cared not what did become of me." Apologizing for her secretive departure, Stafford begged her cousin to send more letters "because the same kindness you have formerly done me in writing to me, I hope you will continue to me although I have acted soe, and be assured it will be a thousand times more welcome." But in her letter Stafford also asked her female cousin for help in rebuilding her female alliances. She wanted to be remembered to her "pretty Coz[in] Nanny, whom I long to hear of" and "to give my Duty to my Aunt and beg her to forgive me and pray for me, and if she is not soe far disobliged as I durst ask one line and receive it from her hand, I should think my self very happy." She even asked for her cousin's help in negotiating reunions with women who had loaned the Staffords money, asking if her cousin would "be soe kind to give my service to Mrs. Stackden when you see her or any body we are indebted [to]," for, Stafford promised, "our intentions [are] of paying them." Stafford believed that regular correspondence with her female relatives and friends would help her to mitigate the depression and loneliness she faced so far from home. This sentiment was reinforced at the very end of Stafford's letter, where she reported excitedly in a postscript that she had just received a letter from some English friends. These missives had changed her entire outlook. Instead of being filled with grief and despair, Stafford wrote that she could "now tell you how much I am rejoiced I have heard from my friends, it has given us new life, and our business goes on with Courage."[93]

Women's descriptions, languages, and understandings of transatlantic friendship and alliance are attested further in a set of letters written by three London sisters, Jane Bradley, Elizabeth Clarke, and Sueanna Perry, who in the summer of 1729 all wrote to their Aunt Lemmon in the Massachusetts Bay Colony. The sisters and their families were of middling status: Bradley was married to a locksmith, Clarke was the wife of "a Clarke [clerk] to a Virginia Merchant in London," and Perry lived "about 4 miles from London and keeps a Publick House."[94] The three women sought to reestablish contact with their aunt via their correspondence. Perry wanted to know about the status of other long-lost family members, and she asked about "my antte that live[d] in white chapell I can nott tell weather shie is living or dead pray antte I begg the favour to tell mee weare shie live."[95] Clarke asked anxiously if Lemmon had sent any letters in the past and hoped for more in the future, hinting that "we shall be very proud to have a letter from you if you will be so kind to do us the favour of writeing to us." Bradley was the least opaque about her desired favors. She wanted to move to New England, and sought Lemmon's advice about both the transatlantic journey and the prospects for work once the family arrived: "My husband is by trade a Locksmith and understands all manner of smiths work and is thought as ingenious a man as any in Town that way. We are informed it's a Business will answer very well in New England and we are much inclined to goe over to try our fortunes but are doubtfull to Venture without you could gives us some encouragement so beg Madam you'll be so good to answer this letter with the first opportunity."[96] Despite the fact that they had never met their aunt, all three women worked very hard in their letters to create a sense of affection between themselves and their new world relative. Bradley professed herself "very joyfull to hear" of her aunt's health and promised she would "pray God it may continue with you." She signed herself Lemmon's "most affectionate and loveing kinswoman."[97] Clarke told Lemmon that "we have often talk'd of you and should have been very glad to [have] had a corresponce with you" and, although having no personal knowledge of Lemmon's children, sent her "Duty's to you and Love's to our Cousen unkown."[98] Perry called Lemmon her "Honored antte" and presented her "humble duty to you hopping these few lines will finde you in good health," signing herself Lemmon's "loving nice."[99] By professing their affections and love, avowing interest in their aunt's health, flattering her with honorifics, and referencing past conversations about her, the sisters attempted to create a transoceanic female alliance.

Prescriptive and Behavioral Texts

Women learned how to craft alliances in significant measure from another genre of early modern literature: prescription. Although printed conduct books for women had appeared occasionally in fourteenth- and fifteenth-century Britain, by the early modern period the genre had been remade. As Ingrid Tague notes in her work *Women of Quality*, "The conduct manual for women began to develop as a genre during the seventeenth century. It evolved out of two separate but related traditions, courtesy books and pious literature, combining the detailed prescriptions for behavior of the courtesy books with the moralizing tone and emphasis on self-scrutiny of the pious literature."[100] Prescriptive guides for women were published in gradually increasing numbers from the mid-fifteenth century on, but in greatly increased numbers in the late seventeenth century and the early eighteenth. Most ladies' guides were published in London, the center of Britain's publishing world, but some were also printed in British territories across the globe, including Edinburgh, Dublin, Boston, and Williamsburg. In the period covered here, Britain's female population became more and more literate: by 1700 up to three-quarters of women in London were able at least to sign their names, and the city boasted a 25 percent female literacy rate overall.[101] The genre of women's prescriptive literature was a marker of the early modern British cultural world, and has been interpreted by historians of early modern Britain as constitutive of modern gender identity (see introduction).[102]

Although they did not always record which prescriptive works they were reading, a few crucial examples illustrate the centrality and popularity of this genre among female readers of the period. In the 1660s Anne Clifford considered prescriptive texts to be so vital to her identity and self-representation as an elite woman that she included one in her portrait: Clifford's *Great Picture* featured her standing in front of a bookshelf that held an "Epitome of Gerards Herball," a reference to John Gerard's popular *The Herball or Generall Historie of Plantes* (1597).[103] Margaret Hoby, an elite woman from Yorkshire, wrote several times in her early seventeenth-century diary that she had "read of the arball," another probable reference to Gerard's work.[104] Women also excerpted portions from prescriptive texts in their household recipe books. The recipe book kept by Anna Cromwell, Sarah Prentice, Mary Park, and Mary Brigham was started in London in the seventeenth century and was so valued by its owner(s) that it was carried across the Atlantic Ocean to the mainland British American colonies. This well-traveled book included recipes attributed to the "Queens Closet," "Digbys Closset," "Salmons *Polygraphices*," and, most tellingly of all, three recipes that the author recorded had been gathered from "Woolly," a reference to the prolific guidebook author Hannah Woolley.[105]

Hannah Woolley, whose works I discuss extensively below, was the first woman to have broken into the largely masculine business of writing and selling cookery and advice books. She was born in 1622 to what was probably a middling-status family. Like many "middling sort" girls, she spent time in service, working as a maid in the home of a "noble Lady," where she learned skills in cooking and also medicine making, in which she boasted that she excelled. She was married twice, once at the age of twenty-four to a man named Benjamin Woolley, the master of a grammar school, and the second time in 1666 to a man named Francis Chaloner.[106] She wrote seven books, and these appeared in print fourteen times. At least three further titles were attributed to her, all of which were printed in multiple editions; in total, an impressive twenty-four books appeared in her name over a period of almost forty years from 1661 to 1700.[107] Woolley's texts had become so popular by the last two decades of the seventeenth century that her name was synonymous with domestic advice and the conventions of ideal female behavior.

Prescriptive texts like Woolley's devoted long sections to philosophies and styles of female friendship and dispensed information on how to make and keep female friends. The first concern expressed in prescriptive literature about women's friendships was that elite women should choose their friends carefully. In the edition of the *Gentlewomans Companion* of 1675 Woolley told young female readers to "be very cautious in the choice of your Companions . . . have a care with whom you associate."[108] And in 1694 N.H.'s *Ladies Dictionary* echoed this injunction, telling its readers that in matters of friendship, "move very cautiously . . . [and] keep to your self a Reservedness. . . . Choice of this kind ought to be made with the greatest Wariness imaginable."[109] Prescriptive authors impressed wariness and caution on their female readers because they worried about the effect that women had on one another. Polite, well-mannered women were good examples for their friends; but if a woman's female companion began behaving badly, these authors believed, it would reflect poorly on both, for "chusing implieth Approving; and if you fix upon a Lady for your Friend against whom the World shall have given Judgment, 'tis not so well natur'd as to believe you are altogether averse to her way of living."[110] Literate women were expected to ponder, carefully, privately, and thoroughly, the individual merits of potential female companions before they trusted them with friendship.

Evidence from women's manuscripts shows that elite women did seem to absorb this rule and that they exercised caution in finding and making friends. But in so doing, women were able to receive sanction and justification for their relationships. Constantia Fowler, whose passionate friendship with Katherine Thimelby I treated above, wrote that she had begun the relationship only at the urging of her brother, remembering that it was his "most fortunate perswadiance, that first maid me write to her . . . for [he] did desire me many times in most sweet wordes, that I would wright often to her . . . and [he] tould me [he] knew I would not repente my paynes in striving to get in to her esteeme."[111] Fowler's comment that she would take "paynes in striving to get in to [Thimelby's] esteeme" was a reflection of the social mores, laid out in prescriptive literature, which mandated that women should build their female relationships slowly and carefully. In the case of Fowler and Thimelby, it took "many letters . . . betwine us of onely complementle frendship" before the two women formed the intense and loving bond that Fowler later wrote of so passionately.[112] This excerpt from Fowler's letters demonstrates the very real practices of female friendship, but it also divulges that Fowler herself used prescriptive guidelines to sanction her alliances. By writing of the careful choice of her friend and by invoking her brother's "blessing" of the relationship, Fowler justifies the strong bond she shared with Thimelby and imbues their relationship with meaning and weight.

Once literate women had made friends, they were expected to be good ones. Reflecting early modern stereotypes that women were naturally unstable and variable, prescriptive texts taught female readers to adopt behaviors of fidelity and constancy in their relationships. *The Ladies Dictionary* advised elite women to "try all manner of ways the strength and constancy of Fidelity" in their relationships with other women, promising that "Friendship well chosen and placed, is a great felicity of Life."[113] By "try[ing] . . . the strength and constancy" of their friendships, women would prove to one another how seriously they took their bonds. And British women did make pledges of fidelity in their manuscript writings, thereby indicating that they generally followed the guidelines laid out in prescriptive literature. In 1672 Mary Sibbald of Clothall, Hertfordshire, promised Lady Hastings of Donington Park, Derbyshire, that even though miles separated them she would remain a faithful friend, for her affections were inscribed on her "heart . . . written with indelible characters." The distance between Hertfordshire and Derbyshire is about two hours by car today, but the difficulties of early modern travel and the fact that Sibbald was nursing a child meant that the two women visited infrequently: "I dare not call it my unhappynesse that I am a nurce but an hinderance of my happynesse that being soe now I am necessarily kept from waiting on your Ladyship whose sight and converse doth still represent virtue and goodnesse to me."[114] Other women made promises about the length and duration of their friendships. In 1674 Elizabeth Lindsey swore to her friend Lady Danby that she was "most senserly yours till Deth,"[115] and in 1671 Bridget Croft closed her letter to her friend Lucy Hastings with the promise that her devotion "will never end but with the life of [me]."[116] Sudden illness or disaster prompted promises of fidelity and constancy from early modern female correspondents. When she discovered that her friend Mrs. Bowman was dangerously ill, Catherine Caryll swore constancy to Bowman, declaring that she would "perfome my promis I will never forsake you pray beleeve what I say I will make out like a constant freind."[117] By making declarations of fidelity, elite women fostered friendships across wide geographic distances, long stretches of time, and when their friends became ill and incapacitated.

Literate women were thus taught to be selective in choosing their companions and to remain faithful and true to their bonds of friendship. As we have seen, scholars interested in the making of modern European cultures have seized on such dictates as a sign that seventeenth- and eighteenth-century British women were conceptualizing themselves in new ways. Historians, literary critics, and theorists have argued that prescriptive guides caused women readers to become self-critical, self-monitoring, and self-correcting subjects. Although the process of self-consideration and self-improvement urged upon early modern women may have been modern, however, it certainly was not solitary. By disassociating modern gender identity from solitude and by recognizing that women of that era were taught to be sociable, loving, and conscientious of others, the nuances and expectations of modern femininity are revealed. Elite women were taught to monitor themselves but were told simultaneously to monitor the actions, words, and attitudes of their female friends, to think carefully, constantly, and critically about the actions and behaviors of other women. The *Lady's New-years Gift* informed readers that to monitor and, if necessary, to censure female friends was "not only natural but necessary. . . . we cannot avoid giving Judgment in our minds . . . [for] an Aversion to what is Criminal, and a Contempt to what is ridiculous, are the inseparable Companions of Understanding and Virtue."[118] Elite women were reassured that to scrutinize the behaviors of their female friends was natural and desirable as well as rational and virtuous.

Their personal papers attest that elite women did, in fact, practice this type of social surveillance. Anne Montagu criticized her niece Lady Hatton in two letters written around 1680 for acting in ways she considered to be "imprudent" and even "disturbed." Hatton's relationship with her husband had been severely damaged—one letter seems to suggest she had lost a large sum of his money—and this terrified Hatton, prompting her to run away from home. Montagu's reply criticized Hatton's behavior as well as her instinct to flee, characterizing her supposedly overly emotional response as a breach in discretion: "I begg of you not to thinke of stirring from Southampton till you see him. . . . if you goe and miss him, your prudence and descretion will bee much called in question." Criticizing Hatton's actions as scattered, volatile, and impassioned, Montagu snapped, "For God sake compose your thoughts, and give not leave to your passion to disturb you." Montagu's command that Hatton should "give not leave" to her emotions reflects the prescriptive dictum that early modern women should control their thoughts and emotions.[119]

Elite women criticized the individual behaviors of their female companions, but they also found fault with other women's alliance networks as a whole. Proof of this type of expansive criticism can be found in a letter written by the elite Scot Margaret Seton to her daughter-in-law Anna Livingston. Seton believed she had caught her daughter-in-law out in a lie: Livingston had written to her mother-in-law that her children "war all in goode [health]," but Seton had heard conflicting reports from their relative Robert Seton, who had simultaneously written, "Your children had bein seik bothe of ye cauld and sum fever." Livingston had hidden the news of her children's ill health from her mother-in-law, and Seton was furious. Blaming the illness entirely on her daughter-in-law's care of the children, Seton wrote scathingly, "I assud [assure] yow [the sickness proceeds] of nothing bot of evill government and will intreat yow to [take] better care of them in tymes comeing." Seton was especially angry because she felt that her daughter-in-law's alliance network had exerted a bad influence on her. She railed that Livingston paid too much attention to the bad or "conjectured" advice of her friends, which she believed had endangered the children. She told Livingston she should stop "looking to everie ones jeld opinion," and instead seek her mother-in-law's advice.[120] Seton said her opinion could be trusted because "praisit be god all o[u]r children here [have] had nathur cauld nor fever this year, [although it] bothe is and has bene exceeding could and tempestuous." Further proof of Seton's capability in child rearing was to be found in Livingston's own son, who was staying with his grandmother Seton; Seton was sure to inform her daughter-in-law that "your sone Hew [Hugh] is in goode health." Seton finished the chastising letter with a further injunction: "on all occasions . . . acquaint me with your estaits."[121]

This type of surveillance and criticism did not always pass unilaterally from the wealthy to the poor, from elder to younger women, or from those of high to those of low status. Women of lower status could and did serve as a check on the behavior of elite women, especially when they felt that obligations of charity and pity had gone unfulfilled. In 1674 a woman named Mary Man wrote to the women of the Hastings family to request their charity. The Hastings women—Lucy, Countess Huntingdon, and her daughters, Mary and Christiane—were wealthy, well-educated, and powerful. The letter gave no context about Man's background, history, or family, but it did disclose that she and her husband were apparently in dire financial circumstances: "For trade ther is none, or that litle that is scars worth the minding, and them that wee ow mony to will not spair us, my husband has bin arested 3 tims this vacation, and redy to be pulld a peesis for mony." Man could see no way out of her financial crisis and said she had been reduced to selling and pawning her family's possessions to pay off debts: "God helpe us wee have noe way but to sell or paune that wee have till wee cann doe it noe longer." Man needed help, and she wrote to the Hastings women in the hope they would take pity on her. But this letter was seemingly not the first Man had sent. In her note Man referred to earlier, disregarded letters and expressed her anger that "my last letters both to my Lady Huntingdon and your selfe, coold have beget nothing but sillens [silence] from you." She reminded the Hastings women that although she "knoe your Honnors as both vertious and religous and full of piety," God himself would be angry at their refusal, for "wer it with mee as it is with you I shoold thinke if I shoold deall soe with any body that God woold [refuse to] bles mee nor any thing I tooke in hand."[122] Man's jumbled pronouns in this declaration, that "wer it with mee as it is with you I should thinke if I should deall soe," are revealing, for they articulate her adherence to the prescriptive ideal of censure and self-monitoring: reflecting on the behavior of the Hastings women, Man found it to be unconscionable. She then applied the actions of the Hastings women to herself, imagining that if she had denied a charitable request, she would have felt guilty. In many ways Man's letter, which invoked the Christian Golden Rule to do unto others as you would have them do unto you, is a perfect example of the type of social surveillance advocated by prescriptive texts. In the letter, Man criticized the Hastings women by focusing attention on their supposedly unfeminine behaviors, that is, their lack of sympathy, care, and support. This attitude adhered to prescriptive ideals, but it had a very real and practical payoff: by chastising the Hastings women, the lower-status Man not only exerted moral superiority over the higher-status Hastings women but also leveraged this position in hopes of obtaining a financial reward.

Prescriptive literature played a critical, complex role in early modern female alliances. It offered a language of friendship to elite women. Availing themselves of gendered stereotypes that women were emotionally fickle and unpredictable, ladies' guides counseled women to forge friendships cautiously and to practice strict fidelity. Furthermore, demonstrating that assumptions about the private, solitary nature of modern identity creation are problematic, prescriptive texts taught women to place themselves in constant community by tracking the actions of their friends. Women did in many cases adopt these guidelines, sometimes for emotional reasons and sometimes surely for practical ones, as they allowed them to create and preserve their female alliances. Like the neoclassical, spiritual, physiological, and epistolary ideas that circulated in other texts, prescriptive literature afforded women a fundamental linguistic framework for articulating and understanding female friendship.

Women could draw on diverse, complex intellectual traditions in thinking and writing about friendship. Although ostensibly excluded from philosophies and theologies of masculine friendship, some women did borrow from classical and religious discourses as well as those on vernacular medicine, letter writing, and prescription in order to elucidate their same-sex bonds. As Anne Dormer wrote to her beloved sister Elizabeth Trumbull, "Friendship is the strongest and neerest tie . . . nature, obligation, and thy owne vertue engage me so many wayes to thee, [that] I may truely say I value thee by many degrees."[123]

2. Noble Presents: Gender, Gift Exchange, and the Reappropriation of Luxury

In the account book she kept between 1687 and 1692 Margaret Seyliard recorded her most valuable possessions. Dividing these objects into two categories, "severall small things that were my Ladys before marriage," and "things bought by my Lady since a Widdow," Seyliard kept record of the objects that structured her life.[1] Portraits of her grandparents and parents, uncles, sisters, and brothers—some of which she proudly listed as having been painted by Godfrey Kneller, portraitist to Charles II—were followed by luxury items such as flaxen sheets, eighteen yards of "coors" (silk) cloth, an image of "The Virgin Mary in a gilt leather Frame," and white marble mortars.[2] Some of Seyliard's cherished goods came from abroad: "A Japan Beaker," "four china Tee Cups," and "Two chocolate cups Red Portugal china." Seyliard occasionally listed the provenance of these objects; the flaxen sheets had been "spun in the house," and Seyliard's silk cloth had been "made out by Mrs. Harrey into Towels & Dresser cloths." But one of the longest entries concerned a gift Seyliard had received. Under those goods she had acquired "since a Widdow" Seyliard included "a wax work head in a glass on a stand, made and presented by my Lady Prat's Granddaughter."[3]

Seventeenth- and eighteenth-century elite women's diaries, account books, correspondence, and spiritual journals contain hundreds of short references to gifts like the one recorded by Seyliard. But the records of exchange in most women's writings are fragmentary at best, for these women rarely recorded exactly why they were given certain items.[4] A typical entry about gifts given or received in an elite woman's diary, account book, or letter consisted of only a few words. Seyliard herself never recorded why the wax head was given to her, and her relationships to any of the donors listed in her account book are almost impossible to determine; this lack of detail might seem to limit the research that can be done on gift objects. It is easier for us to assess the significance of certain objects; portraits, for example, particularly if they were painted by famous artists, are objects we value even today. But Seyliard listed the gift of this handmade, waxwork head (under glass, no less) right alongside her most important possessions. The custom of gift making and giving was a critical part of female sodality, communication, and experience in this period.[5] By gathering together the many fragments of gift references found in women's writings and examining how women constructed and then used these presents, it is possible to read their expressions of the gifts' value in creating or maintaining alliances and to consider the sentiments women attached to presents.[6]

I will consider four specific gift objects that four seventeenth- and eighteenth-century women made or used and then recorded in their writings: a jar of marmalade, a bottle of perfume, a piece of embroidery, and a painted picture. These gift objects have been chosen for their utility in reflecting women's experiences. They disclose the spaces and locations of women's labor: gifts made in the kitchen and those made in the still-room; gifts created in the company of other women; and those made in and for the private closet. But they also illuminate different types and methods of women's work: cooking, distilling, sewing, and painting. Prescriptive literature often divided the manufacture of gift objects according to these categories. And, last, they coordinate with four senses that were crucial to elite identity in the period: taste, smell, touch, and sight.[7] Elites of the period prided themselves on the refinement and cultivation of these senses, which they believed set them apart from people of lower status; female alliances based on the cultivation of these senses were socially exclusive. An analysis of some of the details of the gift objects women made and then exchanged—for instance, their ingredients and composition and the specific skills needed for their correct manufacture—will show that these four gifts were the result of much specialized and gendered work.

Gift exchange has become recognized recently as an important subject of historical inquiry. Charitable donations, posthumous gifts in wills, book offerings, exchanges of scientific specimens, local poor relief, and New Year's gifts have been rich sources of study and have helped to uncover the importance of ritual, sympathy, tangibility, ceremony, and symbolism in early modern Europe and colonial British America.[8] But while these projects have all helped to indicate the meanings and weight accorded to gifts in the seventeenth and eighteenth centuries, no study has treated the giving of gifts as an explicitly gendered practice, and few have explored the special role gifts played in the British world at that time, when new and fashionable consumer goods from across the Atlantic and Pacific flooded British markets; these objects redefined notions of taste and luxury and were a source of new materials for the creation of gifts.[9]

Women who were able to profit from the abundance of these new goods made and then gave away as gifts sugared fruits, embroidered silk and linen, colorfully painted mirror frames, and distilled perfumes. These presents were expensive, but they were also handcrafted, the products of much labor and considerable skill. And since they were made of new, transoceanic products they became expressions of taste, a demonstration of refined and polite cultural norms. I will therefore trace some of what Linda Levy Peck has called "the cultural mentalities . . . that supported luxury consumption."[10] Examination of some of women's "cultural mentalities" surrounding gift exchange proves that women participated in what I call the reappropriation of luxury goods, that is, the manipulation, alteration, and repurposing of finished products. Many scholars have stressed the importance of consumption in the seventeenth and eighteenth centuries, arguing that the proliferation of the "new world of goods" in early modern Europe and its colonies was responsible for the creation of "a new sort of man (and woman): *homo edens*, the consumer."[11] But a growing scholarship on used-goods markets in early modern Europe has begun to undermine the traditional reading of seventeenth-century Britons as obsessed exclusively with the purchase of new goods in the "consumer revolution" of the late seventeenth century.[12] Peck herself argues that the "re-label[ling]" and "demoralization" of luxury goods, such as the kind used by women in the creation of presents, were prevalent in the seventeenth and eighteenth centuries. She contends that British elites relabeled luxury items as "rich, new, innovative, curious, rare, fine, refined, polite, comfortable, and imported" as a way of refurbishing luxury, of making acceptable practices that had previously been considered sinful, selfish, and decadent.[13] We will see how elite women took this practice one step further in reappropriating the goods themselves, by changing them, manipulating them, and adding to them, in order to make their presents morally acceptable.

Most central to the concerns of this chapter, however, is how gift exchange created and maintained female alliances. Creating and then giving presents enabled women to deepen the same-sex bonds they shared with one another. Gifts that were attributable to friends were valued by elite women beyond their market prices, as they were treasured for the time and skill spent in their production.[14] My argument about the valuing of labor in the creation of gifts, rather than emphasizing the weight of consumption in purchasing ready-made presents, has been influenced by Lewis Hyde, whose literary and philosophical anthropology of gift exchange claims in part that the value of gift objects lies in their production, in the act of artistic creativity that is nurtured or exposed during the gift's creation. Hyde argues that such created gifts are always separated from commodities because they engender community ties and positive emotional connections; he claims that this emotional "gift bond . . . precedes or is created by donation and that it is absent, suspended, or severed in commodity exchange."[15] He also genders this practice, writing that the "kind of emotional or spiritual commitment" that is required in "gift labor" is often gendered feminine.[16] I will endorse, historicize, and extend this insight, explicating the bonds, alliances, and friendships generated by those seventeenth- and eighteenth-century elite women who created and offered presents. Early modern British women made and then exchanged gifts in large part in order to cultivate meaningful relationships.

The Gift of Marmalade

On October 25, 1617, Anne Clifford wrote that she "gave [several visiting female friends] some marmalade of Quinces for about this time I made much of it."[17] Clifford's record of a gift of marmalade affords a good example of the gendered and sociable ties that were created when early modern women gave the gift of fruits and preserves.[18] Marmalades, sweetmeats, comfits, and conserves, the sugared and preserved yield of fruit trees, were early modern delicacies. When women gave these objects, they manifested their social position and wealth in two ways: first, in their associations with the fruits themselves and, second, in their extravagant use of sugar. Consumable gifts such as these were meant to signal a woman's culinary acumen, but they were also intended to convey a sociable and affectionate taste. When women gave gifts of fruit and confection, they worked to reinforce the ties, both emotional and social, which bound them together.[19]

Elite girls were taught that the preparation of edible products and especially of sugared fruits was a woman's art. Women worked extensively in gardens watering, weeding, and fruit picking (see chapter 3), but here I focus on women's cooking and preservation of the produce of their orchards and yards. Works of prescriptive literature suggested that a so-called useful woman was one who managed her household's produce carefully and thriftily. Richard Allestree's *Ladies Calling* (1696) suggested that "the art of Oeconomy and household managery [is] . . . the most proper Feminine business, from which neither wealth nor greatness can totally absolve them."[20] But while elite women were encouraged to refine their skills in food production and practice economy as part of "the most proper Feminine business," elite men were, in contrast, actively discouraged from participating in culinary work. Male prescriptive literature is striking in its silence about the preparation of foods.[21] These prescriptive prejudices were borne out in early modern women's manuscripts. Anne Dormer ridiculed her husband for his culinary interests, confessing to her sister that his fascination with cooking was a troubling and aggravating sign of a selfish desire to "please his fancy": "Mr. D is now much taken with all sorts of cookery and spends all his ingenuity in finding out the most comodious way of frying broileing rosting stewing and preserving his whole studdy is to please his fancy in every thing and by runing away from all things that might shew him his errors." Dormer's experiments in food production were quickly and harshly condemned by his wife as lazy and even ruinous, a waste of "all his ingenuity." Dormer equated her husband's cooking activity not with female industriousness but with idleness, wasteful luxury, and indulgence. She was particularly put off by his fascination with sugared confection and fruit preserves, adding derisively, "[He] loiters aboute, somtimes stues prunes, som times makes chocalate, and this somer he is much taken with preserving."[22]

Prescriptive cooking guides dictated which types of women were supposed to cook and in which ways. In these books, higher-status women were allowed to avoid heavy, greasy, tedious cooking tasks, jobs that were supposed to be relegated to under-cook maids or scullery maids. For these unprivileged women Woolley included in her guidebook "instructions for such who desire to be . . . cook-maids in good and great houses," which the author declared was an employment intended for women called drudges and was work which made women "greasie and smutty." These women were told that their "skill will consist in dressing all sorts of Meat, both Fish, Flesh and Fowl, all manner of Baked-meats, all kind of Sawces . . . and making all manner of Pickles."[23] Wrestling with large, heavy beef or mutton haunches, swinging them on greasy metal spits over open, roaring fires, cook-maids and under-cook-maids faced hot, filthy, dangerous work; and the labor of pickling vegetables in huge vats of pungent, stinging, caustic brines was surely both grueling and painful. These were tasks prescribed for women of lower status.

Fruit work, like candying, sugaring, and preserving, was figured differently. Woolley's sections on "Candying, Conserving and Preserving" were considered by the author to be "not only laudable, but requisite and necessary in young Ladies and Gentlewomen," and her book included directions on how to preserve barberries, pears, green pippin apples, black cherries, mulberries, apricots, and gooseberries as well as recipes for "oranges and lemons preserved," and "how to candy all sorts of flowers as they grow with their stalks on."[24] The creation of sugared fruits, herbs, and flowers was designated only for higher-status women. In the first stages of this process, the possession and cultivation of fruiting bushes and trees were a demonstration of the wealth an early modern family possessed. As Stephen Mennell writes, consumables in this period were vehicles for "the expression of social distance."[25] Nourishing horticultural delicacies in England's cooler northern climate was not a feasible activity for individuals of lower status, who, lacking both the means and the architectural structures necessary for horticultural cultivation, typically grew and ate very little fruit.[26]

Elite women frequently gave one another fresh fruit, and when they wrote of these consumable gifts they also, crucially, referenced the personal interactions and alliances they shared with one another. Combining humble self-effacement with an invocation of visits the two had shared in the past, Bridget Croft wrote to her friend Mary Hastings that she had "sent . . . a baskett of very good frute a pleasenter entertainment I am sure in it selfe then my company."[27] In procuring a fruit gift for a female friend, Katherine Oxenden asked her mother to help her obtain the valuable product while also maintaining the pleasant surprise of the gift: "I would desire you to send mee some quinces by the bearer hereof if you have any they are for my Lady Oxinden but shee knows not of my sending."[28] Exchanges of fruit were apparently considered to be so vital to female friendship that when women were unable to supply one another with these gifts they wrote of their embarrassment and disappointment. Anne North apologized to her daughter when she neglected to send her "cuttings" from grapevines, writing that she was "very sorry I did not send you some cuttings of the raison grape which I think is excellent, and bunches so big that every one way a great many pounds."[29] And Elizabeth Wood wrote disappointedly to her mother that, despite her best efforts, her attempts to give her a gift of citrus fruit had gone awry, for she had not been able to find "not one orring [orange] nor one lemon to be got in the town," going on to reassure her that "if ther had bin any you should have had them before."[30]

Early modern women saw fruit as a highly desirable gift, but, then as now, raw fruits had to be preserved if they were to be enjoyed for any length of time. This required enormous quantities of sugar. The amounts of sugar called for in British recipes of the period were an indulgence and extravagance, even for those who had the means to afford them.[31] Sugar had become more widely available in Great Britain by the 1660s, when British West Indian colonies in Barbados and the Leeward Islands shifted from tobacco to sugar production and began shipping greater quantities of the sweet substance to Britain.[32] The product of exploitative transatlantic slave labor, sugar increased in availability during the second half of the seventeenth century, but its consumption in Britain was still restricted by status. Wealthy individuals bought sugar by the loaf, each loaf ranging in weight from three to fourteen pounds. Lower-status families could only afford "scraped" sugar, which was scratched off of a common, store-owned loaf and sold in small quantities inside paper packets. Taxes on the refined product remained high throughout the seventeenth and early eighteenth centuries, ensuring that the confection remained an expensive commodity even in small quantities: "In practice most . . . [sugar] went to the wealthy classes; for the cost of a pound was at least a shilling," a significant expense for most early modern Britons.[33]

This expensive product often was entrusted to women. In her article "The Gendering of Sugar in the Seventeenth Century," Kim F. Hall explains these associations of female identity, medical labor, and making confection, observing that "confectionery provided individual English women with a venue for social and artistic self-expression. . . . it was also an arena where women asserted their own agency and hospitality was visibly a mode of creativity as well as care for others."[34] Sugar was a commodity that could remind women of the ties they shared while simultaneously helping them to create new ones. It had what Sidney Mintz has characterized as "social worth." Mintz determines that "food preferences are close to the center of . . . self-definition," and early modern foods like sugar helped to "validate the social worth of the links that [bound people] together."[35] This was also true of women's experiences in early modern Britain. Sugar work and confectionary drew women together, helping them to form alliances.

Sugar was used extensively in preserving fruits. The prescriptive author Gervase Markham wrote a recipe in 1615 for "Marmalade of quinces red," illuminating the process women would have gone through as well as the ingredients they would have used to create fruit marmalades, jellies, and candies: "Take a pound of quinces and cut them in halves . . . then take a pound of sugar and a quart of fair water and put them all into a pan . . . when it beginneth to be thick then break your quinces, with a slice or a spoon . . . and then strew a little fine sugar in your box's bottom, and so put it up."[36] In this recipe copious amounts of sugar were used both in the mixture itself and for the purpose of forming a light crust around the bottom edge of the finished marmalade. Sugar was the vital ingredient in most early modern preserving and conserving, and a pound of sugar per every pound of fruit was fairly standard in most of Markham's marmalade recipes. Woolley's recipe for "Quince Marmalade" called for the maker to "put white Sugar to it, as much as you please."[37] Considering the character of the British-grown quince, this amount could have been quite considerable; as Martin Crawford states in his article on quinces, "In warm temperate and tropical regions, the fruits can become soft, juicy, and suitable for eating raw; but in cooler temperate areas like Britain, they do not ripen so far. Here, raw quince fruits are hard, gritty, harsh and astringent."[38]

So when Lady Hewytt thanked her sister Dorothy Barrington for the gift of sugared "orringe caks" in 1675, she expressed an appreciation for the gift on two levels. Oranges at that time, like quinces, were sour and small. When Hewytt wrote of the sweet orange cakes, she implicitly recognized and appreciated her sister's wealth by acknowledging the presence of sugar in the orange confection. But, simultaneously, Hewytt worked to reinforce their mutual female ties and skills, praising her sister's unique abilities in the creation of the cakes alongside her polite thanks for the luxury gift: "Deare sister you daily obledge me by your great kindness, I am troubled I can returne nothinge but thankes; these orringe caks I now received . . . are the best I thinke you ever made, none can exceed you in it."[39] In her seventeenth-century writings, the gentlewoman Elizabeth Freke combined the presentation of sugared confection with memory and sororal affection. She noted in her diary that she had sent to her sister in London "a box of suger cakes [and] 30–0–0 to buy her something to remember me by."[40] In mid-seventeenth-century Scotland, Elizabeth Ker wrote to Margaret Scott to offer her both candied orange peels and friendship: "I heve now som mor peils then I had: call for what I here can sarf you in it if ye thenk me your frend."[41] In 1660 Elizabeth Wood told Katherine Oxenden that she would give her confectionery as soon as she could arrange for transport: "I shall send you a few cumfits when wee can send the box for then they will be brought safe."[42] And in the 1680s Mary Leke, when sending a gift of marmalade to multiple women—her much-loved but emotionally fragile sister, her sister's children, and a mutual female friend—took visible pride in and drew attention to the fact that the jam had been her own creation, writing proudly that it was "every bett of my one making." This worthy feat had been accomplished, Leke continued, despite the fact that it had been a bad horticultural year, for "thare is a littel other [fruit] that I fer is very naught for thes year we had very littel frut and what was you will finde was starke naught." Although she felt let down by the produce of her orangery, Leke teased her sister affectionately while also referring to their mutual female friend, a woman named Mrs. Arnald, telling her that "for you thare is sex [six] litel pots but thre [three] are for Mrs. Arnald which I desire you will let stay feall [full]. . . . the pots are marked which are for you and the others for her." Leke continued the joke by reassuring her sister: "I have sent [your children] each a littel pott of marmalett and for fe[a]re that you shud crye for some I have sent you some [too]."[43]

Wealthy women prided themselves on the hard-won produce of their orchards and hothouses and embraced those kitchen tasks which called for the use of expensive goods like fruits, flowers, and sugars. But gifts made of these commodities, because they were so representative of elite status, could also be misunderstood and resented. When fruits and confections were made or given by lower-status women, the activities and products of that labor could be viewed with distrust. An early seventeenth-century cheap-print pamphlet, Stephen Bradwell's *Mary Glovers Late Woeful Case*, related how "an old Charewoman" named Elizabeth Jackson came under suspicion when she "sent Marie Glover an Orange, as in token of kindenes, and the maide tooke it so kindely that she kept it in her hand, smellinge ofte unto it." That a poor woman like Jackson could own—and then give away!—such an expensive object was so inconceivable that it became sinister; and, indeed, instead of acting as a token of alliance and kindness, the inappropriate gift was depicted as a tool of malicious cruelty. Bradwell informed his readers that "afterward the same hand, arme and whole side" with which Glover had held the fruit "were deprived of feeling and moving."[44] Elite confection became suspect in another pamphlet, the *True Narrative of the sorceries and witchcrafts exercis'd . . . upon Mrs. Christian Shaw* (1698). In this text a diabolical elite woman threatened the young Christian Shaw by "promising her Almonds and other sweet-meats." But when she attempted to consume these treats, Shaw was choked and poisoned: "The Girle being seiz'd with sore Fits, something was seen in her mouth like pieces of Orange-Pills [peels], which were Invisibly convey'd thither; she seem'd; in her Agonies to Chew them; and having got them down her Throat, she fell down as if she had been Choak't, strugling with her Feet and Hands . . . and would say, O it was a very sweet Orange-Pill which I got from the Gentlewoman."[45] It is possible to read in this account the type of "inversion narrative" that was prevalent in many seventeenth- and eighteenth-century witchcraft accusations, with the figure of the unnaturally harmful gentlewoman standing in opposition to the hospitality and generosity that was expected of elite women in this period.[46] But fictional stories like *Mary Glover* and *Christian Shaw* are also illustrative of how rigidly elite practices and skills associated with fruits and preserving were assigned to women of high status.

And so when Anne Clifford gave her female friends marmalade in 1617, she was combining preserving and candying with communication and female sociability and with the creation of elite roles and identities. The wealthy, well-educated Clifford (1590–1676) was the daughter of the Earl of Cumberland, and her first husband was the Earl of Dorset. She shared an uneasy relationship with both her natal and married families. Clifford's extensive manuscript papers document disagreements with family members over inheritance issues, estate management, child care, and personal comportment, and her diaries record the many instances in which she "fell out" with her husband and their relatives. In October 1617, when Clifford presented the marmalade to her female friends, she was living on her husband's estate in Dorset. Isolated from the few family members and friends with whom she sympathized, Clifford wrote in her diary of feeling alone and sad, "thinking the time to be very tedious."[47] When Clifford recorded her present of quince marmalade in her personal daily diary, the sentences surrounding provision of marmalade hint at the weightiness of this gift to Clifford and to the greater importance of gift exchange to her own alliances: "Upon the 25th, being Saturday, [came] my Lady Lisle, my Lady ___ [blank in manuscript], my Coz. Barbara Sidney. I walked with them all the wildernesse over & had much talk with her of my Coz. Clifford & many other matters. They saw the Childe and much commended her. I gave them some marmalade of Quinces for about this time I mad[e] much of it."[48] Clifford wrote of the bestowal of the present within the context of a visit, in which three elite women, at least one of whom was a female relative of Clifford's, traveled to Dorset to socialize with her at her home. The women spent time walking together out of doors, talking, and exchanging information. The relationships this incident uncovers are suggestive of alliance and friendly support. And for Clifford this was a positive event, as is evident in the visitors' treatment of Clifford's daughter Margaret, called "the Childe" in the manuscript. As Clifford recorded, the women "saw the Childe and much commended her," suggesting that in addition to walking and chatting together the women may well have exchanged information about child-rearing practices and certainly provided emotional support to Clifford through their commendation of her child. The visit was then recorded as concluded with a gift that was both luxurious and handmade and that Clifford was careful to note was of her own creation. It is also possible to read into Clifford's comment that she had "about this time . . . made much" marmalade an off-handed rejection of luxury; like Margaret Scott's assurance that she had "now som mor peils then I had [previously]," Clifford depicted herself as thrifty and generous, sharing the produce of her labor with her friends when she had excess. By the end of this meeting, Clifford and her female friends had affirmed their alliances, and gift giving was central to the interaction.

The Gift of Perfume

In 1662 Ann Fanshawe recorded in her travel diary that she had received a scented gift from a female friend, the "Abadessa of the Alcantra, neece to the Qween Mother [of Portugal]." Fanshawe wrote that the gift was "a very noble present" and that it consisted of "perfumes, waters, and sweet meats."[49] Perfumes and scents were complex cultural media in early modern Britain. In her recent book *The Ephemeral History of Perfume*, the literary critic Holly Dugan asserts that "scents are cultural materials worthy of historical investigation," and she argues that "early modern English had a precise language of olfaction that described the powerful and invisible interaction between scents and people."[50] When Fanshawe noted the apparent nobility of the gift of perfumes, she flattered the abbess while writing simultaneously of her appreciation for the gift. But Fanshawe's comment was also a reflection of her own self-perceived femininity, taste, and refinement. Exchanging scented gifts—objects such as perfumes, waters, oils, and scented clothing items—enabled women to forge friendships based on what they assumed were mutual sensitivities, tastes, and affinities.

The making of perfumes and scented waters in the early modern period required specialized, expensive equipment. Perfumes, oils, and waters were often made in a still, a teardrop-shaped metal container with a long downward spout.[51] Although today we identify distillery with the creation of alcohol, in early modern Europe stills were frequently used to create perfumes. Scented herbs, spices, and flowers that had been steeped in water or alcohol were placed inside the bulbous body of the still and allowed to simmer over a low heat for several hours. The steam and oil that rose out of the hot liquid collected at the still's spigot, located near the top of the metal bulb. Essential oils and concentrated liquids coalesced out of the steam and dripped down the spout; these materials were then collected in a separate container. Woolley's *Ladies Directory* included a recipe for a "rare sweet water" that required marjoram, basil, lavender, rosemary, muscovy, maudlin, balm, thyme, walnut leaves, and damask roses. Readers were told to distill these ingredients "with a soft fire" and to let the distilled, scented liquid drop on "a little Musk in a piece of laun [lawn]." The resulting perfume, Woolley promised, could be used either "among your cloathes, or mix it with sweet oyles, and burn it at your pleasure."[52]

Many advice books offered women guidelines for the creation of scented presents at home. An author called Hieronymous Brunschwig, whose instruction manual was one of the first books printed in English to be devoted entirely to distillery, provided illustrations for many styles of stills in his *The Vertuose Boke of Distillacyon* (1527).[53] While Brunschwig's sixteenth-century work was intended for both male and female distillers, prescriptive literature intended entirely for women also featured lengthy sections on distilling. Thomas Dawson's *Good Housewife's Jewel* (1596) promised advice on "the way to distill many precious waters." The second edition of this same work, published in 1606, additionally promised to disclose the "most apt and readiest wayes to distill many wholesome and sweete waters."[54] Seventeenth- and eighteenth-century women were expected to use works like these in order to learn how to construct the type of distilling furnaces required to make oils, perfumes, and waters.

Woolley's *Gentlewomans Companion* of 1673 contained a section on distillation, detailing lessons on the extracting of oils and essences from flowers, fruits, and herbs, and this portion of the book was addressed to "Ladies." The association of distillation with elites, especially urban elites, was so strong that Woolley addressed her lengthy section on distillation to "the benefit and study of Court Ladies and City madams." In contrast, Woolley's explanation of the care of cows and dairies was a literary journey "into the Country, [to] find out something worthy the observation of a Rural Gentlewoman."[55] The assumption that urban life was more sophisticated than life in the country and that urban spaces needed fumigation and improve- ment of smell is borne out in women's writings; making a list of "Apparell and necessarys [for] coming to town," Hellena Dering included "2 p[air] of perfumed gloves."[56] But whether they lived in the country or the city, elite women especially were urged to distill alongside their other household tasks, partially because it allowed them to make medicinal waters. Markham consid- ered distilling and scenting an essential skill for elite women and assured his female readers that distilling equipment was an important household item: "I would have her furnish herself of very good stills, for the distillation of all kinds of waters, which stills would be either of tin, or sweet earth. . . . in [stills] she shall distil all sorts of waters meet for the health of her household."[57]

Although promoting health was a central goal, it was not the sole reason that gentlewomen manufactured scented goods. Much prescriptive literature focused on the cosmetic products of distillation. In his *English Housewife* Markham listed eight waters that were to be distilled for medicinal purposes but then went on to relate twelve recipes for items whose purpose was to create a pleasant odor. He discussed perfume and several kinds of soap and even gave explicit instructions on scenting or perfuming items of clothing, such as gloves and jerkins. These were meant to improve the scent of the human body and to create an aura of cleanliness and fragrance. Markham's scented clothes were not merely presentations or objects of worth but also intended to be practical items, used and worn by their owners. His recipe "to perfume gloves" instructed that once the gloves had been scented, the female reader should "let them dry in your bosom, and so after use them at your pleasure."[58] Considering that the glove recipe contained sizable amounts of cloves, musk, rose water, and almond oil, the scent produced must have been highly noticeable; the enjoinder to "let them dry in your bosom" indicates the proximity which this scent was supposed to have to the human body.

Perfumes were lauded by prescriptive authors as desirable products of transatlantic and transpacific trade. Woolley's *Queen-Like Closet* (1672) contained four perfume recipes that utilized goods shipped from overseas: "Perfumed Roses," "Court Perfumes," "Damask Powder," and "Perfume to Burn." Each of these called for the use of Benjamin, also known as Storax (*Styrax benzoin*) or candlewood (*Gomphia guianensis*). *Styrax benzoin* is a scented shrub found in Sumatra, and *Gomphia guianensis* is a type of slow-burning, fragrant pine native to Jamaica and South America.[59] In the early modern period both plants became prized for their use in scented goods and perfumes. Woolley's recipe for "Perfumed Roses," for example, called for her readers to steep rosebuds in "water wherein hath been steeped Benjamin Storax, *Lignum Rhodium*, Civet or Musk." The relative potency of these new goods may have accounted for their popularity; the "three ounces of Benjamin" required in Woolley's recipe for "Court Perfumes" was so strong-smelling that readers were told to "dry them very well and keep them to burn, one at a time is sufficient." Woolley advised her readers to use these exotic perfumes alongside other luxury goods; her recipe for "an excellent Damask Powder" called for two ounces of candlewood and was supposedly "a very fine Powder to lay among Linnen."[60]

Markham's further explanation of the use of scent displays another reason elite women were expected to create and to wear perfumes. Markham insisted that all of his recipes "will make the most delicatest perfume *that may be without any offence*, and will last the longest of all other sweet perfumes, as hath been found by experience."[61] The desire was to scent pleasantly or, literally, as the author stated, to avoid making "any offence" to other people through objectionable body, hair, or skin odors. The abhorrence of unpleasant smells and more important, the appreciation of agreeable ones developed throughout the seventeenth century and the eighteenth as a specialized appreciation and delicacy. Alain Corbin describes a process in which a gradual "repugnance to 'social emanations' " developed in early modern Europe, creating within elite society the perception of a cultivated and heightened sense of smell.[62] Indeed, even the use and appreciation of perfumes was itself a social and hierarchical distinction, for while lower-status, laboring women and men were frequently associated with the smells of their trade, higher-status people were coupled with scents like "perfume, [which was] linked with softness, disorder, and a taste for pleasure, [and] was the antithesis of work."[63] Scent permeated the mental and physical worlds of the female elite so completely that in 1675 the *Gentlewomans Companion* even counseled young female Britons to "preserve those precious odours of your good name."[64]

While pleasant smells were desired by higher-status people of both genders, it was, again, women's literature which discussed the details of constructing scent, while prescriptive sources written for male audiences mentioned nothing on this topic. The production of perfume was understood as a female concern. In fact, the production of scented luxury items was apparently so popular and "fashionable" among higher-status women that some prescriptive authors felt it necessary to curb such behavior; by 1673 Richard Allestree's *Ladies Calling* impressed upon women the need to make sweet-smelling medicines rather than just cosmetic perfumes: "and sure, tho it be a less fashionable, 'tis a much better sight to see a Lady binding up a sore, than painting her face; and she will cast a much sweeter savour in God's nostrils, with the smell of unguents and balsoms, than with the most exquisite odours and perfumes."[65]

Prescriptive works thus recommended, at least in moderation, the practice of making and wearing perfumes. And early modern British women's manuscripts provide proof that they followed this prescription and that they used perfumes as gifts in order to create and maintain female alliances. Ann Egerton's handwritten recipe book included instructions on how to make "a Spanish perfume," which, she wrote, she had learned from her friend Lady Lyinborrow. Egerton's book also had a recipe for scented hair pomade that was called "the Lady Riches Pomatom." Egerton's apparent elite sensitivity to smell (and, specifically, her revulsion to unpleasant smell) can be read out of a recipe she received from a female friend named Mrs. Hews; the recipe simply read, the "Stincking Drinck."[66] For Egerton and her friends, making and appreciating perfumes were activities associated with female sociability. A recipe book shared by two women, Anne Lovelace and Cecilia Haynes, contained similar scent recipes, each attributed to female friends. These included "a resait to make the Ladey Lovlesis fine pomatum" and "My Lady Ogles perfume to burn."[67]

To return to the gift of perfumes that Ann Fanshawe received from her friend the abbess, one can find additional information about Fanshawe's friendly alliances and her sense of her elite identity through close study of the context of her diary entry. Fanshawe (1625–80) was a wealthy, well-traveled woman. She was born in London the daughter of a knight and married Richard Fanshawe, a prominent Royalist and ambassador, in 1644. Fanshawe recorded the gift of perfumes in her diary in August 1662, while her husband was acting as England's ambassador to Portugal. Fanshawe had traveled with her husband to his post in Lisbon and was surrounded by women of different nationalities, languages, and faiths.[68] When she recorded receiving "a very noble present of perfumes [and] waters" from the abbess, she added information about the reason for the gift, writing that the abbess had given her the present "to welcome mee into the country" and that the two remained friends, for "during my abode in Lisbone we often made visits and enterchanged messages to my great content, for she was a very fine lady."[69] Fanshawe's simultaneous recording of the gift with mention of the many "visits and enterchanged messages" the two women shared, references the alliance that engendered the fragrance of scented perfume. This itself uncovers the ties that gifts could create and maintain. But Fanshawe's further comment, that the Portuguese woman was "a very fine lady," as well as her opinion that the perfume was a "very noble present" suggest that Fanshawe viewed the gift as an elite creation. Fanshawe's perfumes were offered with the understanding that pleasing odors could be appreciated and desired by two high-status women of different nationalities. Perfumes were markers of wealth and status and were given with the understanding that the women shared senses of distinction, common sensitivities, and allied tastes.

The Gift of Embroidery

At the end of the seventeenth century Jane Hooke wrote a letter of gratitude to her friend and patron Johana Barrington, who had just sent her a gift of embroidered cloth. Delighted at the present, Hooke expressed her "most humble and harty thanks" for the gift, which she acknowledged was "so much linnin" that she felt unworthy of the present, obliging her to "confes that I com short of deserving any thing good madam."[70] Elites found certain gifts to be pleasant to touch as well as look at, including needleworked book covers, embroidered hats and bodices, needle cases, and clothing, objects which were sewn, stitched, and knitted. This exchange will exhibit gift labor from the perspective of the recipient (Hooke) rather than of the donor (Barrington); and as Hooke was probably of lower social status than her patron Barrington, this will help to illuminate some of the ways in which women's cloth and clothing gifts were used to negotiate differences in status.

In a period in which dress and clothing were determined by socioeconomic status, gifts of clothing betrayed complicated and weighty messages about makers and recipients.[71] As Alan Hunt indicates in his history of early modern sumptuary regulation, objects like Hooke's present were "one of the basic mechanisms that provid[ed] for the legibility of sex and gender."[72] Like gifts of taste and smell, presents of embroidery helped women to construct and maintain social alliances. When receiving needlework and embroidery, early modern women would also have recognized the gift as a product of communal manufacture: women of both high and low status sewed to clothe their friends and families, and they often undertook this activity in groups.[73] Gifts of embroidery therefore both facilitated and provided evidence of women's homosocial networks. But, following Hunt's argument, I will also establish how gifts of embroidery contributed to the identification and regulation of gender in the seventeenth and eighteenth centuries. Sewing was an activity that was supposed to facilitate feminine patience, temperance, and an attention to thrifty utility. A handwrought gift implied that the present was the product of an idealized and productive female community as much as it was of fine thread or cloth.

Women's manuscripts of the era divulge that elite women did associate needlework and needleworked gifts with positive female alliances. When women wrote of embroidered or needlepointed gifts they had received, they often did so with reference to multiple women. When Bridget Cadogan wrote to thank her sister for the gift of an embroidered needle case, she addressed the letter to a mutual friend of theirs, a Mrs. Hays. She asked Hays to communicate her thanks for the gift, which she professed she liked not only for its visual elegance but also because it would make her a more skilled needleworker: "[As for] my scister . . . pray give my moct humble service to her, her pretty presant of the needle booke maks me a very good workewoman and makes mee carefull of my needles."[74] Similarly, when Elizabeth

Montague received an embroidered slip from her cousin Hillary Hatton, she wrote to a mutual female relative in order to convey her thanks. Invoking alliances with two separate women simultaneously, Montague asked her friend Lady Hatton to "doe me the favour to return my thanks to Cousen Hilee Hatton for the slip which I think very pretty."[75]

This sort of evidence is, in itself, illustrative of the alliances created through the exchange of embroidered gifts. But when writing about needlework or embroidery they had received as a gift, women placed emphasis on the fact that the items had been made by someone known to them. The personalized nature of the gift was of crucial import.[76] In October 1711 Elizabeth Freke wrote down a list of her possessions as she was planning a journey to London to settle her will for a final time. Her list recorded objects of value in her household at the time of her departure, but also served as a poignant reminder of the emotionally charged gifts she had received over the course of her life.[77] One subsection of the list was titled "Given me by my dear sister Norton." Freke's method of listing makes clear her high valuation of gifts that had been given to her as presents as she separated items she had been given from those she may have purchased. Freke's valuing of female gift exchange is displayed yet more clearly through her descriptions of the gifts themselves. Descriptive importance was given to those gifts that had been created by, rather than simply purchased by, her sister Norton, and weight was given to those presents that Norton had embroidered. In the midst of a rather dry inventory list of gifts, Freke took the time to write that she owned "6 round stools all by [Sister Norton's] worke . . . 6 couchens [cushions] to them, her work . . . 2 long stools to them," and "1 great easy chair, in her house I left in London." The same was true of embroidered and decorated book covers. Freke recorded in her inventory that she had received "7 New books of my deer sister the Lady Nortons makeing, and her deer daughter the Lady Gettings making." Hinting at the emotional bonds this sort of gift had created, Freke wrote that these were books "wch I prise and vallue for their Authers."[78]

Similar emotional ties were created by the donation of Johana Barrington's gift of embroidered cloth to Jane Hooke. Our knowledge of this donation comes from Hooke, the recipient of the gift. Hooke was a woman who has nearly disappeared from the historical record; we know she was the wife of a Rev. William Hooke, the rector of Upper Clatford, a small village on the outskirts of Andover, England. Only two letters from Hooke survive in Barrington's correspondence, both dating from 1629. After receiving her gift of cloth from Barrington, Hooke wrote to express her thanks. She combined this expression of appreciation with an apology for not writing sooner, confessing that she, "would not have bene thus long ere I had retourned a leter of true thankefullnes had I not bene prevented by weak-enese and sicknes." The combination of gratitude and self-effacement was an attempt to create additional bonds between the women, as it solicited sympathy from Barrington and expressed Hooke's desire for consolation. This impulse was furthered when Hooke continued, writing that she had been a victim of theft. Earlier that week Hooke and her husband had been asleep in their house at night when they were "so scard in the night as we thought with theves." Fortunately for Hooke, the unusual noises she thought had been caused by thieves were actually created by "our maide in letting in young fellowes in to the house at unseasonable howres to riot with them both with our beare and bread." This confusion was exacerbated upon discovery because the servant attempted to obscure her role in the affair by "[coming] up to helpe us cry out theves." Harmless as the imagined thieves turned out to be, Hooke's relation of the story to Barrington, inside of a letter that was ostensibly only a thank you note, evinces the ways in which Hooke solicited pity from her higher-status patron. Decrying the behavior of a servant she judged to be wasteful, articulating her gratitude for Barrington's donation of cloth, and simultaneously reinforcing the idea that she herself was worthy of the gift and deserving of aid, sympathy, and support, Hooke's letter of grati-tude was intended to help Hooke ingratiate herself with Barrington in many ways. Hooke even concluded her letter with an acknowledgment that the gift had strengthened the emotional ties the two women supposedly shared. In thanking Barrington for the cloth, Hooke interpreted the sewn gift as a symbol of their friendship and "love," writing that she was thankful "to have receved such a larg extent of your ladyshipes love."[79]

The Gift of Painting and Decoration

In the aforementioned inventory of household goods kept by Elizabeth Freke, the author-compiler listed another special gift exchanged between early modern women of means: art objects. Freke's inventory included deco-rative picture frames, which she called "pictture sconces," and several portraits. The portraits were of Freke's family members: her father, Ralph

Freke, her sisters Frances Norton and Cicely Choute, and her niece Grace Gethin ("Gettings" in the manuscript). Freke's portraits were not straightforward commissions: she carefully recorded that the portraits and frames had been given to her as gifts by various female relatives, two of whom were subjects of the portraits themselves: Freke's sister Frances Norton and Norton's daughter, Grace Gethin.[80]

Portraits, decorative picture frames, and other paintings were all a type of work that women were encouraged to undertake alongside their embroidery and needlework: art handwork, or the manufacture of decorative objects. Prescriptive literature for women contained many guides on how to make handworked art objects. By following their household advice books, gentlewomen could learn how to create jewelry, decorate chairs, wallpaper rooms, and build picture frames. Woolley's *Supplement to the Queen-Like Closet* promised to provide "some Directions for several sorts of work, which may pleasure you in your Chambers and Closets" and specifically lessons on the "adorning of Closets with several pretty Fancies." These "pretty Fancies" were methods of decorating walls or picture frames and were called either "Transparent Work" or "Puff-Work." Women created pictures and designs out of isinglass, gum, and paint and hung them on their walls for decoration. Woolley told her readers to boil "three quarts full of Isinglass, such as you have at the apothecaries, broken into small pieces, and a small quantity of Gum-Dragon amongst it." Women were supposed to take the resulting slurry and "strain it while it is hot," then to bend a wire "which must be shaped according to the leaves or the flowers you intend it for." The bent wire was to be dipped into the sticky isinglass and gum mixture and then pressed on a sheet of paper. The gum would leave a raised, outline impression of a design, which was then colored.[81]

Color was important. The time and skill required to produce art objects like this signaled that it was an elite practice, but the minerals and pigments used in the manufacture of fine paints were another marker of status. As Lisa Jardine argues in her book on early modern consumption, "Colour itself announced the value and importance of the [painting]. We may be alert to the signal which large expanses of gold and gold-leaf detailing give in a painting. . . . We are no longer attuned, however, to the comparative expense of colour pigments. Paint hues were not perceived as equal."[82] Color, dyes, and paint making were discussed extensively in the gentlewomen's household advice manuals of the period. Woolley devoted a large section of her *Supplement to the Queen-Like Closet* to the creation of colored pigments for painting, giving the paints names like Sea-Green, Grass-Green, Primrose, Damask-Rose, Clove, and Tawny. This elaborate naming system catered to an apparent elite need for and appreciation of diversity in color, and the similarity of some of these hues (sea-green versus grass-green) additionally implied these women had the ability to discern the differences between minute variations in shade.[83] Some color names were supposed to reflect a transatlantic or even transpacific exoticism. Readers were told that to achieve "Orient Red Colours" they were to mix "spirit of salt and smalt," which would make their paint "of an Orient Red colour." The ingredients for the paints were themselves both exotic and expensive. To make paints, Woolley suggested women use saffron, "Brazil-wood," turmeric, date stones, vermillion, cloves, indigo, and the costly "Scutcheneal," or cochineal, a type of cactus insect found only in Mexico and imported across the Atlantic for its use as a crimson dye agent.[84] Even candied fruits were colored: Woolley included instructions on "proper colours for fruitage," which called for elite cooks to use edible paints made of gumwater and rosewater to create colors like "Saffron," "Sap-Green," and "Indian-lake," a name which surely reminded readers of Britain's booming seventeenth- and eighteenth-century trade in both the Atlantic and Pacific.[85]

The association of color with elite status was also carried into fabric dyes. Markham's *English Housewife* taught that homely wool was to be dyed only in basic and easily differentiated colors like black, red, blue, "cinder" (a kind of dark gray), green, and yellow. The ingredients for creating these dyes would have been readily available to most Britons: oak galls, copper, alum, wheat bran, and "old chamber lye." Any further experimentation with coloring wool was, in Markham's view, extravagant and unseemly; he prohibited wool-dyeing readers from using elaborate colors, ridiculing those who dyed wool in the same way they would expensive fabrics like silk or satin as confused and distracting: "The best medly [for wool], is that which is compounded of two colours onely, as a light colour, and a darke: for to have more is but confusion, and breeds no pleasure but distraction to the sight."[86] Making explicit the difference between allegedly high-status and low-status colors, Woolley even urged her readers to "admire but those which are extraordinary in their Colours . . . [for the difference between dull and bright colors is] as much difference as is between a beautiful Lady and a Cinder-woman."[87]

Elite women were expected to use these expensive colors and dyes when hand-decorating gifts. These techniques and materials were used for decorative picture frames; the *Supplement to the Queen-Like Closet* schooled its readers in how "to make pretty Frames for slight Pictures in Black only" and also how "to make Frames for Pictures in work of Satten, Stitch, and the like." The purpose of such work was to produce decorations for rooms in elite homes. Sections titled "Fine Hangings for Closets" and also "To adorn a Room with Prints" ensured that women could create rooms which were "very delightful and commendable. . . . [decoration] makes a Room very lightsom as well as fine." Tutorials in gift-making items such as these assumed that the creator was capable of a certain level of opulence. These decorative gift objects required materials like satin and silk, mother of pearl, coral, and amber. Certainly these were luxury goods, and some of them (mother of pearl, coral, and silk) were products of British sea trade.[88] Crucially, Woolley stressed the importance of manipulating expensive goods in order to shun profligacy. The guide on how "to make Frames for Pictures in work of Satten, Stitch, and the like" told readers to first "let a handsome plain Frame be made of Dealwood, fit for your piece of Work." After this high-quality, expensive, and "handsome" wooden frame had been made for the female artist, she was then instructed to modify it and make it her own by decorating it with "some shells and some mother-Pearl; some Corral and some Amber; some little kind of Creatures make in wax, as Frogs, and such like." And women were particularly instructed to reappropriate older luxury goods they owned to decorate frames with, for example, "pieces of old Neck-Laces and Pendants." The resulting object, Woolley proudly concluded, "will look like a Frame of great price, but it will not cost any great matter."[89] Even when teaching readers how to craft expensive or exotic paints, guidebooks like Woolley's offered ways for wealthy women to seem frugal in their choice of colors; in Woolley's instructions for making a paint called "Spanish White," readers were told to use chalk and alum, that they "may save your Money; for much of that [type of ingredient] is used in all Houses generally."[90]

It may seem initially strange that Woolley would try to persuade her readers to "save [their] Money" or that she would commend an object that "will not cost any great matter," when her books were designed so obviously to promote an elite culture and taste. But this points to exactly the type of reappropriation and removal from consumption that seventeenth- and eighteenth-century British women practiced and valued. By remaking and re-creating luxury goods, elite women were able to bypass accusations of indulgent consumption and instead could boast of their creativity, ingenuity, and skills in housekeeping. One recipe book for women promised its readers they would learn "the Art of Adorning their Tables with a Splendid Frugality."[91] Decrying overconsumption and simultaneously criticizing the high "charges" set by those lower-status women who manufactured saleable luxury goods for their living, Woolley lectured as follows in the *Supplement to the Queen-Like Closet*:

> It is more commendable a great deal to wear ones own Work, than to be made fine with the Art of others; and though one may be envied for it, yet none can have so just a quarrel against them, because it is their Ingenuity; and besides it argues that Person not to be idle, but rather a good Housewife. Any fool may be made fine with Cost, but give me those who can be neat and nobly habited with but a reasonable charge. The World is grown very fine of late years, but it is with so much charge (together with so ill a phansie some have in choosing things) that they look more like Stage-players than fit to come into any Church, or Civil places: Some will plead Ignorance, not knowing how to do these things, but that's a bare Excuse; for if they know not already, they may learn.[92]

Ties between female creativity in art handwork and moral uprightness, ingenuity, curiosity, and keen skill were also made in elite women's own writings. Katherine Oxenden, writing proudly to her mother of her progress on her art handwork, bragged that she was, "entering upon two or three gume flowers and a little fruit (if you please) for the basket," adding coyly that the gift was, "bespoken but not yet made."[93] In mentioning her preoccupation with the gum flowers, Oxenden sought to gain admiration and approval from her mother. Even religious women were praised for their creation of artistic handwork: Jane Barker's poems, which she collected in her self-composed "Book of Verse," included a poetic dedication to "Dame__, Augustine Nun on her curious gum-work." Barker praised the nun for her devotion and skill, tying the female production of art together with domestic British virtues: "We need not to Italion villas go, nor yet Versails, the Toileries, St Cloud, t'admire the works of nature or of art, Since you excell em all in every part. . . . So you bless'd Dames, insensibly dispence, on all your sex your vertuous influence."[94] In addition, women used art handiwork in attempts to secure friendships and alliances. Sometime between 1662 and 1674 Frances Dillon wrote to her friend Mary Dering to thank her for a present of shell flowers. Dillon explained that the gift—decorative seashells that were glued into the shapes of flowers and arranged like a bouquet—was garnering attention, admiration, and even jealousy: "Every one [is] in great admiration of your fine shell flowers and one of them they have by force taken from mee." Dillon flattered Dering through her praise of the gift, but she also used the exchange as an opportunity to spend more time with her friend. Dillon asked if Dering would teach her how to make the shell flowers herself, writing that she hoped "your Ladyship will instruct my dull fancye how to make them up."[95] Celebrating and valuing feminine skills in handiwork, Dillon sought to strengthen her alliance with Dering by asking for her guidance in this craft.

Elizabeth Freke's portraits and decorated picture frames illuminate the early modern social mores which gendered handcraft as an essential feminine skill. Some biographical information about Freke helps to divulge the meaning of these gifts. Elizabeth Freke (c. 1642–1714) was the daughter of Cicely Culpeper and her husband, Ralph Freke, a barrister of the Middle Temple. As a young child Freke lived with her parents in the south of England, in London, Kent, and Salisbury. In 1669 she became engaged to her cousin Percy Freke in London, and they married without Freke's father's permission in 1672. Freke's relationship with Percy was often marked by conflict. They argued over money, their children, and their properties, which were located in Cork, Ireland, and in Norfolk, England. Freke recorded her life in voluminous diaries that make frequent reference to her difficult marriage, but she wrote that she found solace in the company of a few select family members whom she especially loved and trusted: her father, Ralph Freke, and her three sisters, Cicely Choute, Frances Norton, and Judith Austen.[96]

When Freke wrote of the colored, painted, and decorated picture frames she owned, she was careful to note their connections to the women in her familial social network. Freke said she possessed several decorative frames that had been made by her niece Grace Gethin, listing "pictture sconces with glass: Lady Gettings" and "2 pictture sconces of my dear Lady Gettings with glass over them." Freke was clearly proud to own her niece's handwork, but the value she placed on her art objects as evidence of her female alliances was especially evidenced through the portraits she owned. Freke listed five family portraits in her inventory: a "picture of my deer fathers, given me by my dear sister Norton," a "picture of my deer Lady Nortons," one "pictture of my deer sister Choutt drawn by my deer Lady Gettings," two "long pictures" of "my deer sister Norton," and a final portrait "of my d[ea]r neece Gettings her only daughter." Freke, that is to say, owned one picture of her father, Ralph Freke; one picture of her sister Cicely Choute; two pictures of her sister Frances Norton; and one picture of Norton's daughter, Grace Gethin, a woman Freke especially treasured for her own rarity, as Gethin was Norton's only surviving daughter. In this list Freke made special mention of the provenance of two of the portraits. One, the image of Ralph Freke given to Freke by her sister Frances Norton, had been a gift; and one had been painted and then given by one of the members of Freke's female alliance network: Grace Gethin had painted her Aunt Cicely Choute and then had given the portrait to her Aunt Elizabeth Freke.

Freke's valuing, listing, and tracing of these objects is understandable, especially because portraits carried special meanings for early modern Britons. Jennifer Fletcher has argued that, from the sixteenth century on, "an increasingly important function of portraiture was the illustration of friend-ship" and that portraits were habitually "sent as a gift to a close but faraway friend to demonstrate love and esteem, to overcome absence and to stimulate the visual memory." Portraits were thought to be so critical to friendship that they "were often treated like real people—being frequently addressed and kissed." Fletcher gives the example of a woman named Isabella d'Este, whose close female friend "missed her [so] deeply, [she] took Isabella's portrait to table."[97] Jardine's work supports this claim when she contends that portraits and their frames were "designed to be seen in the round, touched and held, rather than seen at a distance."[98] This helps to contextu-alize Freke's notations that each portrait was of a "dear" relative. To Freke, each portrait was laden with sentiment. The pictures were her possessions, some of which had been given to her personally as gifts by beloved family members. They reflected the wealth and status of Freke's natal family, and they served to provoke sentiment and memory, as they were visual represen-tations of the people whom Freke most loved and relied upon. The portraits, especially Gethin's portrait of Choute, served as physical proof of Freke's female alliances. Choute's portrait was a testament to Gethin's own gendered skills in art handwork. It stood for the time that Gethin and Choute spent in one another's company, as Gethin sketched and rendered her aunt's image. And it symbolized the valued relationship shared between all three women:

Gethin (artist and giver), Choute (artistic subject), and Freke (recipient). Choute's portrait quite literally embodied and exhibited Freke's familial and female alliances, strengthening the ties that bound her to those she loved.

Gift exchange was a critical component of seventeenth- and early eighteenth-century elite British female experience. Elite women used luxury presents to convey their similarities with other elite women, their common education, tastes, skills, and wealth. And as these objects were given as presents, they were invested with feelings: admiration for the virtue of the women who had made them; deference and obligation toward givers who were perceived as being superior in status; and sentiment for the friendship the gift was often intended to represent. These women also used their work in creating gifts in order to bypass accusations of profligacy, dissolution, and luxury as they reappropriated luxury objects: sewing expensive fabric into clothing, using discarded jewelry to decorate art handwork, cooking oranges and quinces into marmalade. This work enabled these privileged women to push aside criticisms of their decadence and distanced them from the exploitative, dangerous labor practices—whether in sugar refineries across the Atlantic ocean or in their British manor-house kitchens—which made these splendid objects available to them. Exchanging such handmade gifts enabled women to strengthen their ties to one another and to build and maintain female alliances.

3. Cooperative Labor: Making Alliances through Women's Recipes and Domestic Production

Multifarious alliances were formed between elite women and the lower-status servants, friends, and neighbors with whom they lived and worked. In the kitchens, bedchambers, and gardens of elite homes women from many different socioeconomic backgrounds interacted closely. They baked bread and churned butter; they milked cows and fed chickens; they scrubbed clothing and scoured pots and pans; they distilled medicines and brewed beer. And they undertook many of these tasks together. Study of both elite and lower-status women's activities in elite homes opens a window onto how cooperation and collaboration in labor shaped women's alliances.

For several decades historians of early modern Europe have analyzed the effects of oppressive working conditions, labor conflict, and processes of commercialization in the seventeenth and eighteenth centuries. Much research on the material conditions of early modern workers has centered on artisanal crafts such as baking, weaving, and brewing, and most of it has focused on male labor. Historians have argued convincingly that working conditions inside of artisanal shops were often brutal and oppressive and that the labor performed by both women and men in these spaces was dangerous and repetitive, physically taxing and destructive to the health of workers.[1] Feminist historians have asserted that women's labor—although too often invisible to us now owing to a limited source range—was essential to work-shop success, while remaining similarly onerous and challenging.[2]

As vital as such scholarship has been, it is unfortunate that considerably less attention has been paid to labor performed inside of elite homes in the seventeenth and eighteenth centuries and to elite households as sites of gendered production. Some historians have recognized that the spaces of early modern domestic labor are themselves significant. Amanda Vickery has written that "homes are implicated in and backdrop to the history of power, gender, the family, privacy, consumerism, design and the decorative arts," making study of the home an essential component of any scholarly work on gender, production, and sociability.[3] And some historians have begun to recognize the necessity of studying the interstices of domestic space, labor, and gender identity. As Amanda Flather has argued persuasively in her book *Gender and Space in Early Modern England*, "The acknowledged significance of the links between space, work, and the dynamics of power between the sexes" means that "we need to know a good deal more about the location of [both] male and female work."[4]

But finding evidence of either higher- or lower-status women's domestic labor is extremely difficult. There were many sites of domestic female labor in elite early modern households. Some spaces were indoors, in kitchens, bedchambers, or closets, and some were located in the "domestic exterior," in outdoor spaces such as yards, sheds, barns, and gardens.[5] Many laboring women possessed only partial literacy, and few left records of their work. Elite women did write of their daily labor and activities, but in doing so they often effaced servants, neglecting in their manuscripts to mention the extensive work completed by their employees. The few scholars who have attempted to trace women's domestic work patterns therefore have done so by using very rich, but very limited, source bases. These historians have illuminated in wonderful detail the lives and experiences of early modern British women working in specific trades and in small geographic areas.[6] Their studies are extremely valuable, but they do not allow a comparison of women's labors across Britain and its colonies or over long stretches of time. Nor do they allow us to examine working relationships between women of different educational and socioeconomic backgrounds.

But both higher- and lower-status women's work can be made manifest through three innovative types of primary sources. First, personal household inventories of elite homes offer evidence of the difficult material conditions of women's domestic labor. Second, prescriptive guidebooks for women disclose the ideas and expectations that surrounded and structured women's domestic labor. And third, handwritten medical and culinary recipe books evince literate women's practices of and ideas about collective labor, as these books, written, copied, influenced, and edited by seventeenth- and eighteenth-century British women of varying socioeconomic backgrounds, show how early modern female authors described their work. Taken together, these three types of sources render a new and meaningful history of gendered labor in early modern Britain. Women's domestic labor required the cooperation of disparate people, whose salient differences in social status, age, and training might have occasioned conflicts. Social mores did compel women to cooperate, but successful domestic labor practices could also mean financial, educational, and spatial opportunities for women and their friends. And so very frequently early modern women of higher and lower status forged complex work relationships with one another, negotiating and managing their differences.

Household Inventories

Household inventories, which listed all of the objects that were part of an early modern home, were frequently compiled when an individual died, in order to facilitate the distribution of bequests. But some women wrote or commissioned their own inventories, to keep track of property, remember or sentimentalize their belongings, or protect against loss or theft. Three detailed household inventories compiled in the seventeenth and early eighteenth centuries for three elite women—Anne Southwell, Katherine Perceval, and Elizabeth Freke—provide evidence of women's domestic labor practices.[7] The earliest of these inventories, compiled in London on April 23–26, 1631, is that of Anne Southwell (1573–1636), the daughter of a barrister.[8] Her first husband, who was from Norfolk, owned estates in the early modern plantations in Munster, Ireland. Her second husband was an army captain, and he owned property just outside of London, in Middlesex.[9] The inventory was made when Southwell moved house "from hir dwellinge at Clerkenwell [London] to hir house at Acton [Middlesex]."[10] The second inventory is associated with Katherine Perceval (d. 1679), the wife of John Perceval, a baronet in County Cork, Ireland. The Perceval inventory was compiled at two separate times, in 1665 and 1686. Perceval and her family lived in County Cork on two estates, the first a property called Burton House, just north of the city of Cork, and the second in Kinsale, south of that city.[11] The last inventory examined was associated with Elizabeth Freke (1641–1714) and was a record of the objects found in the kitchen of her house called West Bilney, just south of King's Lynn, in Norfolk, England. The property covered roughly twenty-seven hundred acres and housed six tenements as well as Freke's manor farm. The West Bilney kitchen inventory was written in 1711. Like Perceval and Southwell, Freke had connections abroad. She and her husband, Percy Freke, had owned property in the Munster Plantation, and Freke herself spent portions of her married life there before returning permanently to Norfolk.[12] All three of these women would be classified by modern historians as belonging to the gentry. Their houses were spacious and filled with goods that would have been too expensive for a majority of early modern Britons to own. But Southwell, Perceval, and Freke were not wealthy or moneyed. That all three women had ties to Ireland is not accidental. Ireland was seen as a risky but profitable economic venture in the late seventeenth century, and many middling and gentry families invested there because they hoped Irish lands would enable them to achieve a degree of wealth and status unavailable to them in England. The Southwell, Perceval, and Freke inventories reveal much about women's working conditions in domestic spaces. These sources make it clear that female workrooms in elite homes were unpleasant, difficult spaces for women to negotiate. They were often crowded and cacophonous. They were filled with smells, smoke, and steam. They housed hot, heavy equipment, much of which was hard to handle and was prone to break or malfunction. Inventories prove that it would have been onerous to work in these spaces. And yet, within these extremely challenging spaces, women were expected to—and did— produce the goods upon which early modern elite households depended. Women's work often necessitated female collaboration, and household inventories provide insight into the domestic alliances women forged to facilitate their labor.

Arguably the most challenging domestic space in which servants and their employers worked was the kitchen. In seventeenth- and eighteenth-century England, Ireland, and Scotland, this room was typically inside of the house, but in warmer climates—such as the British West Indies and mainland British American colonies like Maryland, Virginia, and the Carolinas— kitchens were usually located in outbuildings.[13] Wherever they were located, early modern kitchens were commonly hot, smoky, and uncomfortable places to work.

The kitchen's central feature was its large, open fireplace. Attached to the sides of the fireplace were long swinging hooks used for hanging pots and rotating metal spikes used as meat spits. Southwell's inventory listed many metal tools that were in use around her kitchen fireplace: "2 payre of pott hangers for the Chimney" as well as "2 payre of pott hookes, a payer of racks" and "2 spitts." Southwell also owned equipment to manage the kitchen fire itself, such as "a fyre forke," and "a per [pair] of tongs."[14] Freke's inventory of the items in her early eighteenth-century kitchen in Norfolk included many metal pots and pans suitable for use in cooking over large, open flames. She listed in her possession "one brass stue ketle" as well as "one tin sauce pan, one brass skillett, one new coper sauce pan," and "one new brass frying pan." The kitchen possessed several metal cooking utensils, among them "one brass ladle" and "one brass slice." Freke's kitchen equipment included tools for swinging and positioning pots and pans over the fire and tools for tending the flames: "two haks or potts, two iron andiarns [andirons], one iron oven-lid, [and] one great fire shovle."[15] Metal tools like these would have been heavy and difficult to lift, and fireplaces would have been hot, smoky, and dirty. The difficulty of kitchen labor and the expense of the equipment used in kitchens did sometimes cause conflicts between women workers. Freke was apparently so angry that a "Bell mettle skillet" in her kitchen had been ruined by one of her female servants that when she listed it in her inventory she noted bitterly that "the handle of itt [was] brok outt by Amey."[16]

But manuscript evidence divulges that women worked to manage these arduous kitchen spaces and that they tried to make them productive and pleasant. The Yorkshire gentlewoman Margaret Hoby recorded in her diary that she had spent time in the kitchen alongside her servants, an activity she viewed as both sociable and pleasurable; in 1605 Hoby "took order for Househould mattres . . . then into the kitchine wher beinge and with good talke spent the time."[17] Hoby's claim that she was engaged in "good talke" with her female servants suggests that kitchens were spaces in which women could engage with one another in both productive work and edifying conversation. But kitchen conversations were not always high-minded or didactic, for kitchens were also spaces in which elite women and their servants socialized, laughed, and exchanged secrets and gossip. In the late seventeenth century, hoping to facilitate a marriage match between the Hastings and Lille families, a servant named Mungo Kearns reported that an elite woman named Lady Lille discussed matchmaking with her female servants in her kitchen:

"somtims [Lady Lille] gos into the kitchen and talks with [two kitchen maids] Katrean and Katt: [and] tells her that my Lord Hastings is so like her that she must have him."[18]

Household inventories demonstrate that bedchambers, too, were sites of female labor and interaction. Although typically located above ground level and intended for the use of family and servants, early modern bedrooms, called closets or chambers, possessed few of the qualities that today we would associate with bedroom privacy. During the day the rooms were places of female work, and at night they served as sleeping spaces for groups of women. Elite women frequently slept in the same room and often in the same bed as their female relatives, children, friends, and servants. Elite adults, even married couples, habitually shared their chamber with children and servants, who slept on pallets and stowaway beds in the same room.[19] Both at night and during the day, beds and bedchambers alike were crowded, noisy spaces.

Some of the objects that household inventories listed as being in bedchambers uncover practices of communal sleeping. Perceval's inventory, describing the objects in one of her bedchambers at her Burton House residence in Ireland, notes that the room had "four canopy Bedsteads . . . [with] four feather beds and bolsters, [and] four pillows," alongside "two twigg cradles," illustrating that the adults in Perceval's household shared their sleeping spaces with infants.[20] This also meant that bedchambers were sites of early modern child care. Within these spaces elite women and their lower-status servants nursed, entertained, and dressed young children.[21] Sick children were monitored and cared for in bedchambers, which meant that the rooms were sites of doctors' visits, the administration of medicines (often an invasive and messy process in this period), and the bathing and cleaning of the sick. The frenetic nature of early modern bedchambers is detected in Sarah Savage's correspondence. While visiting her adult daughter and grandchildren Savage noted that her daughter's bedchamber was "so full with childr[en] and servants that I can but just Crowd in at Fam[ily] Prayers."[22]

Despite their busy nature, bedchambers, as household inventories make clear, were also places for making food—and especially for making candies, sweets, and other sugar-based products. One of Perceval's bedchambers housed a "Movenry stove for sweet meats," that is, a stove for making confections.[23] In this context "movenry" meant "moveable," signaling that Perceval's candy stove was not for kitchen use alone but could be picked up, transferred to, and used in her bedchamber.[24] Freke's inventory recorded that a "deep box with chocolett, &c." was kept "in my own closett."[25] Evidence from elite women's personal papers also references the creation of confection by groups of women in bedchambers and closets; Anne Clifford's seventeenth-century diary of her life in Dorset mentioned that she made baked goods alongside her female servants in the bedchamber she shared with her young daughter Margaret. Clifford wrote that on February 2, 1619, she "made Pancakes with my women in the Great Chamber."[26] As incongruous as confectionery, sleep, and child care sound, all of these activities were practiced in early modern women's bedchambers. Sugar was an expensive commodity (see chapter 2), and by locating confectionary work in bedchambers elite women may have hoped to keep it from being overused or protect it from being stolen. But with their open flames, teetering brackets and stands, and pots of boiling sugar, confectionary stoves were dangerous additions to bedchambers.

And so were the fireplaces that heated bedrooms. Southwell's inventory of her bedchamber listed two sets of fire tools, one for each fireplace in her bedchamber. These large metal tools included "2 tinder boxes" as well as two sets of "brass Andyrons, tongs, fyer shovel, [and] bellowes."[27] Markedly absent from Southwell's list was a fire screen, which would have provided a shield between the fire and the room. Fires, whether in fireplaces or under candy stoves, made these rooms challenging spaces for women and especially for young children to navigate. Alice Thornton attested to this in her autobiography, writing that in 1659 her young daughter, "my deare Naly," was burned in a bedchamber fire. Thornton remembered that "the child stumble[d] on the harth, and fell into the fire on the rainge with one of her hands, and burned her right hand three fingers of it." Fortunately Thornton happened to be standing close by, "and by God's helpe I did pull her out of the fire by her clothes." The child suffered serious burns on her hand, as "three of her fingers sore burned to the bone."[28] As all of these examples show, women faced serious challenges in their domestic labor within bedchambers and closets. And the spaces of these rooms were themselves uncomfortable, as they were crowded with many pieces of furniture as well as with hot fireplaces and stoves.

But, as in the case of kitchens, evidence from literate women's manuscript papers suggests that some women enjoyed the close, homosocial environment of early modern bedchambers. Alan Bray wrote of early modern men that "if eating and drinking created friendship, so too did sleeping together," and the same concept can be applied to early modern women. In the seventeenth century Anne Clifford remembered that her friendship with her female cousin Frances Bouchier was cemented when the two shared a bedchamber. When the young Clifford misbehaved, his "Mother in her Anger commanded that I should lie in a Chamber alone, which I could not endure. But my cousin Frances got the Key of my Chamber & lay with me which was the first time I loved her so well."[29] Clifford's comment that she "could not endure" sleeping alone signals that co-sleeping and chamber-sharing were both meaningful and normative for early modern women. Clifford's additional remark, that Bouchier's actions facilitated their friendship and "love," demonstrates how bedchambers could be sites for the creation of female alliances.

One further example illustrates the complex bonds that higher- and lower-status women forged in bedchambers. In the late 1660s the diarist Alice Thornton, whose writings cite her many disagreements with other women, recorded a bedchamber altercation she had with another woman's female servant: "Even so was I and my poore child accused and condemned before [Anne Danby] in [the] chamber by her servant [Barbara Pape] in a most notorious manner . . . soe that she railed on me and scoulded at me . . . with the most vile expressions could be imagined . . . soe that I fell downe before the mistres and her maide." The argument between Pape and Thornton ended in violence, when Thornton's "deare husband . . . came to the dore of the scarlet chamber and broke it open, and hearing my complaint, and seeing my condition, did kike that wench [Barbara Pape] downe staires, and turne her out in a great rage."[30] The casualness with which Thornton described her husband's physical abuse of Barbara Pape is chilling, and the story of the conflict speaks to the gross inequalities in employer–servant relations in the period. But Thornton's bedchamber altercation is also illustrative of an eloquent moment of female alliance. Anne Danby was one of Thornton's nieces, and Danby employed Pape as a personal body servant. At the time of the incident, Danby and Pape were living in Thornton's home and were dependent on Thornton's often grudging charity. Danby had a fraught relationship with her Aunt Alice, and when tensions between the two finally erupted it was Pape who controlled and dictated the scope of the conflict. Screaming insults at her employer's adversary, Pape, in a meaningful act, defended Danby's interests and her reputation. Pape broke social norms when she insulted Thornton—early modern servants were expected to be obedient and dutiful—but, much more significantly, she risked her job, her living, and even her physical safety to do so. That Pape was willing to accept those risks speaks to the relationship she shared with her employer Danby.

Another space for women's labor was the domestic exterior, namely, the yards and outbuildings that surrounded the houses of the early modern elite. In the yards and gardens of these homes, women cultivated herbs, fruits, and vegetables. They also brewed beer, washed and mended clothes, cared for fowl and cattle, and processed the eggs, milk, and cream that came from these animals. These outdoor spaces offered challenges unlike those of the interior of houses for both higher- and lower-status laboring women. Many outdoor tasks had to be done year-round, in the sun, wind, and pouring rain. Unfavorable weather conditions made the successful cultivation of crops highly laborious. And in these outdoor "rooms," insects, dust, and domesticated animals would have offered unwelcome intrusions into what was often strenuous, time-consuming work.

The growing of herbs, vegetables, fruits, and flowers was work often undertaken by elite women, aided by their servants. Southwell's inventory listed "a garden line, a spade, a shovel, a mattock, [and] a rake" among the first items Southwell moved between her homes in Clerkenwell and Acton.[31] Gardening and cultivation were topics that women discussed and sometimes complained about with their female friends, relatives, and servants. A woman named Mrs. J. Barrington bemoaned her difficulties in fruit cultivation in the seventeenth century, writing to her daughter that "this colde weather [is] I think freezing . . . [and] spoyling all our hopes of stoare of plums."[32] Cold temperatures prevented Elizabeth Oxenden from securing the seedlings she needed to grow fruits and vegetables, apologizing to her mother-in-law in October 1664 that "those slipes [plant cuttings] that you desire I shall procure . . . [in] the spring people being unwilling to slip any thing in winter."[33] Britain's perennially bad weather was not the only challenge faced by early modern gardeners. Botanical diseases also ruined crops and damaged plants in the period, and elite women sometimes expressed worries about the effects and spread of these blights on fruit cultivation; Elizabeth Boyle wrote to her daughter in June 1683 that "the blast of cherrye trees has reacht as farre as Kent," noting that the disease was "universall as to cherryes" that year.[34]

In the yards of their homes, early modern women also brewed beer, mead, and ale. Brewing was typically done in an outbuilding, shed, or barn.

Household inventories evince that the equipment for home brewing was cumbersome and comprised wooden tubs, vats, paddles, bottles, and kegs. To make beer or ale, grain was allowed to sprout and was then soaked in water; the resulting mash was flavored, cooked, and then strained. Herbs and spices were added when making ale, and hops were added when making beer, ingredients that imparted flavor to the beverage. Barrels, pots, and tubs of all sizes were required throughout this process. Southwell listed "1 pott to boyle meade in" as part of her inventory.[35] Freke's inventory was more descriptive of the process of home brewing, observing that Freke owned "one great mash tubb; with its uti[n]sells" and "one square stand to this mash tub" which was used to hold the tub upright and keep it steady. Freke's brewery also held two "ale stoole[s]," one in the "small beer seller" and one that Freke wrote was housed "in my own seller." Once the ale or beer had fermented and had been strained, the liquid was collected into sturdy barrels and firkins. Freke's brew house included "four half barrels, broad hoopt" and "three new firkins, broad hoop[ed]," all of which, she wrote, were made of oak.[36]

Although historians have discovered that women's professional brewing declined from the sixteenth century on, many elite women continued to brew their own domestic ale and beer through to the early eighteenth century.[37] The authors of ladies' guides asserted that it was an elite woman's responsibility to brew. Gervase Markham's *English Housewife* of 1637 instructed readers that it was "most requisite and fit" for British women to be "experienced and well practiced in the well making of Malt . . . for as from it is made the drinke, by which the houshold is nourished and sustained." Although Markham acknowledged that "many excellent Men-maltsters" did exist, he insisted that brewing was "properly the worke and care of the woman, for it is a house-worke . . . where generally lieth her charge."[38] Markham also explained that brewing was a communal female labor, belonging to "the Housewife and the Maid-servants to her appertaining."[39]

Located a short distance from the main house, early modern dairies housed cattle and accommodated the collection, straining, and separating of milk as well as the production of cheese, butter, and cream. Dairies were crowded places, with bulky equipment and livestock packed side by side. Freke's inventory listed equipment for collecting and scalding milk, all of which would have crowded the space inside of the building. Her dairy housed "one coper furness of a barrel," which was probably used to scald milk, and "one broad cauling keeler with two ears," which would have held the milk while it cooled.[40] The dairy also featured vessels for separating the cream from the milk, such as "one broad milk tray . . . [and] two broad milk bowls," as well as "three great milk pans" and even "four pailes," although Freke noted in her inventory that "two of them must be mended." Most notably, the dairy held equipment used for turning milk into cheese and butter, like "one greatt chees press . . . [and] three cheese vates" as well as "one churn and its dash."[41] Dairies were highly valued not only for the milk, cream, cheese, and butter they produced, but also for their specialized equipment. Southwell made sure to retrieve "2 firkins of butter [and] 2 cheeses" from her old residence during her household move in 1631, but in addition she transported her dairy's "springe wheele," signaling the importance and value she placed on dairy equipment as well as her intention to continue household dairy production in her new home.[42]

Dairying was supervised by higher-status women and executed by their lower-status female servants.[43] After cows were milked, the milk was poured into wide, shallow pans and allowed to sit for forty-eight to sixty hours until the cream had risen to the surface. The cream was then skimmed off and put into barrels for churning, which usually took place once or twice a week in the summer and less frequently in the winter, when colder temperatures inhibited cream from rising. In the seventeenth century most butter making was done with "plunger" churns, which featured long sticks threaded into a barrel; dairy workers would move the stick-plunger up and down rapidly in order to agitate the milk, causing fats to separate from liquids and form butter. These churns had to be operated for approximately three hours to make each batch of butter, and as the cream thickened, the labor became more and more strenuous. Toward the end of the churning process, as the butter coagulated, two workers were required to operate the churn, one to move the plunger and the other to hold the barrel firmly on the floor, making it a necessarily collaborative process.[44]

Despite all of these hardships, elite women's manuscript diaries and autobiographies do provide evidence of women's cooperation and collaboration in the many spaces of the domestic exterior. Margaret Hoby wrote in the early seventeenth century of gardening in the company of her female servants, stating that in April 1601 she "went w[i]th my Maides in to the Garden" and that in July of that year she "went abroad with my Maides that were busie pullinge hempe."[45] Hoby also offered the produce of her garden to neighbor women, writing on April 27, 1601, that she had gone "into the Garden, and gave some hearbes unto a good wiffe of Erley for [her] garden."[46] "Erley" was probably Hoby's abbreviation for Everley, a town about one mile away from Hoby's town of Hackness; this example implies that Hoby built alliances with lower-status women who lived in her vicinity and that she probably shared information about gardening and cultivation as well as supplies with these female neighbors. Even when elite women were physically absent they sought updates about their gardens from female servants and neighbors. While visiting her estate in Dublin in February 1685, Elizabeth Petty wrote home to England, "Nurse . . . must not neglect the Garden in this season." Petty then suggested that the woman she called Nurse should seek the advice and aid of other female servants in this task, reinforcing the idea that gardening was a communal female activity: "Mrs. Price can advise her in this, and get some flowers that will easily prosper."[47] Petty expressed concern about her brewery, writing from Dublin on March 10, 1684, that one of her English female servants was to "be sure to Contrive to have good smale Beere and smale Ale, and well bottl'd by that time we come [back to England]," stating that this task was necessary because members of the family "can not live with out it."[48]

The Southwell, Perceval, and Freke household inventories uncover a new and richly detailed picture of early modern women's labor. Working both indoors and outdoors, higher- and lower-status women cooked and churned butter, cared for children and tended animals, distilled and brewed. This does not mean that all women's work was equalizing, similar, or even satisfying.[49] Social mores dictated that higher-status women perform many repetitive, boring, and exacting domestic tasks because it was expected that "good" elite women would work in this way. And lower-status female servants had to sell their labor to survive, as well as being made to undertake types of domestic work that were more strenuous, dangerous, and unpleasant than those completed by their employers. But some higher-status women did take pleasure in the difficult work spaces they managed and inhabited. And some lower-status women chose to engage with their employers, socializing and talking with them, participating in collective labor, and even occasionally defending their employers' interests and reputations. In these ways, female employers and their female employees shared working relationships and together shouldered the burdens of gendered domestic responsibilities.

Prescriptive Literature

Prescriptive books for women contained lengthy sections on domestic labor. Although ostensibly these texts were intended for elite readers, guidebook authors and publishers marketed their products in sophisticated ways. Prescriptive literature conveyed information in writing but also through images, with detailed frontispiece pictures and in-text diagrams. This mix of text and print was produced to appeal to diverse kinds of female consumers and was intended to instruct partially literate women on the mechanics of domestic labor as well as on the behavior and comportment expected of women who worked in elite homes. Images from guidebooks themselves showed both higher- and lower-status women consuming prescriptive literature. Nathan Bailey's *Dictionarium Domesticum* (1736) features a frontispiece with a female cook seated in a kitchen and holding a book (fig. 3.1).[50] This book is not a symbol of leisure but, like the other objects surrounding the cook—stills, mortars and pestles, jars, drying herbs, beehives, and bottles—an essential tool of her trade.

Figure 3.1. Nathan Bailey, *Dictionarium Domesticum* . . . (London, 1736), frontispiece. © The British Library Board.

The frontispiece of William Henderson's *Housekeeper's Instructor* also illustrates a busy kitchen, one in which several lower-status servants are using guidebooks (fig. 3.2). In the foreground of the image two male kitchen workers carve a roasted fowl. The figure on the left points with one hand to an illustrated diagram in a book, which indicates how the meat is supposed to be cut, and with the other hand gestures toward the roast. The male figure on the right, who wields the knife, looks toward both the book and his companion for guidance. These men are not reading the text of the guidebook but are instead examining its pictures in order to learn how to carve correctly.[51] Women, too, are featured using books in this image. In the background of the picture an elite woman (marked by her powdered wig) offers a book to a female servant (marked by the knife held in her right hand). At the bottom of the frontispiece, an "Explanation" of the image confirms that the picture shows "a Lady presenting her Servant with the Universal Family Cook who diffident of her own knowledge has recourse to that Work for Information."[52] Study of the impact and intent of early modern prescriptive literature must, therefore, include analysis of both the images and the text of these works.

Figure 3.2. William Henderson, *The Housekeeper's Instructor* . . . (London, 1780), frontispiece. Wellcome Library, London.

Elite women and their lower-status employees were encouraged via image *and* text to behave in ways that were considered in the early modern period to be feminine: they were told and shown how to be friendly, pleasant, good-natured, cooperative, and soft-spoken. And this prescriptive literature also taught women to use their supposedly passionate and emotional natures to express love, devotion, and forgiveness toward their fellow female workers.

Ladies' guides counseled workers to exhibit harmony and cooperation in the kitchens of elite households. In her *Queen-Like Closet* (1681) Woolley explained that cooks were to be "quiet in their Office, not swearing nor cursing, nor wrangling, but silently and ingeniously to do their Business." Cook-maids were also told to be quiet and efficient, and Woolley insisted that they "must not have a sharp Tongue, but [one that is] humble, pleasing."[53] Women's positive labor practices were conveyed visually as well as textually in prescriptive literature. The *Queen-Like Closet* has a decorated frontispiece featuring an image of two women working together in a kitchen (fig. 3.3).[54] In this picture the woman on the left of the scene stands over a fireplace; in front of her, pots swing on long chains over the fire, while several fowl roast on spits underneath them. But the woman is not alone in her labor. The female figure working in front of the fireplace has a companion, for another woman is pictured working behind her, on the right side of the scene, pushing pies into a beehive oven with a long wooden paddle. The image itself conveys

Figure 3.3. Hannah Woolley, *The Queen-Like Closet, or Rich Cabinet . . .* (London, 1681), frontispiece. Reproduced by permission of The Huntington Library, San Marino, California.

the studiousness, calm, productivity, and cooperation desired of women working together in kitchens.

A similar image with many of the same themes appeared four years later in another Woolley-attributed text, the *Compleat Servant-Maid* of 1683 (fig. 3.4).[55] This frontispiece highlights an image of a single female figure standing over a fireplace with a long spoon, facing two pots which swing on long chains over the fire. The larger version of the image was back again in Woolley's *Accomplish'd Ladies Delight* of 1685, although it had been altered since 1681 (fig. 3.5).[56] In this edition's frontispiece, two female figures still work cooperatively in a kitchen, but their positions are reversed, with the woman who stands in front of the pots, spits, and fireplace situated on the right side of the scene. Game hangs on hooks behind both women. On the left of the scene the cook-maid's companion, now bending over a dough table, forms pies. Both women perform the same iconic feminine tasks of baking and cooking, producing food for the elite household. This image of harmonious women's kitchen labor was apparently so popular that it came back a fourth time, in 1700, in another edition of Woolley's *Compleat Servant-Maid*, where the lone female figure with the spoon in front of the fire was again used (fig. 3.6).[57]

That all four images were employed for Woolley-attributed texts is significant, but the repetition is all the more remarkable because each text was produced by a different publisher: the *Queen-Like Closet* of 1681 by Chiswel

Figure 3.4. Hannah Woolley, *The Compleat Servant-Maid* . . . (London, 1683), frontispiece. By permission of the Folger Shakespeare Library.

Figure 3.5. Hannah Woolley, *The Accomplish'd Ladies Delight* . . . (London, 1685), frontispiece. Beinecke Rare Book & Manuscript Library, Yale University.

Figure 3.6. Hannah Woolley, *The Compleat Servant-Maid* . . . (London, 1700), frontispiece. Beinecke Rare Book & Manuscript Library, Yale University.

and Sawbridge; the *Compleat-Servant Maid* of 1683 by Thomas Passinger; the *Accomplish'd Ladies Delight* of 1685 by Hannah Woolley; and the *Compleat Servant-Maid* of 1700 by Eben Tracy. On close examination, it also appears the image plates were not sold and reused (a common practice among printers in the seventeenth and eighteenth centuries) but were redrawn and newly carved for each subsequent edition of Woolley's work.[58] The four images were similar but not identical. For example, the 1683 and 1700 versions of the image of the female servant holding a spoon in front of the fire appear to be the same but actually differ in subtle ways. In the earlier image the woman roasts on two spits, while in the later one a single spit is braced over the fire. In the earlier image the wall behind the woman, on which round platters are displayed, holds larger (but fewer) objects than the wall in 1700. These minute but distinctive variations make each of the two image-plates unique. This means that the plates used in the *Compleat Servant-Maid* were not used solely because they were convenient or available, but also because women's kitchen labor, imagined and idealized as productive and harmonious, had become a standard visual trope.

Prescriptive authors offered readers of ladies' guides advice on comportment and behavior not merely in the kitchens but also in the bedchambers and closets of elite homes. In these spaces elite women and their female servants were taught to be friendly, good-natured, and cooperative. Authors of ladies' guides emphasized that laboring women should exhibit feminine love, kindness, humility, modesty, and submissiveness. In her *Compleat Servant-Maid* of 1685 Woolley charged readers who worked as chambermaids to "endeavour carefully to please your Lady . . . be faithful diligent and submissive . . . [and] humble and modest in your behavior." They were told to get along with their fellow employees by being "loving to

Figure 3.7. Hannah Woolley, *The Compleat Servant-Maid* . . . (London, 1683), frontispiece. By permission of the Folger Shakespeare Library.

[other] Servants."⁵⁹ These feminine behaviors were especially encouraged for women who worked with children. Woolley's *Compleat Servant-Maid* of 1683 explained that nurses and child caregivers were to be "always merry and Pleasant,"⁶⁰ and John Shirley stated in his *Accomplished Ladies Rich Closet* (1691) that "a good Nurse" would be "pleasant and cheerful . . . anger must be a stranger to her."⁶¹ But these traits were imposed upon not only lower-status servants. Elite women were also supposed to exhibit feminine emotions of love and kindness while performing child care tasks. In his *English Gentlewoman* of 1631 Richard Brathwaite wrote that elite women should act kindly toward their young charges and that they should both inwardly and emotionally conform to feminine ideals of friendliness and love by taking "no small delight in Educating the young and unexperienced Damsels of [their] sexe."⁶²

These injunctions about female behavior and comportment were reinforced as they were drawn into the domestic scenes that accompanied women's prescriptive guides. Woolley's *Compleat Servant-Maid* of 1683 included an idealized image of a woman caring for children in a bedchamber.⁶³ The picture showed the woman rocking an infant in a cradle while two other young children hovered near her, one tugging on her arm and the other hanging onto the side of the baby's cradle (fig. 3.7). John Shirley's *Accomplished Ladies Rich Closet* (1691) furnished readers with two separate prescriptive examples of women caring for children.⁶⁴ In the first image a woman cuddles a swaddled infant in her arms while simultaneously watching over a second infant in a cradle. In the second image child care was taken outdoors, with the picture of a woman in a garden (another traditional site of female labor, as we have seen) helping a toddler walk with leading strings. In both of Shirley's examples, women were shown in postures that were meant to exhibit docility and calm competence: sitting with children, rocking children, and walking with children outdoors in gardens (figs. 3.8, 3.9).

Other prescriptive books urged practices of communal child care upon women. The tract *Aristotle's Compleat and Experience'd Midwife*, "made English" by a W____ S____ in 1700, proffers two women working together to wrap an infant in swaddling clothes (fig. 3.10).⁶⁵ W. S.'s image of the two women swaddling was adapted into Jane Sharp's *Compleat Midwife's Companion* of 1725, which also shows two women caring for an infant, one woman rocking the baby in a cradle and the other warming blankets in front of a fire (fig. 3.11).⁶⁶ These images might have been intended for lower-status

Figure 3.8. John Shirley, *The Accomplished Ladies Rich Closet of Rarities* . . . (London, 1691), frontispiece. © The British Library Board.

Figure 3.9. John Shirley, *The Accomplished Ladies Rich Closet of Rarities* . . . (London, 1691), frontispiece. © The British Library Board.

women who were employed in caring for elite children. But in these guidebooks, elite women were also pictured as being engaged in child care. Brathwaite's *English Gentlewoman* offered a vignette in which a well-dressed adult woman tutored three female children (fig. 3.12).[67]

Brathwaite's images both showed and told elite women how they were supposed to behave in nurseries and bedchambers. Under a banner labeled "Behaviour," the adult woman in the picture instructs her young charges via a speech bubble that reads, "Loving modesty is a living beawty." Brathwaite's

Figure 3.10. W.S., *Aristotle's Compleat and Experience'd Midwife* . . . (London, 1700), frontispiece. © The British Library Board.

Figure 3.11. Jane Sharp, *The Compleat Midwife's Companion: Or, the Art of Midwifry Improv'd* . . . (London, 1725), frontispiece. © The British Library Board.

book even offered a textual guide to its images, in which "the meaning of the Frontispiece, where in the Effigies it self, together with all the Emblemes, Devices, Features, and Imprezzas thereto properly conducing, are to life described." Brathwaite wrote in his guide that the woman instructing children in "Behaviour" was properly friendly and loving, for she "presents her self . . . with a cheerefull and gracefull aspect," and "by those children she

Figure 3.12. Richard Brathwaite, *The English Gentlewoman* . . . (London, 1631),
frontispiece. Beinecke Rare Book & Manuscript Library, Yale University.

hath about her, she expresseth what she professeth." To Brathwaite the mere
presence of children in the image was a sign that their female caregiver was
feminine, affectionate, and well mannered. Brathwaite's ideal caregiver was
also, not irrelevantly, proud of and owed her excellence to her British identity. He boasted that nurses, governesses, and mothers who followed his
model would display "modest facility, and native liberty" because they
"admi[t] of no forraine fashion."[68]

Moving outdoors to the spaces of the domestic exterior, ladies' guide
authors prescribed that their higher- and lower-status readers maintain qualities of gentleness, love, and docility. Dairies in particular were idealized as a
space of traditional feminine productivity.[69] In prescriptive texts, dairymaids
were taught to be gentle, soft-spoken, and kind. Markham's *English Housewife*
instructed "the milke-maid whilst she is in milking" to "doe nothing rashly or
suddenly about the Cow, which may affright or amaze her" and to conduct
herself "with all gentlenesse." Even the dairy cows themselves, Markham
explained, were to be "gentle and kindely." Anthropomorphizing these
farm animals as feminine beings, Markham insisted that a good dairy cow
should be "affable" as well as "gentle to her milker . . . [and] kind in her own

nature . . . loving to that which springs from her."[70] Accompanying images of women doing dairy work reinforced these ideals. Wolley's *Compleat Servant-Maid* of 1683 depicted a woman churning cream into butter in a dairy; the woman was smiling, imagined as happy to be engaging in what, as we have seen, was in reality a repetitive, lengthy, and strenuous chore (fig. 3.13).[71] John Shirley's *Accomplished Ladies Rich Closet*, printed in 1691, also portrayed a woman standing at a butter churn making butter; in the background, milk jugs and strainers hung on the walls of the dairy, alluding to the figure's productive work in making cream, butter, and cheese (fig. 3.14).[72]

Figure 3.13. Hannah Woolley, *The Compleat Servant-Maid* . . . (London, 1683), frontispiece. By permission of the Folger Shakespeare Library.

Figure 3.14. John Shirley, *The Accomplished Ladies Rich Closet of Rarities* . . . (London, 1691), frontispiece. © The British Library Board.

The image of the churning dairy maid was used a third time in a 1700 version of Woolley's *Compleat Servant-Maid*, again accentuating a woman churning butter in a dairy (fig. 3.15).[73]

Like the images of the woman in the kitchen standing over the fire with a spoon, these images of butter churning were rendered on new plates for each subsequent edition of the book (see, for example, the scale of the dairy-maid in relation to the curtain as well as the size and shape of the curtain itself in the images of the butter churner from 1683 and 1700). By 1727 the illustrated trope of the female butter churner was still being used, in R. Bradley's guidebook *The Country Housewife* (fig. 3.16).[74] Bradley's frontispiece represents women engaged in communal outdoor labor, one woman churning, another wiping out milk bowls, and a third operating a cheese press. Large strainers hang on the wall behind the women. The female workers in Bradley's image are working in an outdoor shed with open walls and a thatched roof; as if to illustrate some of the problems associated with laboring in outdoor spaces, a dog is shown wandering out of the dairy as the women work. In the foreground of the picture a leering man slouched next to a broken cartwheel is drawn smoking and drinking. This portrait of solitary masculine idleness directly contrasts with the cooperative industriousness of the female dairy workers.

Prescriptive guides for women as well as the woodcuts and engravings that accompanied them thus afford crucial evidence of the ideas that

Figure 3.15. Hannah Woolley, *The Compleat Servant-Maid* . . . (London, 1700), frontispiece. Beinecke Rare Book & Manuscript Library, Yale University.

Figure 3.16. R. Bradley, *The Country Housewife and Lady's Director* . . . (London, 1727), frontispiece. The University of Illinois Rare Book & Manuscript Library.

surrounded women's domestic work in elite homes in the late seventeenth and early eighteenth centuries. Intended for consumption by women of many different socioeconomic backgrounds, these guidebooks elucidate the ideologies that structured and informed women's work in elite homes, and they make clear that—despite what we have seen were the difficult material conditions of early modern women's domestic labor—both higher- and lower-status women were expected to work harmoniously and productively together in domestic work spaces.

Manuscript Recipe Books

Literate women's own writings also attest to their activities in domestic labor. The last vignette of this chapter examines lower- and higher-status women's domestic work through examination of a unique primary-source base: manuscript recipe collections. These handwritten books include lists of ingredients and step-by-step directions for making foods, medicines, cosmetics, and handicrafts. In the texts, medical and culinary recipes often appeared side by side. These sources were ostensibly composed by elite women of the period but, as we will see, they were edited, augmented, and impacted by women of many diverse ranks, ages, and educational backgrounds.[75] In the pages of their recipe books, female authors offered advice and aid to the other women in their social networks. They dispensed to friends, neighbors, servants, and relatives information about procuring ingredients and supplies for their homes. They defended female knowledge, space, and education from influences they perceived as threatening, such as that coming from male physicians and authors. And the authors of female recipe books created a sense of gendered community by augmenting, revising, and commenting on the recipes of their friends, employees, and relatives.

The image of domestic female labor as presented in these manuscript books was overwhelmingly positive, and in these sources elite women wrote of their cooperation with domestic servants and other lower-status women. This is not to say that the women who kept and wrote manuscript recipe books blindly, "naturally," or even thoroughly adopted the recommendations on female behavior that were offered in ladies' guides, but through close examination of these sources it will become clear that female authors did internalize, at least partially, prescriptive instructions to be cooperative, loving, and pleasant in the domestic work space. In manuscript recipe books one can find proof not just of female authors making attempts to foster positive relationships within kitchens, bakeries, bedchambers, gardens, and yards, but also of their (sometimes authoritarian) insistence on female collaboration within these spaces. Yet these authors used positive relationships in their own ways and to their own ends. In the pages of their recipe collections, the authors defended traditional practices of women's labor; they advocated the advancement and development of women's skills; they gave advice on managing the crowded, noisy, dirty, and dangerous work environments of elite homes; they offered help in procuring rare ingredients and hard-to-find supplies; they taught their readers how to traverse urban environments and how to negotiate confidently with male practitioners of trades like printing, apothecary, and surgery; and they shared knowledge about the flora and fauna of foreign countries, giving aid to British immigrants in the new worlds of the Atlantic and Pacific.

Manuscript recipe books have finally begun to receive the scholarly attention they deserve and are increasingly recognized as crucial sources for understanding the cultural and social history of early modern Europe. Recipe, or receipt, books afford historians wide ranges of evidence on the consumption patterns of early modern households, on publishing and the book trade, on personal health and vernacular medicine, on the transmission of craft knowledge and skill, and even on the spread of ideas associated with the "Scientific Revolution."[76] In manuscript recipe collections historians have found proof of women's many critical roles in health, healing, and domestic medicine.[77] Women participated actively in recipe culture, sharing their medical as well as their cosmetic, artistic, and culinary knowledge with female and male friends, relatives, servants, and neighbors.[78] And because manuscript recipe books were anthologies, even their composition and assemblage speak to early modern women's alliances.

Recipe books were living manuscripts, typically added to and amended by many people.[79] Women collected recipes from their female and male friends and noted donors' names next to borrowed recipes in their books. Jane Baber's manuscript recipe collection of 1625 included eight attributions from other women, among them a recipe "for the woorms" she had received from her "sister Earnly" as well as another recipe "to macke Puffe proved good Mrs. Cox."[80] Mrs. Carr's recipe book of 1682 featured "Mrs. Canleys Lemmon Creame," and Mary Dacre's book included thirty-four recipes contributed by female friends and relatives, including "Mrs. Sayers Reason Wine" and instructions on how "to make Bear [beer] Brisk and drink as well in two days, as if botled 6 week," which was "Mrs. Staffords receat."[81] Women could exchange these recipes in person, but manuscript evidence shows that they also received them in correspondence from their female friends and relatives. In 1658 Eliza Blennerhassett wrote from Ireland to her English friend Elizabeth Hastings to thank her for a "letter which I receved and the recepts you honoured me with."[82] Anne Lany scrawled a recipe "for Guidiness of the head" on the back of her letter to her friend Anne De Gray, writing in her missive that she was "sorry to hear you're Ladyship can not get rid of your distemper" and that she had enclosed instructions for a medicine used successfully by her sister, who was "cured with this receipt which I shall enclose, and desires you would trie it."[83] Sometimes the women who composed these letters privileged recipes received from friends over those offered by male physicians because of the respect they held for their skills and knowledge: Beatrix Clerke wrote in 1665 that she hoped to procure a recipe from her friend Lucy Hastings, stating that she "doth believe that your Honor's study and practice in phisicke is above our docters."[84]

Although recipes were sometimes gathered individually, many women created their collections by borrowing wholesale from the recipe books of their friends, neighbors, and family members. The author of an anonymous receipt book from 1640 described her method of compilation by explaining that she had excerpted several manuscript books: "the Lady Rayes Receipts," and "the Lady Baeshes receipts" as well as "receipts out of Mr. Ishams Bookes" and "receipts out of the Ld Conaways boake." She also borrowed recipes "out of an old book [of] my Lords Great Grand Mothers."[85] Amy and Mary Eyton's book was divided into similar sections subtitled "these receits following ware given me by Mrs. Moor," and "these receits following are Mrs. Steephans."[86] When Elizabeth Freke accidentally left her book behind while visiting family, she borrowed "my sister Austin's book mine being in Ireland" in order to create a new collection.[87] Female authors took pride in the fact that they were able to collect recipes from respected friends and relations. Remedies and recipes that previously had been tried and tested by close friends were considered to be safer, easier to rely upon, and more apt to work in a culinary or medical crisis. But recipe attributions additionally spoke to a female author's connections and her useful social networks. The book attributed to Lady Barrett featured a nine-page section attributed to a Miss Welldon; that the recipes came from a friend was considered a benefit by the author. She made sure to mention that the recipes in this excerpted section had been tried and proved, writing that "all these last nine leaves are Mis Welldons receits Probatom."[88]

Recipe books were compiled by multiple generations of women over long periods of time, and this facilitated cross-generational alliances. Historians have traced the ways in which early modern British women left legacies of personal papers, household items, and clothing to other women. Amy Louise Erickson argues that bequests of household items show women shared "close ties of female friendship" with their inheritors and that they gave household goods to other women to ensure that the items would be used and appreciated.[89] This argument can be applied to recipe books too. Women made frequent bequests and gifts of manuscript recipe books, and evidence of these exchanges appears in the books themselves. Cisilea Haynes received a manuscript recipe book from Anne Lovelace and commemorated the gift with the inscription, "Lady Anne Lovelace Gave me this Boek Cisilea Haynes

1659."[90] Elizabeth Okeover's recipe book was similarly inscribed, "For my dame Marcy Oke[over] this booke hath been writeing."[91] Anne Dacre compiled a quarto-sized recipe book as a wedding gift for her daughter-in-law Alatheia Talbot in 1606.[92] Mary and Amy Eyton both inscribed ownership marks into their shared recipe book of 1691.[93] And Elizabeth Digby's recipe book from 1650 was handed down to Jane Digby, the daughter of George Digby of Sandon.[94] Usually the books were given by women to other women, although they were sometimes given to men. When Frances Catchmay died in 1629, she asked that her recipe book "be delivered to her Sonne Sir William Catchmay." But even as Catchmay bequeathed the book to her son, she expressed her wish to have it circulated more widely, adding that she was "earnestly desiringe and Chardginge him to lett every one of his Brothers and Sisters to have true Coppyes of the sayd Bookes."[95] To Catchmay, the recipe book was a legacy, one she hoped her children would use and learn from long after she had died.

Recipe books therefore themselves provide evidence of female alliances, but female authors also worked to create senses of community within their collections. Frequently this was done through reference to collaborative labor. Female authors wrote recipes from a communal perspective and referenced in their books the women with whom they worked in elite homes. Mary Bent's recipe book featured instructions on how "to pickle cowcombers the best way," and the author noted that "you may put a little pepper in if you please but we do not." The use of the plural "we" here suggested that, for the recipe's author, pickling cucumbers was a communal rather than a solitary activity.[96] The plural "we" was also used in the book kept by Theresa Herbert and Mary Preston; their recipe for "a fish soupe" advised that "if you think there is not Butter enough add more to it wee generalley use about a pound and a halfe to this quantity." Another recipe in the same book, for "a powder of Mushrooms Excellent for all sorts of sauces and soupes," explained that "some put in pepper, nutmeg, ginger, mace and anchovey but ours is without them."[97] Elizabeth Okeover's recipe book wrote collaborative labor practices into recipes themselves; her manuscript included an entry on "a very good Black Salve," which Okeover had received from her "Aunt E.O." Okeover noted that production of this salve was itself a collective effort, for "there must be two at making it for one cannot do it."[98] And the recipe book from 1692 owned by Lady Ayscough similarly encouraged and reinforced practices of collective female health care in a recipe, "For the Flowing of

Flowers," which was intended to ease menstrual pain. The recipe called for a cloth "dipp[ed] . . . in plantane water" to be applied to the patient's abdomen in order to alleviate cramps. But before the wet cloth was applied, the recipe contributor (a woman named Mrs. Hone) recommended that "one of the maides [should] warm itt a little betweene her hands and then lay itt to the belly."[99] Women thus were taught to rely and call on one another—and in some cases, to demand help—for both the circulation of recipes and the application of them.

That Ayscough's book referenced the skills and labor of "maides" is significant. Women gathered recipes from women of all ranks and stations and noted these contributors in their manuscript books. In Anne Brumwich's recipe book was a contribution from a local magistrate's wife entitled "a receipt of Alderman Langhams wife of a sere cloth almost for any thinge as aches, swellings, spr[a]ins, soares, bruses, cuts to draw and heale if not an hot humour."[100] And Elizabeth Godfrey's recipe book included a "recipt for a cancor in the brest," which had "cour'd [cured] Mrs. Finches maide."[101] Many other women collected recipes from servants who lived and worked in their homes.[102] Mary Dacre's book, compiled over thirty years from 1666 to 1696, included several recipes she had gleaned from wet-nurses. A woman named "Nurse Colman" provided recipes for "a Rare Purge" and "for a hoarsness or cold," as well as "to make an exclent Lime watter." A second woman, playfully called "Nurse Barefoot" in Dacre's text, contributed recipes for "posit Drinck in a feeavor" and for "an Exelent thing . . . to chere the sprits, for the scurvey, to procure a good Apitete, and to take after an inflamation."[103] A woman named "Nurs Blicotts" contributed a "cure for a cutt" to the book kept by Mary and Amy Eyton,[104] and a "Nurse Barrett" offered "a spechell Oyntment, good for all bruces, swellings, pains and the siatteca" to Mrs. Head's recipe collection.[105]

Recipes were collected as well from women outside of the home.[106] Sometimes recipes were acquired from urban laborers: Mary Chantrell's receipt book of 1690 provided instructions on "how to scower lutestrings and . . . sarcnett [sarcenet, a soft, thin silk] hoods" and was attributed to a laundrywoman whom Chantrell had met in London. Chantrell wrote that "the woman as give these two receapts, I knowed her to gett the greatest part of her Bread by them in London a great parte of her life," signaling that Chantrell had talked with the woman about her life and livelihood and that their relationship was amiable enough that the laundress was willing to give, or to sell, evidence of her methods to Chantrell.[107] Other recipes show the extent to which elite women relied on the help and labor of lower-status women to procure ingredients. Mrs. Carr's receipt book from 1682 said that "a wound drinke for any fistula, sore brest, leprosy, or any Manner of Runing sore in any part of the body" was made with fresh herbs, "but," she explained to her reader, "if you have occasion to use this drink in winter you may buy the herbs ready dryed of the herbwoman all the winter long."[108] The advice of aged persons was also welcome in recipe books; one anonymous collection from the mid-seventeenth century included a recipe from "Old Mis Lancstone, for one that hath a cough of the lungs or a cough a long time."[109] And Chantrell's book offered a recipe for "an ointment for an each [ache] or scrinkeng [shrinking] of the senues [sinews]," which had been "approved by an old woman who was grown crooked in her hams."[110] All of these examples illustrate the great degree to which elite women came into contact and worked with women of all kinds, both within their homes and in shops and markets.

Elite women thus counted on lower-status and aged women for advice and aid, but there is evidence that elite women also used their recipe collections to advance female independence. Women's recipes allowed them to share knowledge about acquiring materials and ingredients, navigating through urban spaces, and negotiating with male shopkeepers.[111] Many recipes encouraged women to purchase supplies in London, which had large numbers of apothecary shops. "M.B.'s" recipe of 1640 "to whiten the Teeth" called for "the stones of crabbs," and readers were told that "you may buy [them] at the Redd Crosse in Cheap side a drugist."[112] An anonymous mid-seventeenth-century woman's book recorded that "Vatican Pills" could be purchased from "the Apothecary that makes them . . . in the old Bayly in London at the signe of the three blacke lyons, his name is Smith."[113] And Mary Chantrell's book had a recipe for "an Excellent Coole pummatum [pomatum] for the face," with ingredients that could be purchased "in See Lane in Holbourn."[114] Some manuscript books even supplied women with lists of fair prices. Anne Lovelace told readers of her recipe book to purchase saltpeter "at houndsditch in gravell lane in London" and explained that "it may be had for 4 shilings a bushel."[115] Instructions like these enabled women to negotiate and claim urban London as their own. That women shared this knowledge with the members of their alliance networks is also evidenced in their recipe books. Anne Brumwich's book highlighted a recipe for a lotion that was said to prevent hair loss, and the ingredients for this lotion had to be purchased near Gray's Inn, London, at "a Chymist a dutchmans in high holborn neare Grayes Inn field." The author was careful to record that she had received the instructions from a female friend, for the lotion was "Mrs. Trusells receipt."[116] From Gray's Inn to Cheapside and from the Old Bailey to Holborn, early modern women used the information they gleaned from the recipe books of friends and relatives to traverse urban space. This knowledge was surely both useful and empowering. By furnishing women with information about reliable dealers, fair prices, and shop locations, handwritten recipe books allowed female recipe authors and their readers to share vital knowledge with one another and assert their independence in London's streets and alleys.

Recipe books certainly enabled women to take advantage of rare ingredients available in urban spaces like London, but they also allowed women to gain new knowledge about the properties and efficacy of foreign recipes and practitioners. Some women boasted of the information they acquired from people who seemed alien or unusual: an anonymous seventeenth-century recipe book, possibly compiled by a woman named Mrs. Baesh, included instructions on how to make "an excellent Salve to heale any wound or sore, taught by a Jewe" and a recipe for a "salve made by an Egiptian good for any wound."[117] Elizabeth Digby's recipe book from 1650 boasted of a "medicine for those that have lost the use of their Limbes with the gout, or other diseases." Digby claimed that "with this did an Italian helpe Margarett lying bed-rid at London." This Italian healer was "one of the Kings servants wives," and her Mediterranean unconventionality apparently lent credibility to the recipe, for Digby went on to write that "many more have beene helpen since with the same [recipe]."[118]

Other recipes were made noteworthy by their exotic ingredients, products that mostly had come from around the world. Eager to take advantage of products that were being discovered and cultivated overseas, many women sought to incorporate transatlantic goods into their culinary and medical repertoires. Mary Dacre's recipe book adapted an old recipe on how to make "Mrs. Rigamores Pectorall Decoction" to take advantage of new world ingredients. Dacre wrote, "If this drink does not quite cure the stomack, you must anoint it with oyle of tobacco."[119] For Dacre, new and fashionable products like tobacco improved the recipe, increasing its efficacy. The recipes in Freke's late seventeenth-century commonplace book called for ingredients from across both the Atlantic and the Pacific: she included a recipe for

"Tobacoe Salve" which was "good for all wounds" and also provided a description of "Tea, or Thee." Freke explained to her readers that "this shrub grows in Japan . . . the goodness of it is known by itts Fragrantt Arrimatticall smell," and she proudly exhibited her expertise on this foreign plant by stating knowingly that "one pound of Good Tea is worth A hundred of Bad Tea."[120] One of the recipes in Jane Newton's receipt book appealed to trans-pacific tastes even as it celebrated British thrift: it taught how "to Make Mango of Mushmillions [muskmelons]," which Newton promised "shall eate as well as any India Mango that we give two shillings or half a crown [for]."[121]

Recipe books helped women who emigrated from Britain to the West Indian and mainland British American colonies adapt to their new environments. A collection of recipes now called the Charles Brigham Recipe Book, held at the American Antiquarian Society in Worcester, Massachusetts, was transported from England to the British American colonies by one of its many contributors. This collection shows how recipe book authors used their books as adaptive tools. A woman named Anna Cromwell started the Brigham book in 1650, and the collection includes ownership marks from at least three other women, all of whom added to, revised, and amended the book through the late eighteenth century. References in the early pages of the book show that it was originally compiled in England, while later references show that the collection was continued in Massachusetts.[122] Close study of this remarkable source shows how recipe authors used their books to learn about and use the new plants, animals, and foodstuffs available to them after emigrating to the Atlantic colonies. The recipe "to sauce a turkie like stargion [sturgeon]" suggests that one of the authors learned how to cook new world breeds of animals, like turkeys, by preparing them in the same way as fish eaten in Britain. Other recipes celebrated the new plants that were at colonists' disposal; one recipe "to cleanse a skurffy skin" instructed practitioners to "bath the place where the scurff is with spirit of nicotiane," a reference to *Nicotiana tabacum*, or tobacco. Another recipe in the same book, for a makeup called "incomparable cosmetick of pearl," crowed delightedly about the availability of this precious commodity in the colonies, noting that "this is one of the most exelent beautifiers in the world this oil if weel prepared is richly worth seven pound an ounce in England."[123]

The information that early modern British women circulated in their recipe books also enabled them to take advantage of the knowledge of male professionals. Information acquired from male physicians and alchemists was reproduced and appropriated in women's medical manuscripts.[124] Lady Barrett's recipe book suggested "four receits [that] was taught me by a distiller," one of which was "the Led Life Water or Water of Life."[125] A recipe book that belonged to a mid-seventeenth-century woman boasted that she had borrowed a recipe "for the wormes to be given to a child," from a "Dr. Chambelaine" and that she had seen its effects proven on "a child of 3 yeares ould."[126] Anne Brumwich's book included a recipe "for eyes that have skins or mists before them" which had been "commended by Do[ctor] Thurberwell an Oculest."[127] This practice was also used for culinary recipes: the book compiled by Amy and Mary Eyton listed a "receipt for Pottage" that the author wrote had been "given me by my Lord of Ormonds Cook."[128] Occasionally women's own expertise in traditionally masculine fields was celebrated; Anne Lovelace's recipe book of 1659–63 included an entry on "extracting the oil from Feathers," which had been invented by "Mrs. Jane Richards [who] rec'd 20 Guineas from the Society of Arts for this."[129]

Women who had male relatives employed in the formal practice of medicine appropriated their recipes for their own use. Sarah Palmer's recipe book had instructions on how to make "the syrup of wort," which she had collected from "Dr. Fulwoods sister." Palmer declared of the recipe that "Probatum est, Docter Fullwoods sister gave mee this."[130] Mrs. Head, the daughter of a doctor named Sir George Ent, used many of her father's recipes in her own manuscript recipe book. Head recorded a medicine that was "ordered for [daughter] Ketty, when she was about a year old and in a consumtion by my father." Another recipe, with "Camomel and Seafery flowers of each a purgil, aniseeds and juniper berries of each half a dram, [and] a little peece of liquorich stick" had been "proscribed by my Father for my husband."[131] Mrs. Head recorded and appropriated her father's recipes, placing them alongside her own medical inventions in her manuscript recipe book.[132]

Although women did adapt professional medical knowledge to their own use, many women's recipes worked to defend female knowledge in health care and medicine by criticizing the actions of male doctors. The book compiled by Mary Preston and Theresa Herbert presented a recipe for "The Rumatism Water" which had "cur'd Mrs. Throckmorton when al[l] the docter left her of[f]."[133] Elizabeth Okeover told her readers that an "ointment to strengthen the legs and back" in children was most efficacious accompanied by a bloodletting. She warned that although she felt it "necessary the

Child be let blood in the eares," it was a course of treatment "disapproved of by some phisitians." "Yet," Okeover asserted, "I have found by experience that the cure is more difficult with out it."[134] Anne Brumwich's recipe book listed ingredients for "a soverain powder to cuer the stone," which the author wrote "hath been proved by the Lady Digby." This recipe was lauded in the book as being better than instruction or care provided by male doctors, for although Digby "could never find ease by noe meanes that docters could use," the author wrote proudly that Digby's medical invention "hath freyed her from all her terrible fites and keeps her fre from paine."[135] And Elizabeth Digby's own book from 1650 listed a recipe "for the winde in the Stomacke," of which the author bragged that "this being knowne will breed health, and hinder gaine to the Phisitian."[136]

Mary Chantrell's book even included two recipes that had saved women when male doctors could not; the first, "a perfect cure for the dropsey and scurvy . . . hath cured when the ablest dockters in London hath left of dead persons." And the second, "for a cancer in the breast," had apparently "dissolved a cancer in Mrs. Hartops Brest wich was designed to have beene cut of[f] by Mr. Hobbs."[137] The claim in this recipe resonates with findings made by Seth LeJacq, who has documented gendered resistance to amputation and surgery in his excellent article "Butcher-like and hatefull." LeJacq argues convincingly that early modern British surgeons' tools were figured as masculine, and in cheap-print lampoons their "razors" were depicted as threatening to the virtue of female patients.[138] Recipes like Chantrell's therefore allowed women to praise their own efforts in curing and protecting female bodies—and especially intimate, sexualized parts of the female body, like breasts—from the incorrect diagnoses and threatening amputations of male physicians.

Women worked to separate and defend their manuscript recipe collections from recipes in print. Some women copied recipes from printed books into their manuscript collections, adapting and claiming them as their own. Elizabeth Freke copied information about "trees, herbs, and roots" from Gerard's *Herball* into her recipe book but made the information her own by noting that it had been "collected, and abstracted by me Eliz: Frek for my own use: March the 22 1700."[139] Other women adapted recipes from female authors: Lady Ayscough's recipe book furnished instructions for "an excellent astringent sirrupe" which the author had gleaned from "Mrs. Wooly," probably a reference to the popular Woolley.[140] But several manuscript books

claimed their superiority to printed collections. An early eighteenth-century
book compiled by Mary and Jane Hammond held instructions on how "to
presarve Damisons," with the addendum, "I can ashure you this is the best
recect you can have if you look over all the bookes."[141] Jane Newton's manuscript collection of 1675 bragged that her recipe for "Partridg Potage" was "a
thing never yet in Print." Newton privileged her handwritten collection for
its inventiveness, and she went on to promise her readers, "I shall give you
the best directions for the making them when I treat of bake meates which wil
bee thereafter given you."[142] By asserting their own knowledge, creativity,
and capability, female authors of manuscript recipe books set their works
apart from printed recipe collections.

Despite assertions of community, creativity, and cooperative labor in
women's texts, evidence of conflict between women in the domestic work-
place sometimes appeared in recipe collections.[143] Women disagreed about the
ingredients for recipes and argued about the best techniques to use in cooking.
The recipe for "My Lady Bradshaw's Posset" inside of the Mary Bent recipe
book noted a correction, for the inscriber wrote in the margin of the book that
although Bradshaw's original recipe called for the use of wine, "I pute ine a
quarte of gooseberry and halfe a pound suger in sted of the wine to every
gallon."[144] Similarly, the original owner of the Mary Bent book had a recipe
for "Portegall Cakes" which called for the cakes to be formed into a size "the
bigness of half a crown." But a later owner of the book corrected this, crossing
out these instructions and writing instead that the cakes were to be placed in
"petty pans and bake them in a modrit oven."[145] Some recipe collections even
expressed criticism or outright dislike. Later owners of the Mary Bent recipe
book added reviews of many of the book's original recipes. Sections on how
"to Make an Oyster Pye" and how "to Pott Beef Like Veneson" were both
deemed "not good" by later owners of the book, who scrawled their negative
opinions in the margins next to Bent's recipes.[146] These corrections demonstrate that women did sometimes disagree in the pages of their recipe collections, but the notes surely also suggest that female recipe writers believed their
notations, emendations, and marginalia would be taken seriously and read
carefully by future owners of their manuscripts. All of these examples prove
that women devoted an enormous amount of time to reading, editing, and
revising the recipe collections of their female friends and relatives.

But the clearest evidence for the inscription of female alliances into
manuscript recipe books comes from the conversations women wrote into

their books. As recipe books were passed from owner to owner, women engaged with one another in the margins of their texts. Crammed into the borders of recipe books, tucked next to and around the edges of the recipes themselves, these comments provide evidence of the opinions and tastes of each successive owner. This practice of commentating certainly demonstrates how women internalized idealizations of female cooperation and collaborative domestic labor. But the practice attests as well to the living character of early modern recipe books, their use by diverse and successive owners, and the accumulative nature of their creation.

Some female authors created conversations in their recipe books by inscribing and excerpting personal correspondence directly into their collections. Elizabeth Okeover copied a portion of a letter alongside a recipe for a "Cordiall Tinckture good for a rheumetisem" into her manuscript book; in the letter, one of her cousins urged Okeover's daughter Betty to "be pereswaded to make tryal of these things I hope thay would doe her a great deal of good."[147] The book created by Anne Brumwich included a recipe for "the stone an ilectury [electuary]," which was "sent and recommended by my Lady Cavendish who writt May the 24 1716 . . . to Mis Hussey at Bloxham."[148] The Charles Brigham Recipe Book features a recipe on a loose folio along with a note from the donor: "I commend to you that precious salve called diacaleitheos or diapalmeum this salve quickly heals wounds."[149] The recipient of this "precious salve" tucked the entire letter into the binding of the recipe book, perhaps to serve as a reminder of the donor's friendship as well as a record of the recipe's benefits.

The best example of letters that were excerpted directly into recipe books comes from Elizabeth Freke, whose commonplace book included a recipe entitled "to make Lodunum." The recipe was accompanied by a long narrative which provided the recipe's provenance and explained how Freke had acquired it. Freke wrote that it was actually "the Lady Powells Receitt" and that it had been "sent me by my sister Austen in my distress." Freke then mentioned the recipe's efficacy and safety, for her sister "has taken of itt neer two years her selfe." Freke added the date, writing that her sister Austen had "sent [it] 1712." Freke then went on to copy a long portion of Austen's own letter into her recipe book:

> I have sentt my deer sister the receitt of the Ladynum; as I make itt
> . . . to master the humour; (which I hope my deer sister itt will doe)

both in your head and back. My Lady Powell, who gave me this receitt says she had bin dead many years since butt for it. . . . my Daughter Judith when shee takes itt has often the benifitt of putting her into asleep for six or eight howers together tho' in the collick. . . . I have a neighbour by me tells me she takes itt twice a day. . . . all these informations I give my deerest sister thatt you may see itt is a safe thinge and nott be affraid of itt . . . butt for all thatt I wrightt itt my deer sister with pleasure hopeing itt may doe you good, and then itt is butt a small penance to purchas to ourselves a little ease whilst we live in this world.[150]

This inclusion worked in several ways. By using phrases like "deer sister" and "deerest sister," Austen expressed her affection for Freke as well as her worry about Freke's illness and her hope that the recipe would afford her sister "a little ease whilst we live in this world." But in addition Austen's letter attested to the recipe's legitimacy by specifying the many women who had used it. The laudanum had been made and safely consumed by Austen herself as well as by Lady Powell, Austen's "Daughter Judith," and an anonymous female neighbor who enjoyed the medicine so much that she "takes itt twice a day." The testimonies of these four women were cited by Austen so that Freke would "see itt is a safe thinge and nott be afraid of itt." Freke was encouraged thereby to trust the opinions and medical knowledge of this community of women, all of whom had made the recipe for themselves and found relief through it. Freke felt so reassured by this inscribed alliance that she used Austen's words in her own manuscript book, where they would have served as a reminder of sororal affection but surely also of the care and authority of her network of female friends.

As this vignette has shown, elite women's manuscript recipe books provide much evidence of women's labor in domestic work spaces. The authors of these collections were elite women, but the recipes inside of the books were unmistakably influenced, edited, and contributed to by women of many socioeconomic backgrounds. The image of collective female labor presented by recipe book authors was overwhelmingly positive, a reflection of the mores that characterized women's guidebooks, which sought to persuade female workers to adopt feminine behaviors of kindness, productivity, cooperation, and gentleness. But even as they adhered to prescription, elite recipe book authors worked to advance their own interests and agendas, promoting female space, knowledge, education, and financial and commercial independence.

Early modern female alliances were not the sole privilege of wealthy women and their equally affluent female friends and relatives. In the kitchens, chambers, and yards of their homes, elite women forged complex and sometimes contested bonds with female servants, neighbors, and friends. Recovering evidence of these relationships is extremely difficult. But early modern women's efforts in collaboration, cooperation, and shared labor are made manifest in household inventories, prescriptive texts, and manuscript recipe collections.

4. Hot Spring Sociability: Women's Alliances at British Spas

This chapter marks a turning point in my examination of women's alliances in early modern Britain. Women constructed social ties in their homes, in reading, thinking, and writing about the meaning of friendships and alliances; in the exchange of handmade presents for their friends; and in the challenging domestic labor they performed alongside other women in the kitchens, bedchambers, and yards of elite houses. But women also created and maintained homosocial relationships across the urban spaces, national borders, and oceans that constituted Britain's early empire. One of these urban spaces in the seventeenth century and the early eighteenth was the hot spring spa. Spa cities such as Bath, Epsom, and Tunbridge have been recognized by scholars as historically significant sites in early modern Britain. Focusing mainly on the late eighteenth century, historians, literary critics, and scholars of art, architecture, and design have shown that these cities were extremely popular in the period, hosting hundreds of visitors each year.[1] Women and men of both high and low status traveled to spas seeking cures; elite visitors additionally enjoyed opportunities to socialize with one another in the gardens, pump rooms, bowling greens, and ballrooms for which spas became famous. Spa cities were vibrant spaces in the seventeenth and early eighteenth centuries, long before the Georgian period that most modern scholars have focused on; and spas, in addition to being gathering places for people of both sexes, were sites of same-sex sociability, as both women and men undertook distinct activities during their sojourns.

Excerpts from the letters of three women who were writing from spas to their female friends at home give one a sense of the ways in which spa activities were gendered. Writing to her mother between 1676 and 1678, Katherine Perceval privileged the health care advice from her female friends over that of the spa doctors, insisting that she "dare not advise with the Doctors here . . . becaues I think I am better provided with the advice my worthy good freinds supplied me with in their instructions to me when I parted from you."[2] Growing angry that male socialization intruded on time that should have been spent more profitably on health concerns, Anne Dormer complained in letters written between 1685 and 1691 that by accompanying her brother to the spa she had incurred unwelcome obligations among his social circles: "I had littel benefitt this year going with my brother who loves a great deal of company which to me that want rest was very inconveneint and expencive too."[3] In a letter to her sister in 1682 Mary Leke mocked a male cousin's behavior at the spa, expressing her hope that bathing women would be more interested in meeting together to "scold" men rather than flirting with them: "I fancy my Cozen Coot has had plasent sport att Ebsem [Epsom baths] I wod give aney theng that he was knoen and that all the yonge wemen he made love to . . . wold gett togather and scold at him."[4] As Perceval's, Dormer's, and Leke's letters evince, early modern women held complex assumptions about the purpose and function of British spas. Seventeenth-century spas may have been imagined by some early modern Britons as spaces for heterosexual flirtation, but in a time when homosocial interaction was the norm for many women, spaces like the spas, where women chose to participate extensively in homosocial activities, deserve fresh study.[5]

Spas throughout Britain, but mainly at the largest, most popular spa cities of Bath, Tunbridge, and Epsom, were described and experienced by early modern women in many ways. Testimonies from women's diaries, correspondence, and household account books reveal that spa cities, despite their relatively small size, had visible and authoritative female populations and catered to women's activities and priorities.[6] Women at the spa facilitated same-sex sociability by drawing on feminine knowledge of medical care, cookery, and handcraft to create and deepen their female alliances both by talking and writing about healing the sick, making food, and producing works of art, and by joining with other spa-going women in these activities. Spas served as crucial sites for gendered identity creation. My analysis of identity creation in early modern spas is influenced by the work of Miles

Ogborn, who, in his *Spaces of Modernity*, urges scholars to seek out "the specific sites in which subjects are formed."[7] Like Ogborn's Vauxhall Gardens, British spas served as a site in which subjects were formed; but many of the spa's subjects were women, who, through their activities at hot spring cities, contributed to the creation of a new, modern femininity. Femininity was created in the late seventeenth and early eighteenth century in part through the acts of sociability women undertook at spas: by visiting and taking the waters in tandem, by exchanging medical advice and providing child care, by providing physical and emotional care for others, and by sharing experiences of illness and disease.

An image of the city of Bath drawn by Thomas Johnson in 1675 illustrates what spas looked like and how they functioned (fig. 4.1). This extremely detailed pen-and-ink drawing depicts the King's and Queen's Baths, the two largest pools in Bath's spa complex. Throughout this chapter I will examine this image in detail. By comparing vignettes from this image with corroborating documentation from female-authored correspondence, diaries, and account books, I will explore the gendering of spa cities and the creation and maintenance of female alliances within them. Johnson's image helps to illustrate what a typical bathing experience was like in the late seventeenth and early eighteenth centuries.

Spa Practices

To "take the water" in the early modern period meant to seek its effects both internally and externally and for extended periods of time. Women and men stayed for weeks or even months at a time in spa cities in order to seek cures. In 1717 Grisell Baillie, a gentlewoman from Scotland, traveled to the English city of Bath for several months, writing in her diary that she "was 9 weeks at bath from 8 Aug till 8 Octr." Her long stay was perhaps predicated on the length of time it took her to travel between Scotland and Somersetshire, for she noted that she was "9 days on the roads . . . going and coming from Bath." In March 1729 she made the journey again, remarking that this time she was on the road "16 days to Bath."[8] Once travelers arrived in spa cities and began their health regimes, they bathed frequently. It was common to swim, soak, and walk slowly within the baths. Stone benches or seats were built into the walls around each pool, and bathers reposed on these, "generally set up to the neck in water." The stone seats could be adjusted to the

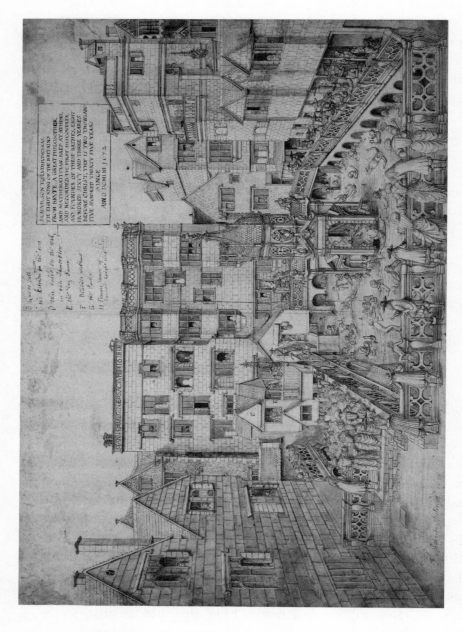

Figure 4.1. Thomas Johnson, "The King's and Queen's baths at Bath, looking West," 1675. © The Trustees of the British Museum.

height of the individual bather; one female spa-goer reported, "If you thinke the seat is too low they raise it with a coushon as they call it, another Stone." But, she reassured her readers, this was not uncomfortable, for "the water bears you up that the seate seemes as easy as a down coushon."⁹ Those who sought the benefits of bathing without risking full submersion could utilize aboveground pumps. In this case local workers could be paid to siphon water mechanically onto a patron's affected body part—a lame leg, a sore arm, or even a head: "I saw one pumpt, they put on a broad brim'd hatt with the crown cut out, so as the brims cast off the water from the face . . . they have two pence I thinke for 100 pumps."¹⁰ Johnson's print confirms this practice, depicting the figure of a man activating a pump by pulling on a long pump handle. In the print this building is marked by the letter "E" and is identified in the accompanying key as the "Dry Pump" (fig. 4.2).

Visitors to the spas also drank the waters, filling glasses and ceramic bottles at street-level pumps which purportedly gave access to fresh liquid, that is, not already paddled in by bathers. But their drinking the water didn't mean that early modern patrons considered it to be pleasant or even

Figure 4.2. Detail, Johnson's "Baths."

palatable. Bath's sulphurous water was said to be "very hot and tastes like the water that boyles eggs, has such a smell."[11] Despite its distinctively unpleasant smell and taste, drinking natural spring water was so popular that sometimes bottles of it were transported to people who were unable to travel to the spa cities themselves. Celia Fiennes reported that the waters from Tunbridge Wells were often consumed away from the spring site: "Many has it brought to their lodgings a mile or two off and drink them in their beds, nay some have them brought to London which is near 40 miles; they have the bottles filled and corked in the well under the water and so seale down the corks which they say preserves it."[12] Declarations in other women's papers suggest that deliveries of this sort were a fairly common practice. Mary Parker, Lady Fitzharding, wrote from London to her spa-going friend Sarah Churchill, Lady Marlborough, that although she didn't "design to drink the waters" at Bath, she was advised "to take some waters hear which the dockter says will doe me as much good."[13] Declaring that water from a spring at Rousham had been good for her health, Anne Dormer wrote that she had been able to drink it without traveling, for "the spaw water . . . had been sent downe before I went from home."[14] And in 1716 Grisell Baillie paid £1.03.06 for "12 botles Spa water" to be sent to her home in Scotland.[15]

For a majority of cure seekers, however, there was no substitute for visiting the source. Johnson's image of Bath immediately assaults the viewer with the busyness of these baths. His view of the King's and Queen's pools depicts men and women crowded together on the promenades and avenues overlooking the waters and depicts people swimming in the waters. This seems at first to match the physician Edward Jorden's assessment that the baths were "bear gardens . . . where both sexes bathe promiscuously" and the Anglican clergyman William Harrison's claim that seeing the steaming and frothing pools of Bath reminded him "of the Resurrection," where bathers "appear so nakedly and fearfully in their uncouth, naked postures."[16] But in the case of many women who wrote about their spa experiences, spa pools were rigidly segregated by sex. Celia Fiennes, a singlewoman who traveled extensively on her own and wrote enthusiastically about her experiences, is one of the best sources for understanding the daily patterns and routine behaviors of female bathers who pursued homosocial activities at the spas. Fiennes, who made many of her travels in the company of other women, outlined her bathing procedures at the Bath spa.[17] Contrary to Jorden's mixed-sex "bear gardens," at Bath, Fiennes insisted, men and women "keepe their due distance," not least for fear of being chastised by a watchful "Serjeant belonging to the baths" who was employed by the City Corporation to make sure that "order is observed. . . . [he] punishes the rude."[18]

Women and men swam separately in the pools. Fiennes wrote that male bathers frequented the middle of the pool, while female bathers generally stayed on the outer edges: "The middle has seates . . . for the Gentlemen to sitt and round the walls are arches with seates for the Ladyes." Although Fiennes admitted that the baths were crowded, she explained that women swimmers hired female water guides to help govern each bathing session. These chaperoning women, one stationed at each elbow of a female bather, kept the patron upright while she was in the pool, "for the water is so strong it will quickly tumble you down."[19] To completely protect a female spa patron from the press of the swimming crowd, Fiennes reported, it was usual to hire "2 of the men guides [to go] at a distance about the bath to cleare the way" during an aquatic perambulation.[20] The use of bath guides was also refer- enced in Grisell Baillie's account book, as Baillie wrote of paying nine shillings for "guids" while on a visit to Bath in March 1729.[21]

As for clothing, Harrison's cry of a "naked" or "uncouth" scene from Revelation found no purchase in Fiennes's accounts. Fiennes remarked that men wore "drawers and wastcoates" while swimming, while female bathers were mummied in multiple layers of flannel, linen, and starched and pleated canvas: "The Ladyes goes into the bath with garments made of a fine yellow canvas, which is stiff and made large with great sleeves like a parsons gown, the water fills it up so that its borne off that your shape is not seen, it does not cling close." To avoid the embarrassing risk of being seen in wet, clingy (and therefore inappropriately revealing) garments after ascending from the bath—Fiennes scolded elsewhere in her diary that "wett garments are no covering to the body"[22]—she assured her readers that in the city of Bath stringent clothing rules were imposed, all of which assured bathers of suffi- cient degrees of privacy: "When you go out of the bath you go within a doore that leads to steps which you ascend by degrees, that are in the water, then the doore is shut which shuts down into the water a good way, so you are in a private place, where you still ascend severall more steps, and let your canvass drop off by degrees into the water, which your women guides takes off and the meanetyme your maides flings a garment of flannell made like a nightgown with great sleeves over your head, and the guides take the taile and so pulls it on you just as you rise the steps, and your other garment drops off so you are wrapped up."[23] Fiennes's version of bathing is reflected in Johnson's drawing. Although Johnson's baths are crowded, they are organized and sexually segregated (fig. 4.3). Bathers are not depicted touching one another except in a very few instances, and when they are, these people are in same-sex pairs. Johnson even draws women guiding one another while walking in the bath.

Spa Sociability

For many women, spending time in female company rather than with men was a critical component of the experience of visiting the spa, both in the water and out of it. Fiennes recounted that sociable diversions on the grassy lawns at Tunbridge Wells were also segregated according to gender, for "the Gentlemen bowle [but] the Ladies dance or walke in the green."[24] These separate activities were copied at Epsom, where on the verdant Upper Green Fiennes found "Gentlemen bowling [and] Ladyes walking."[25] That early modern women sought female company when attending the spa is also visible in their correspondence. When Katherine Perceval traveled to France in 1678 in order to improve her health and to visit some of the country's famed mineral spas, she was accompanied by her daughters Helena and Katherine as well as their maid Betty Willis and their housekeeper Deborah Fowler; all five women took cures during their French sojourn.[26] In 1680 Mary Dering requested that her daughter accompany her to Tunbridge Wells and talked to her of inviting a mutual female friend on their visit: "I cannot brag much of my health so I feare I must see the bath before I come to London but if I dow, I hope you will come to mee and I know Mrs. Fenton will not be unwilling to come to mee there."[27] In 1695 Katherine Manwaring, informing her friend Frances Hastings of the attendance of three of her female relatives at Bath, wrote that she "had a letter from my Neice Baules and she thinks she shall goe to [Bath] the end of this month my sister Chos and my Neice Betty are with her."[28]

Figure 4.3. Detail, Johnson's "Baths."

A brief comparison of these women's homosocial spa experiences with those of Samuel Pepys, a famous male diarist, will help to demonstrate that interactions at the spa were often segregated by gender. Pepys was a frequent visitor to hot springs in Bath, Tunbridge, Epsom, and Barnett, where he often socialized with other men while seeking cures for constipation and his persistent gallstones. When Pepys visited the hot spring at Barnett in 1664 he went with his longtime friend, servant, and companion William Hewer, writing on July 11, 1664, "I and Will [went] to see the Wells, half a mile off, and there I drank three glasses, and went and walked and came back and drunk two more."²⁹ Pepys made another visit to Barnett with his cousin William Joyce, when he went "to my cozen W. Joyce's, who presently mounted too, and he and I out of towne . . . thence forward to Barnett, and there drank."³⁰ Three years later, in July 1667, Pepys visited Epsom to drink from its well and wrote that while drinking the waters he was able to socialize and conduct business with other men: "We got to Epsum by eight o'clock, to the well; where much company . . . I did drink four pints, and had some very good stools by it. Here I met with divers of our town, among others with several of the tradesmen of our office."³¹ The next year Pepys visited the city of Bath with his wife and some of their friends; upon their arrival on June 12, 1668, Pepys toured the city in the company of a man, their landlord: "We come before night to the Bath; where I presently stepped out with my land-lord, and saw the baths, with people in them."³² Watching the bathers was an activity that Pepys enjoyed again a few days later with his male friend Mr. Butts. The two men walked through the city and observed people bathing in the pools, where both men took note and talked of the socioeconomic status of the bathers: "Up, and with Mr. Butts to look into the baths, and find the King and Queen's [Baths] full of a mixed sort, of good and bad, and the Cross [Bath] only almost for the gentry."³³

Pepys enjoyed socializing with men while in spa cities, but the clearest proof of his practices of spa homosociability occurred in Epsom, where he made several visits with his friend, rival, and frequent bedmate John Creed. In July 1663 Pepys and Creed took a short vacation to Epsom together. Pepys wrote that he and Creed "resolved that . . . we would go to Epsum. So we set out." When the men arrived at the spa city they "could hear of no lodging, the town so full." They finally found a small room to share, which Pepys called "a lodging in a little hole we could not stand upright in." But Pepys and Creed were not dissuaded by the size of their room and "rather than go further to look we staid there." The two men dealt with the close quarters with friendly intimacy and good humor, as Pepys recorded that "by and by [we went] to bed, where, with much ado yet good sport, we made shift to lie, but with little ease, and a little spaniel by us." Although the limited space meant that Pepys got "little ease" in sharing a bed with Creed, he enjoyed the friendly intimacy, or "good sport," it afforded with his friend. The next day, after taking the waters, Pepys and Creed amused themselves by wandering through the countryside, when Pepys "took him to walk up and down behind my cozen Pepys's house. . . . I led him to the pretty little wood behind my cozens house, into which we got at last by clambering, and our little dog with us, but when we were among the hazel trees and bushes, Lord! what a course did we run for an hour together." Romping and playing in the woods made the men "all bewildered and weary and sweating," and the two decided to lie down for a nap together: "Creed he lay down upon the ground . . . and going and lying by Creed an hour [we rested]."[34] Walking the city as a flâneur, conducting business with tradesmen, horseback riding through the country-side, running and roughhousing in the woods, and sleeping out of doors were activities traditionally or stereotypically enjoyed by—and in many instances, allowed solely to—early modern British men. For Pepys, the expe-rience of taking the waters was tied to acts of masculine homosociability.

Women at the spa likewise undertook activities that were traditionally or stereotypically enjoyed by women. Elizabeth Harley's papers offer some insight into the ways women could use the spaces of the spas. Her account book from 1687–88 has accounts she kept during time spent at Tunbridge Wells. They show how Harley's purchasing patterns changed while she was at the spa, for these accounts were bracketed not only by those kept at Harley's home of Brampton Bryan on the English–Welsh border, but also, even more usefully, by those she kept while visiting London. Comparing her accounts from London with those from Tunbridge, we are able to ascertain how Harley's lifestyle in London and in Tunbridge differed not only from her everyday life on her country estate, but also from each other. They suggest that, for Harley, Tunbridge functioned very much as a space for female–female activity. The accounts indicate that while at the spa Harley was surrounded by women. She was with women when involved in elite entertainment and play, writing of distributing money on one occasion "for Mrs. P [Harley's cousin Mrs. Partridge] and hir made to see the popet sho." But Harley's accounts also reflected the gendered demographics of the spa city's laborers. Harley's disbursements were divided into two categories: money that was paid and money that was given, that is, what was allotted in payment for goods or services as opposed to what was offered for charity. When Harley paid for services she merely listed the object purchased and the amount, but when she gave in charity she either mentioned the beneficiary by name or identified them in some other way. While this is interesting in and of itself—it implies that Harley perhaps associated herself more intimately with those she sponsored charitably—it also divulges the gender of the people with whom Harley engaged. One recipient of Harley's wealth was her maid Selwood, issued money "for a faring," or to attend the spa city's fair or festival; other recipients included, "a pour woman that cut her nose."[35]

Harley's account books also record that a majority of the people with whom she interacted were other women. She gave money to fourteen women over the course of her stay, but on six occasions only were her disbursements to men. This stands in stark comparison to her activities in London, where funds were distributed equally between male and female recipients.[36] Further, the women with whom we can document Harley interacting, while usually of lower social status, varied in their employment. Some, like the woman with the slashed nose, were probably indigent poor, but other recipients were occupied in labor associated with the city, such as money "given to the made whare I loged" on two separate occasions. When Harley closed her reckonings at the end of her stay in Tunbridge, she offered money to all of the servants and tradespeople with whom she had interacted on a daily basis. Seven of the nine were women, and all seven were recorded by Harley as being "goodwives," implying that they worked in the city rather than being supported by its charity. Even on those rare occasions when men were named personally by Harley, they were associated with women. Harley offered money to "Goodey Forms boys" and to "Goodey Ward . . . her son."[37]

Harley's book suggests that while patronizing the spa elite women could choose to bathe, eat, entertain, and do business within a largely female community. Spa cities were places where the female population was larger than the male population, and female residents of spa cities were socioeconomically diverse and widely visible. In his study of Georgian spas, Peter Borsay has written that one of the "most striking characteristics of resorts was the female profile of their population," both among members of "the service sector, with its high demand for female labor, especially as domestic servants," and also among the "large numbers of affluent women visitors and residents."[38] Confirmation of the popularity of spas among women can be found in some manuscript sources as well. Pepys noted in his diary, for example, that he saw "much company come; very fine ladies," when he visited Bath in June 1668.[39]

While statistical data on the female populations of spa cities are scarce, two brief examples from Bath hint that the city was populated largely by women. Bath's poor and needy were frequently employed by the City Corporation and given jobs that required close interaction with visitors. Bath had two almshouses, St. Catherine's Black Alms and St. John's Blue Alms (named for the color of the robes the inmates wore), which partnered with the City Corporation to supply the city with a labor force. In the early seventeenth century these almshouses accommodated nearly three times more women than men, with fifty-five female almsfolk to nineteen males. This sort of data matches population studies done by David Souden, who shows that sex ratios in southwestern counties like Somerset, where Bath is located, were skewed dramatically toward women.[40] Almshouse records attest as well to the visible presence of poor women working at the spas and in the city: washing clothes, caring for swimmers, and cleaning public buildings. This was work required by those who ran the almshouses and was intended to act as recompense for inmates' upkeep.[41]

The second example comes from Bath's highly visible female presence in trades which guaranteed interaction with visiting bathers: between 1640 and 1740 many women applied to the Bath Corporation for deeds to run businesses in the service industry. These records show that women ran boardinghouses and confectioner's shops, bake houses and millineries. One woman oversaw a slaughterhouse and another a coffeehouse, while a large number of women applied for deeds to manage brew and public houses.[42] Women's correspondence corroborates this practice. In 1651 Mary Haton Helsby visited Bath and wrote to her friend the Lady Smith that "there be manie millaners of good report (& some bad) but . . . I want none of them as yett."[43] A map of Bath drawn by Joseph Gilmore between 1694 and 1717 confirms the large number of women working in the city's service industries. Around the margins of his map Gilmore drew small pictures of some of Bath's lodging houses. Twenty-three houses with rooms for rent to spa visitors appear on Gilmore's map, and six of these were recorded as being run or managed by women. Gilmore advertised "Mrs Savils Lodgings Nere the Hot Bath, Abbey Church" and "Mrs. East's Lodgings in the Abbey Green." A woman named

Ms. Childs ran a lodging house in High Street, and three women managed properties on Westgate Street; this cluster of women's boardinghouses were run by "Ms. Toop," "Ms. Pocock," and "Ms. Granfield."[44] Westgate Street, only a tenth of a mile in length, was a street on which many women lived and did business. The Bath City Corporation deeds register that a woman named Elizabeth Gay leased a stable on Westgate Street in 1647 and that Mary Stoughton leased a public house called the Rose and Crown in the same location in 1661.[45] That Westgate Street was home to three of Bath's landladies and several businesswomen over the course of fifty years is perhaps indicative of the spa city's gender divisions.

Despite the general popularity of spas in the seventeenth and early eighteenth centuries, some women did not want to undertake visits to hot spring cities. In their writings early modern women who were ill or incapacitated expressed fears about the discomfort of leaving home, traveling to the spa, and undergoing intense medical regimes. An elderly Scottish woman named Mrs. Bruce wrote to her female friend in 1707 that she was unsure about "agoeing to the Bathe." Her husband wanted the couple to take the journey, and "Mr. Bruce apears to be not only ernest but posative to heve me go thear." But Mrs. Bruce was not convinced. She explained that she was "alltogether agenest it for I'll be a vere trublesome carige . . . as bot dead weght [as but dead weight]." Bruce's advanced age and her physical immobility made her nervous about traveling from her home in Kinross, Scotland, to Bath. She also expressed embarrassment about bathing in public, explaining that the thought of swimming in the baths "apears to me a thing unpraktekable wethuet mekeing a beas figeuer [without making a base figure], and as I thenke wan had much beter not go atall."[46] Other women reported that drinking and swimming in the spa waters made them feel exhausted and sick. In 1691 Anne Dormer's father encouraged her to go to Tunbridge Wells to improve her health. She complained that her stay at the spa had been "a tedious time" and that the visit had been detrimental to her health, for "I cann scarce say the water did me any good, it pass't so ill, and it purg'd me so much, that I look like a gridiron."[47] Katherine Moore wrote in July 1678 that her mother had been injured by drinking spa waters in France, recounting that "my mother took the waters 7 days but they did not doe her any good. . . . I beleive they would have done her much hurt we all saw she was much the worse for it."[48] Other women, even after completing a bathing regime, found the results of the spa visit to be inconclusive. Henrietta Borlase confessed to her friend Lady Alltom sometime between 1660 and 1680 that she could not tell "what good I receafed by the bath." Borlase admitted, "I find my sellfe much better than I was but cannot say I am quite well for I have som pane still."[49]

Early modern women may have registered their hesitation and skepticism about the benefits of spa visits, but, critically, even when women did not wish to visit the spas, some sources show that they could at times prevail upon one another to do so. Elizabeth Shirley wrote to her niece Lady Norse in 1694 that Norse's mother was "really very ill and you know Madam has allways had so ill helth." Shirley encouraged Norse to tell her mother to visit the spa, for "her life I beleve will not be long. . . . I hope you will prevall with her to use the Bath."[50] When Frances Hastings miscarried in August 1692, her husband, Theophilus, wanted her to visit the spa to regain her health. He wrote to his mother-in-law Anne Leveson that he was "under very greate concern for my wife who misscaried on Saturday with much pain hath bin very weake." But Frances was unwilling to make the trip to visit the spa. Theophilus explained that while "myself and all her friends perswades her to goe to the Bathe," his wife "hath hitherto obstinatly refused itt." Appealing for help, he ceded his ostensible control over his wife to his mother-in-law, explaining, "You hath authority sufficient to prevaile with her to doe a thing so necessary for her health."[51] Theophilus Hastings acknowledged that it was women, not men, who held the "authority sufficient" to make decisions about matters relating to health care and spas for other women.

Spa Activities

Spas had large, visible female populations, and they were places where women undertook same-sex activities like bathing, shopping, discussing health regimes, and providing medical advice and encouragement. But documentation that spas functioned as feminized spaces can also be found in the very visible presence of children.[52] The sort of leisure activities frequently offered at spas promoted childlike activity and fun. Bowling greens, dances, raffles, and lotteries in addition to puppet shows and toy shops featured prominently at spas, and these entertainments were enjoyed by both children and adults.[53] Grisell Baillie's children and servants often accompanied her on trips from their home in Scotland to Bath, where they spent sizable sums of money on entertainments. In August 1716 Baillie recorded that she had spent

£8.10 "for expence of Publick divertions at Bath" and a further £4.10 "to Raffles at Bath." Much of this entertainment money was spent on her two young daughters, Rachel and Grisell. She gave money "for Musick books to Grisie" and £1.7.6 "to Rachys poket."[54] Some children themselves even served as sources of spa entertainment: Celia Fiennes reported that the city of Epsom held amusement races every Monday afternoon, featuring either "boyes, or rabbets, or piggs."[55] The spa was understood, even by young children, to be a site featuring fun, play, and toys. In August 1690 Theophilus Hastings and his wife visited Tunbridge, leaving their thirteen-year-old son George behind at home. George wrote to his father, hoping "the waters doe agree well with your Lordship and will cure you of the headake" and asked for a present from the spa, hoping that "your Lordship will bring me something from Tunbridge."[56] This playful atmosphere extended into the spa pools. In Johnson's drawing, among the many busy figures soaking in the water are some engaged in play: two people float in tandem with their limbs locked around each other. In another part of the image two feet rise jauntily from the surface of the pool. Early modern print sources confirm these practices: Thomas Guidott's *Register of Bath* commented that an adult man named Edward Shepheard, a joiner, was frequently occupied "swimming in the Bath, and diving for farthings as Boys use to do" (figs. 4.4, 4.5).[57]

Spas were certainly seen as sites of youthful fun and play, and children themselves were visible and active spa patrons, both in and out of the water. Shepheard's practice of "diving for farthings" was apparently de rigueur among young spa-goers; male visitors to Bath wrote of paying to have boys dive for coins in the depths of the large pools, a diversion which was enjoyed by John Leland as well as by Pepys.[58] Johnson's work documents this, showing the figure of an elite man carrying a walking stick and a sword who

Figure 4.4. Detail, Johnson's "Baths."

Figure 4.5. Detail, Johnson's "Baths."

Figure 4.6. Detail, Johnson's "Baths."

is flipping a coin from his fingers while naked children clamber to retrieve it (fig. 4.6). Yet the drawing portrays many children in the spa pools, and not all of them are represented as amusing wealthy men by diving for coins. Several children are shown swimming in company with adults. In one vignette two small children cling to the buoyant shoulders of an adult swimmer. Nearby, another small child clutches at the back of a swimming adult, receiving a ride through the pool (figs. 4.7, 4.8).

The sight of children cavorting in the pools was not an unusual one, but sources also suggest that children took the waters in their own right and

Figure 4.7. Detail, Johnson's "Baths."

Figure 4.8. Detail, Johnson's "Baths."

that they underwent health-care regimes. The spas were a refuge for sick children and infants who were brought to the springs for therapy, often by their mothers. In 1689 Elizabeth Harley professed her reluctance to leave her household duties for a visit to Stoke, but she wrote that she eventually decided to undertake the trip on behalf of her child: "I was willing to cum because the weather was prity fare and my poor little babeye not well."[59] Grisell Baillie recorded in her household account book that her daughter Rachel received treatments at spas and bagnios on a regular basis. In November 1715 Baillie paid six shillings "for Raches going to the Baino to cup," and in July of the next year Baillie observed that the treatment was repeated, and again she paid six shillings "for Rachys Bathing and cuping at the Banio."[60] Other medical treatments—in this case, cupping, a type of phlebotomy—were often combined with spa regimes.[61] Sometimes young patients' treatments were conducted in the company of other spa-goers. Mothers and their children were often treated simultaneously. Dr. William Simpson reported on a Scarborough spa treatment prescribed to Mrs. Mary Bateman of York, who was cured of "a scorbutick cattarrhe," described as "rheumes, which had swelled up her face and eyes." Immediately after this entry he listed one for her daughter: "The daughter of the aforesaid woman (of about ten years of age or more) had an Erisipelas or Inflamation in her legg, called vulgarly the shingles."[62] Some doctors even sought to treat infants literally *through* their mothers. In 1693 Dr. Thomas Guidott wrote that the son of Richard Ford, an apothecary in Bath, received mineral water therapy at only sixteen weeks of age by "sucking the Mother, who drank the Bath waters, received cure, and made the same effects as if the Child had drunk the waters himself."[63] This reinforces the idea that early modern health spas were sociable places and catered to the mutual, even simultaneous, treatment and entertainment of mothers and their children.

Female care of and interaction with children at the spas was especially stressed in early modern children's own writings. In 1687 the siblings Anne and Henry Petty, whose mother, Elizabeth Petty, Lady Shelburne, had been called away to manage the family's lands in Ireland and, perhaps unexpectedly, could not accompany them, visited Epsom under the watchful eyes of their mother's female friends. While it may initially seem strange that the Petty children were sent to take the waters on their own, as there is no intimation that they suffered from a specific physical complaint, their lavish entertainment at Epsom renders spas as places which not only supported the labor of rearing children, but also catered to their well-being and entertainment. One of Elizabeth Petty's friends, a woman the children referred to as "Lady Blundell," took Anne and Henry "to the wells, where we saw all that that place did afford the danceinig Raffleing Toy Shops Lottery etc." After this excitement, the children wrote that another one of their mother's friends looked after them when "my Lady Caverly carryed us home in her coach." These amusements continued over the course of the visit, as the children wrote that "there was a horse race and my Lady Mordant let us her Coach to go see it," and later that yet another "coach carryed us to . . . see the pupite show the bowling green and all that was to be seen at that place."[64]

That Elizabeth Petty's female friends took so much time to entertain the children, and did so with such frequency, suggests this was an activity common to the spas. In the letter, four women are mentioned as having spent time with the children: Lady Blundell, Lady Caverly, Lady Mordant, and a Mrs. Rouse. These women not only accompanied the children to special entertainments such as puppet shows and horse races, but also spent time socially in their company, talking and visiting with them. The children wrote that this was a frequent event because while in Epsom they "went and call'd [on] my Lady Blundell (whom we see every day)." The care these women took with the children was noted by the young Pettys, and they made sure to inform their mother that her absence did not hamper their social engagement: "My Lady Blundell is as kind to us as if your Ladyship was here we could not be better but for your Company." Moreover, it appears that Blundell paid close attention to Anne and Henry Petty's physical health. She advocated that they lengthen their stay, insisting that since she couldn't "tell wheather the air will doe us good in so short a time," it might be better if the children's vacation was extended. Overall, the visit was so genial and the time so well and happily spent that the children assured their mother, "Wee are as well here as if we were att home. . . . [everyone] is as kind to us as can be imagined and we eate and lye very well."[65]

Attestation of practices of child care at spas demonstrates how these cities enabled women's experiences and occupations. But early modern women also claimed the spaces of the spa—and reinforced their senses of feminine gender identity—through the creation of handcrafts at the baths. Two types of handcraft that were created by early modern women who visited the spa were confection, which included sugared fruits, preserved spices, sweetmeats, and candies; and decorative art handwork, displayed in this instance through the painting, gilding, and embroidering of frames and mirrors. As we saw in chapter 2, confection and decorated objects were multivalent objects. When women exchanged such articles with their female friends, the goods conveyed information about women's identities, educations, and the early modern ideals of femininity to which they were expected to adhere. But confection and art handwork were also items through which women expressed their claims to the spaces of spas as well as the recognition that they could create a female culture, language, and identity within these sites.

Thinking, writing about, and making confection were popular activities among women at spas. While visiting the baths women traded both medical and confectionary receipts with other female patrons. Recipe exchange was a common activity among women in any locale, but many spa-goers noted carefully in their manuscript recipe collections when recipes had been gathered from friends at the baths—and many of these were for sweets and candies. Joan and Joanna Gibson recorded a recipe in their manuscript collection for "How to make Lemon Cream," which, they wrote, had been given to them by a "Mrs. Bowes at Bath 1702."[66] And in the margins of Elizabeth Freke's commonplace book of 1684–1714, the word *Bath*, along with a date, appeared next to several of her accumulated receipts. The Bath recipes Freke collected included sugared "Bath Cakes," a favorite and iconic treat in the city and such confectionary as "Bath Tarts," "Cheese Cakes a dozen," and "To make Puff Past[ry]," all of which, Freke wrote, she learned in Bath in 1712.[67]

This type of notation is itself significant. But the recipes women like Freke and the Gibsons collected while visiting spa cities had an additional special characteristic: they all called for large amounts of sugar. This is perhaps due to the fact that spa cities were themselves associated with the consumption of confection and baked goods. Celia Fiennes reported an unusual prevalence of sweet bakery and confection at Bath, explaining that the city was known for its "little Cake-houses where you have fruit Sulibubs and sumer liquours to entertaine the Company that walke there."[68] This was also the case at Epsom, which boasted several "shops for sweetmeats and fruite."[69] Some of these confectionery shops were so close to the hot water springs themselves that, as Fiennes explained, the activities were almost combined: "There is a house built, in which the well is . . . where people have carrawayes sweetemeates and tea etc."[70]

The consuming of sugar was an integral part of a spa experience, both outside and inside of the pools. Samuel Gale and Ned Ward both witnessed women who swam through the spa waters towing small candy-filled containers. While they soaked in the bath the women tied enameled and japanned wooden bowls to their arms with ribbons, which allowed the bowls to float on the surface of the water and afforded their owners ready access to therapeutic sweets. Treating this practice as a routine part of female medical practice in the seventeenth century, the Bath commentator Ward explained that "the Ladies with their floating Jappan-Bowles, freighted with Confectionary . . . Wade about like Neptun's Courtiers, supplying their Industrious Joynts."[71] Gale explained the decorated vessels were kept close at hand not for sustenance but for medical purposes, "in case the exhalation of the water should be too prevalent."[72] In Johnson's print the practice is confirmed by the presence of the figure of a woman holding aloft small receptacles suitable for carrying food and drink (fig. 4.9).

This custom was so pervasive that spaces within the baths themselves were named after those female-dominated rooms in early modern households in which confection was either created or consumed. The area directly underneath the statuary in the middle of Johnson's image of the King's Bath is labeled "the Kitchen" (fig. 4.10). Fiennes confirmed this nomenclature in

Figure 4.9. Detail, Johnson's "Baths."

Figure 4.10. Detail, Johnson's "Baths."

her diary, writing that the area, "they call the Kitching in the K[ings] bath . . . is a great Cross with seates in the middle and many hot springs riseth there."[73] Another of these spaces was "the Parlor," a water-filled, walled room just off the Queen's Bath. Within this enclosure Johnson draws women clustered together in conversation (fig. 4.11).

Confectionery was a sought-after commodity at spas at least in part because of the widespread use of sugar in early modern medicines. When early modern women recorded consumption of sugared products at spas, they were enacting their feminine knowledge of health care and medicinal remedy. Natalie Zemon Davis argues that women gained a sense of identity

Figure 4.11. Detail, Johnson's "Baths."

in caring for others. When women invented and manufactured medicines, when they practiced the trade of midwifery, when they provided health advice to others, and even when they tended the ill, Davis writes, they found a "vocational identity" as well as a sense that they were part of an educational lineage and historical tradition.[74] Privileged among medical labors, the production of sugared foods required detailed skills, spoke to a specific kind of education, and in the early modern period was a uniquely feminine task as well as a fundamentally genteel one. In addition, as we saw in chapters 2 and 3, sugar work was expected and desired of higher-status women.

Proof of women's work with and consumption of sugar, sweets, and other exotic transatlantic and transpacific goods at spas can be found in their manuscript records. In July 1716, during Grisell Baillie's and her daughter Rachel's visit to a spa in Scotland, Baillie listed in her account book the purchase of exotic, imported goods alongside her daughter's bathing treatment, writing that she had paid "for spermacity 18d., Lozanges 2s., saffron 3s.6d., Baino Rachel 6 [shillings] and spice 1s.6d." Baillie regarded the spa as a place to buy confections like "Lozanges" as well as rare items like spermaceti, a whale fat used in the production of medicines, "spice," and "saffron," all of which came from overseas. A month later, in August of that year, the pattern was repeated when Baillie visited the city of Bath and bought sweets and imported goods, such as "8 lb. green Tee," "Modera [Madeira wine]," and "ginger bread."[75] Elizabeth Harley was an avid consumer of exotic goods and sweets during her stay at Tunbridge spa, and the purchases she recorded in her household account book hint at the extent to which women undertook confectionery projects while seeking hot spring cures. At Tunbridge, Harley purchased ready-made confections as well as ingredients commonly used in the production of candies. According to her account book, Harley, like Baillie, purchased tea at the spa, but she also laid out money for wafers, herbs, candied or dried lemon peel, sweetmeats, a "chis cake and p[e]ars," peaches, apples, preserved nutmegs, and a seed cake. She purchased flummery, a sweet milk porridge, on three occasions and, most suggestively of all, about triple her usual consumption of sugar: "2 pound of dubel refine shuger" on one day and "Shuger . . . and [two] Wouden shuger box[es]" on three other occasions. This contrasts with the accounts she kept at London. On a visit to the capital immediately preceding her visit to Tunbridge, Harley purchased sugar only once, in a single one-pound increment.[76]

Moreover, elite women who traveled to hot spring cities spent much of their time in the manufacture of nonedible luxury goods such as decorative mirrors, ornamented picture frames, and painted or embroidered silks. These, too, spoke to an elite, feminine knowledge and identity. Part of an elite woman's education comprised training in crafts and handwork, and women frequently produced such items in order to give them as gifts to friends (see chapter 2). To highlight the way that this process worked within spa cities I'd like to return to Elizabeth Freke's papers. In her personal manuscripts, Freke collected recipes in order to convey her culinary, medical, and fine art techniques, and she claimed these recipes were "for my own use and most of them experyenced by mee Eliza Freke." Freke was careful to name alongside each recipe "the authers from whence I had some of them collected." This kind of attribution was characteristic of Freke's manuscripts, which comprehended recipes from more than forty of her female friends and relatives.

In addition to the confectionery recipes she had learned "at the Bath," the spa portion of Freke's book recorded skills she had acquired in painting, craft, and handwork during her visit. Among these were detailed rules for mixing pigments and preparing painting surfaces. During her sojourn at the spa Freke wrote that she had learned how to make a "scarlett [paint to use] upon wood" which contained ingredients such as white and clear varnish, carmine, and vermillion. Freke inscribed lengthy instructions on how to properly combine these expensive ingredients while making red paint, noting, "Your fine red you doe not grind." Instead, Freke wrote that paint makers should "mix a drop of gum watter and spring watter" to smooth the pigment. When ready to paint, Freke explained, the handworker should not "wett your colers to much" but should mold the paint "with your pencil against the side of your gally potts" in order to achieve a desirable consistency. This entry she marked with her initials, writing that she had "learned [this] at Bath by EF: 1712." The instructions were so specific that Freke even suggested the reader should "buy the coulers at the couler shops att St. Lukes head, neer St. Clemments Church." On the same page, she went on to note a fair price for which one could expect to purchase the pigments.

Another set of handwork recipes in the Bath portion of Freke's account book was "learned by my Daughter Freke at the Bath." This indicates that Freke's daughter had accompanied her on the spa journey and that the two women had taken part in some of the same leisure activities during their hot-water sojourn. Under the words "to painte on Satten," Freke wrote that her daughter had been taught the following: "When you have painted any thing, before you end itt you must . . . darken your worke by goeing over itt often; which yet you must doe with a light hand and shade itt as you would doe needleworke."[77] This divulges not only the detailed, exacting nature of Freke's instruction—implying that the conversations and time spent on the subject were lengthy—but also the degree to which this information was exchanged between women. Freke had been given the recipe by her daughter-in-law and then had written it into her book, signifying the pair's shared knowledge and appreciation of handwork skills. But even more revealing was the language Freke (and, by extension, her daughter) employed. She and her daughter equated the satin-painting technique with a method of embroidery. Freke's notation in her manuscript recipe book that handworkers who painted satin should "shade itt as you would doe needleworke" proved she had received her information from people who understood what this meant. The statement was a relevant reference point only to people who were skilled in needlework themselves. In early modern Britain, needle workers were almost exclusively women.

In this single but extremely illustrative example one sees that spas were spaces in which female cultures, skills, and languages were cultivated and appreciated. Freke's entry for satin painting shows how some of the hand-worked objects produced at the spa facilitated female discourse. Freke's instructions tied her painting activities to her needlework, a material object

that historians have shown worked to augment female agency, express political power, and even showcase female alliances.[78] Although she wrote that
her recipe book was for her "owne use," Freke's manuscripts were hardly a
product of one woman's experience. Early modern women habitually read
and exchanged recipes; reflecting the importance and even privileging of
female kin, women's wills bequeathed their receipt books to cherished family,
neighbors, and friends. Freke's many recipe attributions to other women as
well as her daughter-in-law's salient presence in the book's pages made her
receipt book a product of Freke's female community. Her instructions were
therefore not just a reminder to herself but also a guide for the women who
might own, read, and learn from the book during her lifetime and after her
death. Within the space of the health spa, Freke formulated a female language
made up of words and references that would have been understood and
appreciated by other early modern women. And by speaking to other women
through the pages of her book as well as by instructing them in a gendered
language Freke announced her feminine identity.

Few scholars have studied what spas were like before they became a popular
Georgian diversion. As Sylvia McIntyre acknowledges in her study of
Georgian spas, "Our impression of Bath in the late seventeenth century is
obscured by the tendency of later [Georgian] writers to disparage the past in
order to praise the present."[79] Despite their enormous popularity with both
women and men, Restoration spas and the gendered activities that took place
within them have largely been ignored by scholars of early modern Europe.
I have attempted here to alleviate what McIntyre called the obscurity of the
Restoration spa by exploring the intersections between sociability and care
of the body in late seventeenth-century health cities. But, crucially, I have
worked to recover women's own voices and perspectives on spa life and
sociability, validating the view that spas were sites of feminine identity
creation and that women used their gendered experiences of child care,
confectionery, handwork, and the provision of health care at spas in order to
enrich their female alliances.

5. Yokemates: Female Quaker Companionship in the British Atlantic World

In the summer of 1729 a British American woman named Susanna Heath Morris (1682–1755) was shipwrecked off the coast of Holland while on a voyage from America to Europe. Morris was a Quaker minister from Pennsylvania who was traveling to preach about her faith.[1] But Morris had not made this perilous journey alone. She was traveling with a woman named Sarah Lay, whom she described as "my comfortable Companion." Morris believed that she shared a special religious bond with Lay, one so intense that the emotions engendered in their relationship would sustain them both in frightening, life-threatening situations. As Morris's and Lay's ship approached Amsterdam, Morris remembered that "at night the wind grew boisterous and the mariner young and unskillful so that we got fast on a sand bed." Broken, leaking, and stuck on the sandbar, the ship began to sink. In this moment, Morris reported, Lay "held fast hold on me." Clinging to her companion in the stormy sea and facing what both women thought was certain death, Lay pledged her devotion to Morris, declaring that "if she then must die she would go off with me." This intense commitment was possible, Morris believed, because of the religious bonds the two women shared, for "the living Lord was a comforter to me and my dear companion Sarah Lay and that we were so in fellowship one with another."[2]

Lay and Morris were Public Friends, traveling preachers who traversed Britain's earliest empire in order to spread the message of Quakerism.[3] In this time period Quaker women traveled by ship, on foot, and by horseback across enormous distances: to visit the British American colonies of Long Island, Rhode Island, Massachusetts, New York, New Jersey, Maryland, and Pennsylvania; the British West Indian colonies in Antigua, Nevis, and Barbados; and throughout the British Isles, in England, Ireland, Scotland, and Wales. Some made three or four transatlantic voyages over the course of their lifetimes.[4] These early modern itinerant Quaker women described their voyages in very specific ways, writing of them as "sufferings" undertaken for Christ's sake. Many of them were poor, uneducated, and of lower social status and endeavored to mitigate the hardship of travel through companionship with women of their same faith. Traveling women formed a prominent part of the colonial British American and colonial West Indian landscape, and female alliances helped them negotiate travel and emigration through the spaces of Britain's earliest empire.

Quaker preachers frequently wrote of and published chronicles of their travel, participating in what was a well-established literary genre in early modern Britain: the sufferings narrative. Although Quaker women carefully situated their own stories in relation to this popular literary genre, their written accounts were reflections of the actual adversity faced by female Quaker travelers. Itinerant female ministers, who were frequently viewed as rootless and "masterless" as well as heretical, were treated by most non-Quakers with scorn and unease and sometimes with outright hostility and violence.[5] But by describing their ordeals in print and by positioning themselves as feminine sufferers, these women attempted to gain the sympathy and pity of their readers. Homosocial relations were central to these female Quaker missionaries. During their travels they sought solidarity with and solace from other women. Although female Public Friends occasionally traveled with men, they more frequently undertook their extensive, often transoceanic, voyages with women, who acted as their religious partners and fellow travelers. These itinerant women wrote that their female companions sustained and succored them during arduous missions.[6] They valued female companionship and believed that the spiritual society they shared with their female companions heightened their religious experiences. Female Quakers called their travel partners yokemates, figuring them as devoted, long-term companions who shared an identity of religious purpose.

Quaker Women and Sufferings

Female Quaker ministers were prolific writers. In the latter half of the seventeenth century nearly four thousand texts by Quakers appeared in print, and 5.7 percent of these were written by female Quakers; even more texts were dictated by women or featured them as the main subjects. As Catie Gill has argued of Quaker women authors in this period, "[In] print culture, female Quakers had few rivals."[7] The early Quaker texts, printed and circulated widely throughout America, Britain, and the West Indian colonies, were part of a deliberate campaign to disseminate positive information about the faith. Kate Peters has written, "The early [Quaker publishing] movement should not be dismissed as a disillusioned spiritual remnant of the English revolution, but was rather a purposeful campaign which sought, and achieved, effective dialogue with both the body politic and society at large."[8] This campaign to persuade nonbelievers of the legitimacy of the Society of Friends was especially necessary for women because Quaker publications functioned as vehicles for expressing authoritative female perspectives and speech. Conscious of the hostility of most early modern Britons to female Quakers, printers and pamphleteers struggled to make female Friends' public presence acceptable.[9] Quaker women themselves wrote and published in accordance with this goal, but also because they believed the exercise to be essential to their faith. This was especially true of Public Friends, the women who traveled and preached in order to publicize Quakerism throughout Britain and its early colonies.

The physical challenges undertaken by traveling Quaker women and the literary works they subsequently published about their voyages were intended as "testaments for truth."[10] Believing that the most genuine followers of Christ suffered in his name, Quakers felt that their physical torments and spiritual tribulations identified them as Christ's true adherents. Any affliction a preacher might experience in the course of a mission was thus to be offered to public view because it was a testimony of religious devotion and a lived example of faith.[11] This style of Quaker writing, the sufferings genre, provides evidence of early Quaker women's experiences in traveling and preaching. Drawing upon fifteen printed tracts composed by traveling women as well as supplementary manuscript correspondence and personal diaries kept by these Quakers, I will show that, while their texts adhered to the standards of the sufferings genre, the works nonetheless constitute meaningful evidence of Quaker women's actions in travel and divulge the very real hardships faced by early modern women who traversed the British Atlantic world. By describing their activities in preaching and proselytizing as suffering, Quaker women not only strove to advertise and promote their faith but also worked to cast themselves as "feminine" victims deserving of pity, sympathy, and support.

Historians usually have associated the type of bodily religious torment promoted in the sufferings genre with Quakerism's early, enthusiastic, and "convention-defying" phase.[12] It is certainly true that the introduction of "quietist" practices in the 1670s as well as the formal certification of female preachers allowed traveling Quaker women a certain kind of authority within their community.[13] But charismatic and bodily religious suffering was crucial to the lives, writings, and female friendships of traveling Quaker women. As late as the 1750s the actions of Public Friends were considered to be strange, and their motivations unknowable, even sometimes to fellow Quakers.[14] Repetitious, wide-ranging travel was dangerous and painful in this period. Quaker preachers faced hostility well after the Act of Toleration was enacted in 1689, and within Quakerism writing of missionary travel as an experience of dedicated and profound suffering continued as a prolific, popular literary genre throughout the seventeenth century and the eighteenth.[15]

Although the sufferings genre was a recognized literary convention, the stories told by Quaker women in their writings were reflective of actual events in their travel and preaching. As Gill emphasizes, "Sufferings narratives are a particularly rich source of information on the persecutory treatment of women by Quaker opponents, and because these texts reveal the level of hostility [faced by Quaker women preachers], they are relevant for establishing the obstacles women faced when taking a public role in Quakerism."[16] The correspondence and published narratives written by Quakers do evince some of the continuing challenges faced by women who joined the Public Friends. These sources illuminate the many very trying experiences of early modern Quaker women in Britain's first empire and also represent the ways in which these women envisioned their struggles and how they grappled with the difficulties and trials they believed were inherent to their missions.

Procuring funds for their missions was a central theme of Quaker women's travel narratives. Public Friends were discouraged from relying solely on the hospitality of non-Quaker strangers whom they might encounter in their travels. This meant that Public Friends were dependent on either their own funds or the international network of Friends' Meetings to sustain them in foreign territories. All Quakers were encouraged to offer hospitality to Public Friends in the form of food, clothing, and transportation.[17] This probably reinforced a sense of Quaker community and was intended to highlight every individual Quaker's appreciation for the work of the Public Ministry; it also granted Public Friends a degree of safety during their travels, allowing them to maintain their distance from potentially hostile strangers. And, crucially, it served to make traveling Friends look more respectable, keeping them from incurring heavy obligations or debts to non-Quakers and therefore helping them to avoid accusations that they were beggars or vagabonds.

But Quakers were not so numerous in the early modern Atlantic world that this type of charity was enough to sustain Public Friends on their missions. In her memoir, the seventeenth-century Quaker Barbara Blaugdone announced proudly that "in all my Travels, I traveled still on my own purse, and was never chargeable to any, but paid for what I had."[18] This was an exceptional case, for most Quakers had to persist through financial straits during their journeys. When Katherine Evans and Sarah Cheevers were imprisoned by the Inquisition in Malta in 1658, they were forced to use their own money to buy food for themselves in jail; living on extremely small rations, the pair found that "our money served us a year and seven weeks, and when it was almost gone the friars brought the Inquisitor's chamberlain to buy our hats." Refusing "[to] be chargeable to any," Evans and Cheevers wrote self-assuredly that they would not "sell our clothes nor anything we had." But with no funds to pay for food and drink, the women "did eat but little for three or four weeks" and became so malnourished that the prison staff "said that it was impossible that creatures could live with so little meat as they did see we did."[19] In 1657 the Quaker widow Anne Burden visited the Massachusetts Bay Colony, which had strict laws outlawing Quakerism. At the time of her arrival Burden's savings consisted of thirty pounds "in goods."[20] But when she was discovered by the authorities, Burden was thrown into prison and told she would be exiled to England; seeking financial solvency, she "desired that she might have liberty to pass for England, by Barbadoes, because her goods were not fit to England." Presumably this meant that Burden's wealth existed in the form of finished goods, items which were of little value in metropolitan Britain but carried much higher value in the more remote West Indian colonies. Burden requested that the Bay Colony officials allow her to sell her property in Barbados before continuing to her exile in England. Denied this request by the Massachusetts officials, Burden was apparently unable to recover her losses. Forced into traveling without funding or supplies, Burden was even taken advantage of by sailors. It seems "these rapacious people" demanded "six pounds ten shillings" for the trip to England and a further "seven shillings for boat-hire to carry her on shipboard."[21] Burden wrote that she was left destitute. Quaker women ministers continued to face such misfortune through the eighteenth century, as Susanna Morris wrote that during her mission to Scotland in 1745 "at times my poverty was great."[22]

Even if a traveling minister was able to secure at least some funds for her travel, she faced continuing scrutiny from her fellow Quakers, and her behavior and preaching were constantly evaluated. In the earliest days of the ministry George Fox received reports of preachers' behavior. Ministers were watched carefully to make sure they were representing properly the tenets of Quaker belief. A woman named Agnes Ayrey was recalled from her travels in the 1650s when it became known that she was "not serviceable to go forth, for lust and filth and darkness rule in her." And in 1658 complaints were similarly leveled against Mary Howgill for preaching "confusion" as Quaker doctrine; it was said that Howgill "hath been much in these Counties of Essex suffolke and norfolke wheare she hath done hurt for she ministereth confusion amonge friends."[23] Sometimes traveling female Friends were even monitored and criticized by other Quaker women. In 1685 Mary Ellwood and Margery Clipsham offered a critique of the public activities of Susanna Aldridge, declaring that Aldridge's "thundering is from an unholy mountain, and her trumpet gives an uncertain sound." Evaluations of preaching women were largely bureaucratized by the turn of the century: in 1695 the Morning Meeting in London was responsible for admonishing Elizabeth Redford, who had encouraged Friends to cease paying taxes to the government.[24] Censure and criticism from within the Quaker community thereby made preaching in public onerous for some Quaker women.

In the eighteenth century the criticisms of Public Friends continued, albeit in different forms. Quietist women in the Public Ministry harshly criticized themselves and often wrote of their fears about preaching correctly. Some of these women exercised self-discipline in the Meetings they visited by staying silent, despite the fact that they may have traveled enormous distances to reach isolated communities in which to preach.[25] The exercise of silence was itself expressed as an almost bodily form of suffering. Blending ecstatic Quaker terminology with quietist impulses, the British American Quaker Elizabeth Hudson Morris wrote that during a "meeting at Burris" at which she was expected to preach publicly she instead stayed silent. Comparing her silence with a physical burden, Morris admitted that her "companion had the principle service for through my backwardness I sat under the burden of the world." Her silence was not only painful to Morris herself but also a punishment for the female Friend in her company, for "[my silence] made hard work for my companion." Hudson Morris also remembered "a hard silent meeting" in the town of Youghal in which "great . . . were my sufferings."[26]

Female ministers may have found it difficult to gain permission to leave on a mission, and they may have found the constant process of critique and the evaluation of their activities to be daunting. But the most common fear that female Public Friends expressed was that of travel itself. Journeys to colonial British America or the West Indies were expensive, and many Britons who immigrated to the colonies were often forced to indenture themselves in order to pay for their passage. For these Britons, the hellish trip—in leaky, cramped vessels on which passengers suffered from disease and malnutrition, shipwreck, and piracy—was usually endured only once, in permanent emigration. Voyages for other reasons were viewed by most seventeenth- and early eighteenth-century Britons with pity or distrust; in 1727 even the well-traveled and wealthy Virginia merchant Robert Carter noted of a fellow merchant that "poor Isaac Lee [has a] strange inclination to travel the remote parts of the world."[27]

The perceived strangeness or danger of long-distance travel in that era was not lost on traveling Quaker women. Immediately after revealing to the members of her American Meeting that she desired to undertake a mission from Pennsylvania to England, the traveler Elizabeth Hudson Morris felt dread at the thought of her journey, professing that she had no idea how to convey her divine message while traveling: "After the meeting great exercise of soul fell upon me. I had promised and I could not go back yet how to perform knew not."[28] Other women worried about transgressing gender norms; emphasizing her "naturally" quiet character, Barbara Blaugdone remembered that when God "called me forth to labour abroad," she had "stood so in the dread, awe and fear of the Lord . . . for I was never hasty nor forward."[29] The Irish Quaker Mary Peisley Neale wrote that her female companion "seemed affrighted about going" on their joint mission in the eighteenth century, "and wept considerably."[30] The traveling ministry was understood to be so dangerous that it was even used by some Quaker women as a rhetorical foil against unwanted or onerous tasks. Around 1670, when Elizabeth Stirredge worried that God had asked her to bring negative testimony against a respected man in her Meeting, she prayed desperately that she would instead be sent "to a Nation of a strange Language, whose Face I never knew."[31]

Worse still, calls to missionary travel were often resented by the family and friends that a woman left behind. As Cristine Levenduski has argued of eighteenth-century American Quakers, the itinerant lifestyle necessitated by the Public Ministry was seen as "problematic in a culture emphasizing family stability as the basis for community solidarity."[32] Seventeenth- and eighteenth-century Quakers valued both family stability and community solidarity, and the demands and nature of the Public Ministry challenged these values. Elizabeth Lloyd Pemberton was saddened by the loss of a female cousin and her husband to missionary work, writing of her dissatisfied resignation to her American cousin Deborah Moore, "We were happy some time with dear Cousin Norris, but soon deprived. . . . we all courted their way with us as earnest as possible; but could not prevail—you draw the strongest that side [colonial British America], so we have lost our hope of keeping them, and must now wish them a happy voyage and joyful meeting with you—and we must be content; we canot enjoy all happiness in this world."[33] Such complaints were intensified when traveling women left behind a husband or children. Some female itinerant preachers did face resistance from their families when revealing their decision to undertake a traveling mission. Elizabeth Webb (1663–1727) recorded that when she revealed to her husband her "concern on my mind to go to America, and asked him if he could give me up," her husband's cautious reaction was that "he . . . hoped it would not be required of me." When Webb "told him it was," she acknowledged that the news "seemed a little hard to him at first."[34]

Female Quakers understood that making a religious journey meant taking large risks with their health and personal safety. During the voyage she made between 1697 and 1699 Elizabeth Webb wrote that she had experienced physical exhaustion, as she had become "both sick and lame. For I had traveled hard beyond the ability of my body and with heats and coulds and wet and dry."[35] Long hours spent traveling outdoors caused some women physical pain and illness, but travel by sea was perceived as even more challenging. The very early years of the movement involved preaching in England, Scotland, and Wales, but as early as 1660 a majority of traveling Quakers had focused their attention across the Atlantic. Long journeys at sea were made uncomfortable by unfamiliarity with oceanic travel, poor rations, bad hygiene, and cramped living quarters, and these were often intensified by the spinning, nauseating misery of seasickness. Margaret Ellis wrote that "during the voyage [from Philadelphia to England] my Companion was sickly most part of the time," a months-long illness that was alleviated only when the two reached shore.[36] Joan Vokins was also prone to seasickness and frequently complained of her struggles with it in her memoirs. On her initial transatlantic voyage from England to America, "in the first Vessel thatever I was in," Vokins wrote miserably, "Sarah [her companion] and I are both Seasick." On another sea voyage to New Jersey, Vokins remembered the Atlantic's rough seas and stormy weather, writing, "The Winds being boisterous, and the foaming Sea in so great a Rage . . . Elizabeth Dean, that then travelled with me, was very sick."[37]

But the discomforts of life onboard ship seemed small in comparison to the truly life-threatening dangers of piracy, shipwreck, and drowning, all of which made Quaker women especially nervous about undertaking oceanic travel.[38] Among the first wave of traveling ministers, the lives of three prominent female Friends were cut short by accidents at sea. The ministers Sarah Gibbons, Mary Weatherhead, and Mary Clark all undertook a voyage to New England aboard the Quaker-owned ship *Woodhouse* in the midseventeenth century. Although the tiny ship arrived safely in colonial British America after its initial voyage across the Atlantic, within a few years all three of the women had drowned: Clark and Weatherhead were shipwrecked on a subsequent voyage, and Gibbons's canoe sank off of Providence, Rhode Island. Their travels as well as their watery deaths were well publicized and underscored the dangers of sea travel to many missionary Quaker women.[39]

Both female and male Quaker ministers wrote of their fears of dying at sea in their sufferings narratives. Feeling himself sicken aboard the *Samuel* while en route to London from the West Indies in 1675, William Baily tried to reconcile himself to the idea of a burial at sea: "Shall I lay down my head upon the waters? Well, God is the God of the whole universe; and though my body sink, I shall swim a top of the waters."[40] Susanna Morris became so fearful during one of her transatlantic voyages that she worried she was receiving a providential message from God. Dreaming one night of ship-wreck, Morris panicked, thinking she was receiving a vision of her own death: "Soon after I got out to sea something of a weight fell on my mind, and I dreamt our ship would be lost; and there remained on my mind, a solid weight for fear it should be so. . . . again I dreamt the same, and was . . . fixed in the belief of the truth of it, and thereby I dwelt in a fearfull tossing of Mind . . . [thinking that] the Lord was pleased . . . to make it known to me only that we should assuredly suffer shipwreck and I believed it was the lord that discovered to me what he intended to do by us."[41]

Sea voyages were thought to be especially dangerous for women trav-elers, who were sometimes victimized when ships experienced distress or disaster. Barbara Blaugdone, sailing from England to Cork in 1655, became the victim of rumors about witchcraft while at sea. During a storm the sailors fixated upon Blaugdone, citing her status as both a Quaker and a single-woman as a source of bad luck: "When the tempest was high, the seamen said that she being a Quaker was the cause of it, and they conspired to cast her overboard."[42] This was not the end of Blaugdone's troubles aboard ship. During another storm her ship was cast on a rocky shoal and began to sink. The crew abandoned ship, leaving Blaugdone behind: "Barbara who was still in the cabin . . . almost stifled by waves that beat in upon her." Escaping to the deck, she yelled for the crew to help her, but they had deliberately aban-doned her and were by this point safely ashore. Perhaps perversely, the sailors then encouraged Blaugdone to jump from the floundering wreck and to attempt to swim for safety, "but being entangled in the ropes in leaping down, she was drawn from them again." Close to drowning, Blaugdone was finally able to ride "a wave [that] came rolling and . . . she was thus caught again, and drawn to shore." Yet Blaugdone's troubles at sea were still not over: while on another journey, this time from Dublin to Limerick, she recorded that while "at sea [she] was robbed of all that she had, by a priva-teer."[43] Oceanic travel, not exaggeratedly, was figured as both dangerous and frightening by many early Quaker women.

Blaugdone's description of her interaction with a privateer was reflec-tive of another frequently expressed concern in women's travel narratives: the fear of warfare, robbery, and piracy. Piracy was not uncommon in the early modern Atlantic, and the knowledge that boats were often overtaken and their passengers assaulted and robbed caused Quaker female mission-aries much mental torment. Elizabeth Hudson Morris became worried about piracy while en route from her home in America to England, and when her ship encountered a foreign boat at sea, she reported, "I found my mind very uneasy about her [the strange vessel] and expressing my thoughts to my companion found we were of one mind respecting of it."[44] In 1745, when Susanna Morris's ship approached the Isle of Man on a trip from Ireland to England, she "saw a vessel which appeared to be an enemy, sailing sometime one way, sometime another way, almost round us." Morris noted that this activity "shocked" her into extensive prayer.[45]

Sea travel was clearly challenging for many early Quakers, but female Friends also wrote of encountering problems upon reaching their destinations. Delivering their spiritual messages proved to be difficult for many women ministers, especially when it meant interacting with those non-Quakers whom they suspected, with good reason, of being hostile. This was a prevalent theme in Quaker women's writings even through the mid-eighteenth century and was often expressed by traveling women as a fear of difference. Quaker women mentioned their strong desires to stay among Friends, who shared their national, racial, socioeconomic, and religious backgrounds. Susanna Morris wrote that her voyages through Holland caused "heavy burdens . . . it being a place where the conversation amongst Friends is mostly by an interpreter, they being a people of an unknown tongue to us which was harder for us to find out to speak what was in our minds."[46] Margaret Ellis struggled to balance her missionary work with impulses to stay among Friends of similar social status. On one occasion she found herself "drawn in my Mind to visit some Meetings . . . near the Iron Works . . . to the Forge Men." Realizing she would have to preach to men who worked at refining metal ore in sweltering, dangerous, filthy conditions, Ellis blanched, confessing that the call "was much against my will." She found a sympathetic ear in her traveling companion, who said she was "of my mind that it was hard to go to them."[47]

Quaker women may have found it "hard" to preach to ironworkers and to people of a different nationality, but they faced many more hindrances in delivering their message in places like the West Indies, where they were confronted by the practice of slavery. Although most Quaker abolitionism dates to the nineteenth century, the accounts of seventeenth-century female Public Friends reveal a persistent discomfort with the practices and ideologies of enslavement. During Alice Curwen's yearlong mission to Barbados in 1676–77, the female minister felt compelled to share communion with enslaved Africans. When Curwen discovered "a widow-woman in Barbados that had negroes to her servants, who were convinced of God's eternal truth," she delivered an angry lecture to the wealthy widow. Curwen was furious that the woman had refused to allow her "convinced" slaves to attend Quaker Meetings. But accosting the widow and demanding access to the slaves didn't seem to have the effect Curwen desired, for "when I did speak to her she did deny me." Revealing that she was of humbler origins than the elite, plantation-owning widow, Curwen worried that "the highness of all sorts of people [in Barbados]" meant that they might "trample upon [her] little testimony."[48]

The first wave of Quaker missionaries to reach the West Indies tried to make preaching to slaves an important part of their work. As early as the 1650s Joan Vokins said she had gone "from [Antigua] to Nevice [Nevis], and an honest Widow went along with me, who was very helpful to me; and we had good Service amongst the Blacks and Whites."[49] But the "good service" of Quaker women like Vokins was not usually appreciated by white plantation owners. In 1676 the deputy secretary of Barbados, Edwin Stede, passed "An Act to prevent the People called Quakers from bringing Negroes to their Meetings," which outlawed Quakers from interacting with slaves whom they did not own. The law decried the fact that "of late many Negroes have been suffered to remain at the Meeting of Quakers as hearers of their Doctrine, and taught in their Principles." Stede and his compatriots, probably worried that the Quakers were spreading egalitarian ideas to enslaved persons, felt that proselytizing to slaves could mean "the safety of this Island may be much hazarded." Accordingly, the Barbadian lawmakers forbade the practice and, in a further preventative measure to limit the spread of Quakerism in Barbados, effectively outlawed the ministry of traveling Public Friends, declaring that "no Person or Persons whatsoever, That is not an Inhabitant and Resident of this Island, and hath been so for the space of Twelve Months together, shall hereafter publickly Discourse or Preach at the Meeting of the Quakers."[50] Quakers considered these West Indian laws to be both immoral and unjust.[51]

Itinerant Quaker women faced similar encumbrances when ministering to both enslaved and freed black populations in mainland colonial British America. When the minister Margaret Ellis traveled to Philadelphia in the early eighteenth century she felt called to "visit" with black Philadelphians, to preach to them and speak with them about her faith. But Ellis was unsure of how to accomplish her task. Slavery had been present in the area since 1639 in the South River settlement owned by the Dutch. Slave populations increased when Pennsylvania became a British colony, and by the 1680s many wealthy Quaker merchants and particularly émigrés from the West Indies owned slaves in Philadelphia.[52] Yet despite the fact that slavery was an acknowledged and visible feature of Quaker life in early Philadelphia, the Society of Friends' attitude toward preaching to slaves in the city was ambiguous. Although Philadelphia's Friends had been encouraged to bring their slaves to Quaker Meetings since 1696, black Philadelphians, whether free or enslaved, were largely segregated from white Friends, as they were not permitted to join Meetings as full-fledged members.[53]

When Ellis felt a desire to preach to black Philadelphians, she met with an uncertain legal and spiritual situation. Learning that a black funeral was going to be held near the home where she was staying, Ellis found her "concern soon discovered to me," believing that the funeral afforded a valuable opportunity to interact with members of the city's black population. Her first instinct was to find a female Friend to accompany her. She stated that although "a concern rested on my mind for some time to visit the Negroes [at a funeral]," she was at "a loss for a Companion" and worried that she could not go without the support of another woman Quaker. She sought out a female companion to help ease the encounter and asked for the opinion and help of other female Friends, "so I step'd to a Friends house in the way and told them I wanted company to go to the Negro's Burial." But when Ellis's compatriots discovered that she had been "called" to preach to black Philadelphians at a funeral, they discouraged her. The particular cultural space in which Ellis proposed to introduce her ministry was contested; as Gary Nash has argued, free and enslaved black Philadelphians were "a people whose long tradition of reverence for ancestors made proper burial rites highly important." Nash writes that as early as 1699 Philadelphia's black population successfully campaigned "to preserve the remains of their friends and kin in an area that was theirs alone." Furthermore, the black burial grounds in Philadelphia served as sites for relatively free expression and cultural autonomy; legislation from the period indicates there were complaints about "the great multitude of Negroes" who gathered at these spaces in an allegedly "Riott[ous] and tumultuous manner."[54] Echoing Nash's findings about the insularity of black burial rituals and grounds, Ellis's coreligionists discouraged her from the mission by warning her that "non[e] used to go [to black funerals] but them selves." Their discomfort with the situation palpable, Ellis's friends nonetheless finally agreed to her request, and Ellis noted that "two Women friends sayed they would go with me if I must go."[55] Although Ellis's mission was not entirely acceptable to her compatriots, her work was finally accomplished, but only through the aid of other female Friends.

But all of these difficulties paled in comparison to the physical punishments many Quakers received from hostile outsiders. From the time the movement was founded, members of the Society of Friends faced legal and social persecution for practicing their faith. Punishments were leveled against both female and male Friends, but female Quaker missionaries were treated with acute violence. Female Public Friends were imagined by many seventeenth- and eighteenth-century people as having abandoned their husbands and families in order to travel and therefore were thought to possess dangerous and aberrant loyalties. Seeing the devil acting in Quaker itinerancy, the Boston minister Thomas Weld wrote of female Quakers as early as 1653 that nothing less than "a sinfull neglect of their families and callings . . . [is] apparent in their constant wanderings up and downe."[56] These condemnations were repeated in Britain. Reserving a single, bland defamation of men while heaping sexualized insult upon women, one English magistrate "call[ed] men rogues, and the women whores, jades, carrions, and damned bitches."[57]

Physical punishments meted out against early modern female Friends were brutal and painful. While undergoing their three-year imprisonment by the Catholic Inquisition in Malta in 1658 the Quaker companions Katherine Evans and Sarah Cheevers wrote of experiencing heat stroke, dehydration, and starvation. The high temperatures and lack of air in their prison cell apparently caused the women's hair to fall out. Evans additionally described that "our skin was like sheeps Leather," and, as a result of fly bites, the women's "faces and . . . heads . . . were swollen as if [they] had the small-pox."[58] Other sufferings faced by Quaker women were direct and corporal. William Sewel recorded in his *History of the . . . Quakers* (1717) that on their arrival in the Massachusetts Bay Colony the septuagenarian Elizabeth Hooton and her companion were identified as witches, forced to walk "two days journey into the wilderness, among wolves and bears," and then abandoned. Sewel explained in detail how, over the next several years, the two women faced "much scurrilous language," imprisonment in a "stinking dungeon, where there was nothing to lie down or sit on," and exposures in strange forests, "where were many wolves, bears and other wild beasts, and many deep waters to pass through." After escaping to Rhode Island in 1664, Hooton returned to New England, where she was attacked by a Massachusetts jailer, who beat the aged woman repeatedly "with a three-stringed whip."[59]

Texts like these stressed the perilous hazards Quaker women faced during their journeys. By describing female Friends as sufferers, Quaker authors—both male and female—feminized female missionaries. Sometimes this gendering of Quaker women was quite overt. In *History of the . . . Quakers* (c.1717) Willem Sewel depicted most of the women in his book as suffering, feminine, and fragile. In describing the Quaker companions Anne Coleman, Mary Tomkins, and Alice Ambrose, who were sentenced to being whipped naked in Dover, Massachusetts, in 1662, Sewel emphasized the weak, "tender," and feminine nature of the women: "Cruel indeed was this order [for punishment]; because to whip these three tender women through eleven towns, with ten stripes apiece at each place, through a length of near eighty miles, in bitter cold weather, would have been enough to have beaten their bones bare."[60] The Quaker William Edmundson similarly recounted in his published *Journal* that a traveling female preacher named Anne Gould, "being a tender woman, was much spent" when he encountered her in the course of his own mission in the 1650s.[61] Imagery of feminine weakness and the suffering of female Public Friends persisted through the eighteenth century. Such portrayals were employed even by female Quakers themselves; they resorted to early modern stereotypes of femininity in order to solicit sympathy and empathy from readers of their texts. Elizabeth Ashbridge (1713–55), a preacher from Cheshire in the Welsh borderlands who traveled both to the mainland British American colonies and to Ireland, claimed of her companion and herself that nothing short of "a miracle" had allowed "two poor weak women . . . to lay down their lives in the cause of truth."[62] Even Susanna Morris, the formidable traveler who survived her shipwreck in Holland, counted herself among "the weaker sort of [God's] people" and recorded that she was grateful that her God "had and has still a good regard to the Humble and lowly altho' handmaids."[63] Elizabeth Webb, an English Quaker who traveled throughout colonial British America, stated simply, "Had I been a man I thought I could have went into all corners of the land."[64] When Quaker women ministers represented their travels as sufferings, they documented the many very real incidents of hardship, privation, and physical torment that were inflicted on members of the Society of Friends in the seventeenth and eighteenth centuries. But in describing their experiences these women also worked to position themselves as feminized sufferers for Christ, deserving of pity and toleration.

Quaker Women and Their Yokemates

Female Quakers deliberately drew on gendered stereotypes about women in order to make their actions seem acceptable to non-Quakers. By positioning themselves as righteous sufferers, traveling ministers wrote in their narratives, they were able to overcome the hardships and obstacles they faced over the course of their missions. But female ministers wrote as well of mitigating the many trials they faced in their journeys through the development of religiously supportive partnerships with other women.

Quaker women often referenced the power of female homosociability. When Margaret Ellis initially received the "call" to Quakerism, she remarked that she was fast asleep, visiting a Quaker home fourteen miles distant from her parents' house. She recalled that "one night in bed lying between two Women Friends I heard my name called very distinctly which awakened me out of my sleep." Attentive to what she perceived was a divine message, Ellis "got softly out of Bed, put on my Cloaths and went out into a private place in the Barn to pour forth my Spirit before the Lord." When she had finished communing with God "several hours [later]," Ellis "returned to the House, washed myself and went among the Friends." During breakfast Ellis's private conversion and religious rebirth were observed and interpreted by another female Friend, a Traveling Quaker who "seemed to take more than ordinary notice of me, and spoke saying where had Margaret been for she looked so innocent as if she had been newly born."[65] Ellis's account highlights the continuing importance of female society to the Public Ministry of women Friends. Ellis made a point of mentioning that she was lying asleep between two female Quakers before she experienced her vision. Ellis's bodily proximity to her coreligionists was important to her recollection of the event; lying between two women who respected and supported her religious choices made it seem to her as if the bodily intimacy of her fellow Quakers allowed her to be more receptive to God's call. Ellis, whose parents were unsympathetic to her Quaker leanings, clearly treasured the rare experience of staying and socializing with female Friends. This intimate nearness to other Quakers and exposure to their society seems to have heightened Ellis's vision.[66] After the visionary experience was over, it was again the perception of female Friends—specifically, of a Public Friend—which allowed Ellis to acknowledge her call, to validate it and discuss it among women of her new faith.

For Quaker women in the Public Ministry, a female companion was a necessity, and many women could not contemplate undertaking travel without the presence of a female Friend. When Elizabeth Webb felt called to journey to British America in 1697, she contracted with God about her service. She promised that if she was supplied with the few provisions she considered to be necessary for travel, she would freely devote her life to missionary work. In Webb's eyes these necessities were not food or shelter, health or a safe passage, but harmonious female companionship: "I covenanted with the Lord that if hee would be pleased to make way for mee and give me a suitable companion I would give up my days in his servis."[67] Webb's declaration was significant, for Quaker women believed that female companions could offer doctrinal advice, provide care during illness, share financial burdens, and give succor during imprisonments and after physical punishments.[68]

The promise of having a sympathetic partner with whom to share the physical, social, and emotional burdens of the traveling ministry was so compelling that it sometimes forced female Quakers to accelerate or change their plans. Joan Vokins was so desperate to procure a companion for her voyage to the British American and West Indian colonies that she asked the London Meeting for help; although they supported her desire to travel and furnished her with documentation attesting to her worth as a minister, they were unable to find anyone who was willing to accompany her. Vokins eventually was forced to travel with a number of women who were undertaking voyages for their own reasons, some of them even non-Quakers.[69] On a voyage to Ireland in 1720 Deborah Bell rushed onboard when she was made aware that "a Ship lay . . . ready to sail, and a young Woman suitable to accompany me in that Voyage was gone down, in order to imbark." This coincidence was both so desirable and so fortunate that Bell wrote she "looked upon it as a providential Opportunity; so I hastened to the Pill [tidal inlet] that Evening, and met with her."[70] Susanna Morris complained that because she "had not freedom [from God] to Except of" any of the Quaker women who had offered to accompany her to Ireland, she was forced to "leave it, till I came to the sea port"; she had to compromise at the last minute on a "Woman, for my Companion, although not a Minister."[71]

When Quaker companions were forced to part, the breakup of their partnership often caused them to suffer serious emotional distress. When Mary Peisley and her companion separated, Peisley was disconsolate. Calling her partner a "second self," Peisley made it clear that she and her companion had shared a mental and spiritual connection: "What now adds to my trials is that I have got no second self to whome I might disclose my joys my griefs etc., my dear and endeared companion has left me."[72] Elizabeth Hudson Morris faced a similar dilemma when her companion became too ill to travel. Hudson Morris debated whether or not to continue her mission, for the thought of solitary travel brought her into a "low and deeply bowed state," wherein she confessed that she "set out on [the] journey under great weight of spirit, for [I] had no companion to bear a part . . . in this so great an undertaking."[73] This sentiment was echoed by Hudson Morris's sickly partner, Jane Hoskins, who confessed that in addition to her debilitating illness she was despondent without her companion's presence: "The want of thy company makes everything insipid. . . . I could get no sleep from the time thou left me . . . to be left alone was hard and more than I could bear."[74]

The female Public Friend's intense desire for companionship is no better illustrated than through the early eighteenth-century example of Elizabeth Ashbridge, a young Quaker woman who was kidnapped because of her desire for female companionship. In her memoirs Ashbridge wrote that as a young woman she was approached by "a gentlewoman, lately arrived from Pennsylvania . . . [who] was intending to return." Interested in visiting the colony, which was a recognized haven for Quakers, Ashbridge was told that she would be the strange woman's companion, and Ashbridge "soon agreed with her for my passage." What Ashbridge failed to realize was that she actually had been tricked into becoming the woman's indentured servant. Ashbridge, the daughter of a ship's surgeon, was probably familiar with the workings of boats and the nature of seaports, but she protested that she had been victimized because of her young age, which meant she was "ignorant of the nature of an indenture." Taken into a private room, "that it might not be found out," she was pressured into signing unfamiliar paperwork.

At this point Ashbridge's better judgment started to exert itself. Why, she wondered, had "this [been] done privately"? Her captors attempted to soothe and convince her—not with money or sweets or fancy clothes but with a promise of female friendship.[75] Ashbridge was "invited . . . to see the vessel in which I was to sail. I readily consented, and we went on board, where there was another young woman." Speaking eagerly with the compatriot who she was told would share her voyage, Ashbridge was thrilled to learn that the girl "was of a respectable family, and had been brought there in the same way as myself." So content was she in her new friend and so "pleased with the thought that I should have such an agreeable companion in my voyage," Ashbridge became blind to the suspicions that had haunted her over the signing of the indenture contract. She soon became engrossed in conversation with the young woman, and it was not until much time had passed that she noticed that "my conductor went on shore, and, when I wished to go, I was not permitted." Panicking, Ashbridge admitted that "I now saw I was kidnapped." Ashbridge and her respectable female friend were "kept a prisoner in the ship three weeks" without any way of reaching their friends and family on shore. At last the young woman imprisoned with Ashbridge was able to escape, for "my companion was found out by her friends, who fetched her away." Now alone and desperate on the ship, Ashbridge said that she "was kept close for two weeks, but at length [I also] found means to get away."[76] Ashbridge's story has resonance with some transatlantic captivity narratives from the period; however, while a captivity narrative can be read as "a ritualistic journey of salvation, a passage through suffering and despair toward saving faith," Ashbridge presented her own story as a tale of feminine naiveté, innocence, and youthful susceptibility.[77] Her story makes clear how desperately female Quaker missionaries searched out female alliances with companions they believed to be trustworthy, who were "agreeable," and with whom they believed they could share good conversation.

Female Friends also provided spiritual, physical, and emotional support during the corporal punishments to which early Quakers were often subjected. After a weekly meeting Barbara Blaugdone and a coreligionist named Mary Prince were walking "arm in arm" back to their homes when they were physically assaulted: "As Mary Prince and I was coming arm in arm from a meeting . . . there was a rude man came and abused us, and struck off Mary Prince her hat, and run some sharp knife or instrument through all of my clothes, into the side of my belly."[78] Later in her account, Blaugdone wrote that she had endured further sufferings while being incarcerated and whipped; this punishment was witnessed by a fellow female Quaker, a woman named Ann Speed, who "was an EyeWitness of it, and she stood and lookt in at the Window, and wept bitterly." Speed's expression of sorrow and sympathy was intensified when Speed later "came in and drest my Wounds."[79]

Blaugdone was careful to note specifically Speed's role in her experience of suffering. Speed had not only washed, poulticed, and bound her friend's injuries, but also stood as an important "EyeWitness" to the event. And Speed's emotional reaction to watching Blaugdone suffer under the whip was intertwined with the evidence of her doctoring. The fact that Speed had "wept bitterly" intensified the impact of her later physical succor. Some traveling women sympathized so greatly with the sufferings of their partners that they wrote of their desire to share pain and even death. When told that her companion had been killed while undergoing the torture of being pressed by stones, Katherine Evans professed that it was "a great trouble to me, because I could not suffer death with her."[80]

Traveling women continually recounted how their female alliances sustained them through the many trying hazards of their travels. But female Quakers also insisted on the singular importance of companionship to the missionary work itself. Female companions could help to mitigate the hostility female Friends faced when they preached to non-Quakers. Joan Vokins was momentarily stymied when she confronted a priest after his sermon and asked him, " 'What Church that was that [women] should not speak in?' and he did not answer me, but went away." At risk of losing her quarry, Vokins reported proudly that "a Woman Friend that was with me took hold of him, and said, My Friend, answer the Womans question."[81] For Vokins, the presence of another female Quaker was not just a matter of companionship and support, but also an integral aid in evangelization, successfully allowing her to challenge Catholics and Anglicans and giving her a means of reinforcing her Quaker sense of authority.

Quaker women also stressed that, when companionship had been divinely blessed, missionaries could share a single doctrinal message, even in dire circumstances. When Sarah Cheevers was imprisoned in a separate cell from her companion Katherine Evans, the two women claimed a mutual and spontaneous religious understanding. Cheevers reported triumphantly, "When we were separated, we spake one and the same thing, being guided by one Spirit. They would go from me to Catharine . . . bid[ding] her speak as Sarah did, and so she did to their condemnation."[82] And Quaker women believed that this kind of mutually supportive, unified bodily and spiritual partnership would be a guide and example to others, even into the eighteenth century. Jane Hoskins (1694–1764), whose widely ranging travels incited her to take six companions over the course of her life, insisted that when partners were in clear communication both with each other and with God, their messages would be amplified: "I am persuaded where companions in this solemn service are firmly united, in the true bond of christian fellowship, it must tend to confirm the authority of their message, testifying their joint consent to the doctrines they teach, to comfort, strengthen, and support each other, through the many trying dispensations which in the course of their travels they have to wade through; this being the real case, judge how great must be the disappointment when it happens otherwise."[83] Hoskins's insistence that good companionship "confirm[ed] the authority" of the Quaker preacher and that female partners, through "joint consent to the doctrines they teach," were able to present a more unified and powerful theological message reinforces the argument that Public Friends understood their relationships to be built on a spiritual kind of sociability.[84] Hoskins was resolute in her belief that her faith and even her sense of Quaker doctrine were strengthened by the relationships she had with other women. But her final clause, expressing her worry about "the disappointment" when female companions fought with one another, hinted at a reluctance to admit to conflict between Friends and a fear of acrimony within partnerships.

Despite distinct efforts to promote companionship as special, loving, and harmonious, signs of antagonism between partners did appear occasionally in Quaker texts. Hoskins, a seasoned, loyal, and confident missionary preacher in many respects, wrote that she experienced "heavy and painful" religious exercises on a discordant journey with her partner Elizabeth Hudson Morris: "[I] hitherto underwent many closer trials and provings in my pilgrimage through life . . . [but] this visit was attended with some of the heaviest and most painful exercises of any I had ever before performed."[85] Hoskins's and Hudson Morris's conflict apparently arose out of the fact that they felt they spent too much time apart. In her account Hoskins admitted that Hudson Morris traveled alone during most of their shared mission, undertaking her own religious activities. On their return to America, Hudson Morris faced criticism from Friends in her home Meeting for what was seen as an abandonment of her companion.

Hudson Morris also clashed with her later companion Ellen Rebanks when it became clear that Rebanks was spending too much time in the company of another woman. Spilling out the intimate details of their rancor into her public memoirs while simultaneously claiming to resign their differences to God, Hudson Morris made her jealousy and suspicion about the rival Friend obvious:

> [The] satisfaction which was wont to be betwixt . . . [us] in our travels in each other's company grew less, which I attributed to her removal of affection to one who joined us to visit about two weeks meetings, who did me great unkindness. . . . any part of those unpleasant hours I spent with my companion, which till after this time were as few as I believe ever any had who traveled together as long as we did [were unbearable]. . . . tis not always consistent with the Divine will to indulge us in the choice of our helpmeets. . . . I have reason to believe it would have been best for us to have parted. . . . I never after found our spirits united in [the] gospel labor . . . which made us truly dear to each other and helpmeets indeed. And I was in hopes it would have revived again, especially when the friend parted from us who I thought the principle impediment to our fellowship as formerly, but this I leave only say, I had a bitter cup to drink during her being with us.[86]

It is telling that quarrelsome confessions like those of Hoskins and Hudson Morris are very rare in published Quaker texts, and records of this kind of conflict are almost impossible to find. Love, concord, loyalty, and a shared sense of spiritual purpose were expected and privileged in Quaker women's descriptions of their traveling partnerships. Positive companionship was central to the experiences and expectations of female Public Friends and was meant to be a counterweight to the missionary necessity of suffering for God's truth.

Female Quakers favored a spiritual kind of female sociability. In the narrations of their travels, the religious nature of Quaker female friendships was given primacy. This phenomenon is visible in the language traveling women used to describe their companions. Female Quaker travelers referred to their companions as their yokemates or "yokefellows."[87] Yokemates were teams of draft animals, ideally pulling in tandem with unified effort and purpose. But to speak of two people as yokemates in early modern Britain was also to invoke domestic harmony and spiritual equity within heterosexual marriage. William Whittingham's *Geneva Bible* (1561) warned its readers to "be not unequally yoked with the infedels [i.e., nonbelievers], for what felowship hathe righteousnes with unrighteouesnes? And what communion hathe light with darknes?"[88] Thomas Becon's *Golde[n] Boke of Christen Matrimonye* equated *yokemate* with spiritual and marital homogeneity: "To drawe one yoke is a maner of spekyng . . . to yoke the selves together in wedlock." If a man married someone of a different religious persuasion, he risked "giv[ing] over himselfe unto such thynges, as may alienate hys mynde from God and his trueth."[89] The term had gained even more popularity by 1655, when William Gouge's prescriptive *Domestical Duties* repeated the idea, teaching that believing (meaning religious) husbands and wives could do one another mutual good through shared spiritual beliefs, which was beneficial "both for their own sakes, and also for the sake of their yokefellow."[90] Richard Allestree's *Practice of Christian Graces, the Whole Duty of Man* (1658) proclaimed that "husbands and wives are mutually to pray for each other, to beg all blessings from God, both temporal and spiritual, & to endeavour all they can to do all good to one another, especially all good to each others Souls, by stirring up to the performance of duty and disswading, and drawing back from all sin." Allestree maintained that this sort of mutual religious persuasion and support would make spouses "true yoke-fellowes," and, furthermore, he insisted that a yokemate relationship was "of all other the truest, and most valuable love. . . . if the love of husbands and wives were thus grounded in Vertue and Religion, 'twould make their lives a kind of Heaven on earth."[91]

Working to create a sense of "Heaven on earth" was an enterprise that resonated strongly with Quakers, who placed so much importance on embodying a lived example of good behavior and God's truth. This is perhaps why many early Quakers adopted the term *yokemate* to describe their own intimate relationships with their husbands and wives. For these individuals, a yokemate was someone with whom they shared a common faith as well as a lifelong bond. In 1655, for example, the Quaker John Camm distinguished his wife as "a faithful yokefellow unto me" and wished "prayers to the Lord for her."[92] The yokemate terminology was apparently so commonly used by seventeenth-century Quakers to describe their heterosexual marital partners that it was eventually turned against them in satire. The *Academy of Compliments*, from 1640, included a mock letter from a Quaker elder in which the man prostituted a young Quaker girl to his fellow elder and friend: "Having been accustomed to the Use of a Yoke-Fellow, thee mayst have some yearnings after Creature-Refreshment. . . . I doubt not but she may prove a Help-meet for thee upon both Accounts, being possessed not only of Youth enough to set an Elder agog, but having besides a considerable Stock of what the World calls Fortune, besides what she expects from Pennsylvania."[93]

Known for their manipulation of early modern gender stereotypes, Quakers also used *yokemate* to describe their same-sex spiritual partners and insisted that the spiritual and emotional bonds they shared with these travel partners were equal to those shared by husbands and wives.[94] Phyllis Mack found that the "emotional bonding of male traveling companions, or 'yoke-fellows,' was described with an intensity as great as, if not greater than, that found in their letters to their own wives."[95] This term was prevalent as well among traveling Quaker women. Writing many years later of her travels in 1723, Jane Hoskins remembered her friend Elizabeth Levis, the woman who had accompanied her on a long, dangerous journey to Barbados. She described her companion by identifying their enduring religious and emotional bonds: "I always preferred her for the works sake . . . I hope the love which subsisted between us when young, will remain to each other forever; mine is as strong to her as then." Appropriating the phrase that was so commonplace among male Friends, Hoskins added, "In all [our] journeys and voyages we were true yoke-fellows."[96] Katherine Evans named her companion Sarah Cheevers variously as "my dearly beloved Yoak-mate in the work of our God," "my dear and faithful yoke-fellow," "my dear yoke-fellow in the Lord's work," and even "my dear and faithful Yoke-fellow, Sister and Friend," who she contended was "worthy to be embraced of all friends forever."[97] Cheevers responded in the same language, referring to Evans as "my dear Yoke-mate K.E."[98] If the female Quaker's nomenclature for her female companion was motivated by ideas similar to those professed by male Quakers, each woman was speaking here not only of the religious parity she and her companion shared but also of their intense and lasting emotional commitment.

The use of the term *yokemate* in this context is one that has puzzled certain literary critics and historians. Mack avers that Quaker women's writings are often problematic to analyze because "the observer who seeks to understand the seventeenth-century religious visionary finds a group of women and men whose sensibilities ultimately elude the tools of the modern scholar."[99] It is not easy to pin down precisely the "sensibilities" that were possessed by Quaker women and men who called their partners yokemates. Some scholars have posited that Quakers employed the term in a deliberate rejection of Anglican heterosexual marriage. The literary critic Rachel Warburton, for example, holds that Quaker missionary women used the word to transcend any heterosexual bonds they might have shared with men.[100] But does this truly capture the sensibilities of early modern Quaker women?

Quaker authors, as we have seen, highlighted and privileged the sufferings faced by traveling Friends in order to prove their membership among God's chosen ministers, and female Quaker travelers negotiated the practice of suffering through companionship with members of their own faith. The female Public Friend's use of the term *yokemate* should therefore surely be analyzed according to this special Quaker sense of spirituality and theology. Criticizing modern historians for imposing their secular biases on early modern religious subjects, Brad Gregory writes, "An action that might look non-religious and that could be interpreted plausibly in secular terms might have been motivated by and understood by its protagonist in religious terms."[101] The Quaker female missionary's use of *yokemate* might at first glance seem to be an exercise in erotic, literary, or matrimonial defiance. But to stress exclusively this interpretation is to deny the resolute spirituality of Quakers and to ignore the sacred autonomy so volubly defended by the female protagonists whose experiences have been uncovered here.

It is more useful to focus on the religious nuances of the traveling Quaker women's terminology, to follow Gregory in asking, "What did it mean to them?" When Becon wrote of women and men "drawe[ing] one yoke," he was invoking an image of plowing which would have been familiar to most people in seventeenth- and eighteenth-century Britain, the West Indies, and mainland colonial British America. Women and men were expected to labor for God, to pull together religion's plow. The repeated claims made by traveling female Quakers that their yokemates helped them to bear burdens are undoubtedly reflective of this sense of shared, burdensome religious vocation. Traveling Quaker women referred to their companions as yokemates because, through their emotional succor, these women shared the extensive and extreme burdens of ministerial suffering. Susanna Morris recalled that during the trials of her ministry she "went through heavy burthens, and I believe my good companion also."[102] When the minister Deborah Bell praised her companion Mary Richardson, she did so by explaining that Richardson had helped to bear her burdens, describing their relationship as one in which they "travelled together this long Journey in much Love and true Unity, always being willing, according to the Strength given, to help to bear one another's Burthens." This produced for the couple proof that they were God's favored ministers, legitimating their spiritual message through "an humble Sense of the divine Goodness we had been favoured with."[103] And when two suffering Female friends found themselves succored and comforted together, a shared sense of redemption strengthened their bonds. Mary Peisley Neale wrote of her companion Elizabeth Hutchinson in 1748 that "we were comforted one in another, and enabled renewedly to bless the name of the Lord."[104] Similarly, in describing the bonds shared between Friends, Mary Penington (1616–82) explained that true bonds of Quaker female alliance were those borne out of both shared spiritual suffering and shared redemption, praising those individuals "who had known our unjust sufferings respecting our estate, and many others of our trials, and had compassionated us: (we had suffered together, and had been comforted together)."[105]

Female Quaker yokemates gave one another a sense of solidarity and support. The study of both printed and manuscript sources, dictated or written by early Quaker women travelers, illuminates the many arduous experiences Quaker women faced when traveling and preaching for their faith in the seventeenth and eighteenth centuries. In many instances Quaker women authors—and those male authors who supported the work of female Public Friends—wrote of their experiences as sufferings and deliberately cast themselves as feminine victims deserving of pity and support. But in these writings Quaker women authors also claimed that they received succor from their female companions, the same-sex yokemates who shared their journeys. Seventeenth- and eighteenth-century Quakers believed that female alliances were critical to their ministry and spiritual growth. Women companions, who shared a sense of burdensome vocation and spiritual identity, granted female Public Friends the sympathy and support they needed to undertake the many sufferings of religious travel.

6. Reconciling Friendship and Dissent: Female Alliances in the Diaries of Sarah Savage

When Sarah Henry Savage contracted smallpox in March 1688, she felt isolated and alone. Newly married, Savage had been living on her husband's farm in the north of Wales for less than a year when she came down with the debilitating disease. Savage was certainly grateful that the disease's progress within her own body had been gentle; this outbreak of smallpox had caused several deaths in the neighborhood, and Savage believed that God had been gracious in sparing her life. But, confined to her bed and unable to work, Savage was miserable. Her sadness did not abate when she was "visited by several neighbors" who came to talk with her and keep her company. Finding their conversation stultifying and banal, Savage was not comforted by this community of women but "bewail[ed] the drowsiness of my converse." She ended the visit as soon as she could and turned to a letter that had been sent by one of her sisters. Here she found spiritual inspiration and vigor: Savage wrote in her diary, "By non of their visits was [I] so much refreshed as by a Pious Letter from Sister A."[1]

Savage was an early Presbyterian. By the 1680s, when Savage was inscribing her entries about the smallpox into her spiritual diary, members of her denomination were Dissenters, ejected from the national church and persecuted for their refusal to conform to officially sanctioned forms of Anglicanism. These beliefs structured Savage's relationships with people. As Patricia Crawford has argued in her study of Dissenting women, "No

Dissenting wife or daughter could be a member of the town's social elite. Nonconformist women experienced social ostracism. Since women in communities depended on the support of members of their own sex in their daily household tasks and domestic emergencies, the loss of neighbourliness was a handicap."[2] But as Crawford also notes, "Women's private losses—of former homes, of friends and neighbors, of income and of social status and respect—have been little acknowledged."[3] Detailed study of Savage's life, experiences, and written works affords a close case study of one woman's experiences with Nonconformist religion, female sociability, and neighborhood relationships in late seventeenth- and early eighteenth-century Britain. Savage's faith plays a large role in this examination of female alliances. Her life was structured around the same gendered practices of sociability experienced by many of the women featured in this book, yet her Nonconformist beliefs prevented her from participating in the kinds of social, alliance-building activities practiced by most Anglican—and even some Quaker—women. Study of Savage's struggle to reconcile her daily work and her local relationships with her Nonconformist religious beliefs and practices allows one to understand Presbyterian sociability more fully. But this analysis also works to reinforce the presence and character of female alliances as evidenced throughout this book. Savage denigrated the kind of sociability practiced by a majority of the women with whom she came into contact. Typing most female visits, conversations, and entertainments as vain, wasteful, and superficial, Savage strove to incorporate Nonconformism into any sociable interactions she experienced with other women. For Savage, the benefits of alliance were rendered better in a ritual of the mind rather than that of the body, in religious books and on the pages of her diary rather than in physical performance. Yet even as Savage mocked and criticized supposedly typical forms of female sociability, she reinforced the visibility and importance of these practices in the lives of most elite British women.

Savage's diaries help to demonstrate as well the overall significance of female alliances in this period because they were written by a woman whose social connections directly affected the health and safety of her family.[4] Like many elite women, Savage relied on her female friends to give advice, medical aid, and financial support; but for Dissenters, who faced the loss of ministerial livings and the threat of imprisonment in the late seventeenth century and the early eighteenth, this need would have been more acute. As we will see, even after institution of the Toleration Act of 1689, Dissenters like

Savage found their chapels demolished and their families repeatedly harassed and attacked.[5] Dissenting families therefore often required extra financial, legal, and even medical aid; but Savage's religious beliefs isolated her from the community in which she lived and distanced her from those who might have offered help. Tensions were made worse by Savage's gender. As Patricia Crawford has observed, "The position of women even worsened after the Glorious Revolution," when fears about women's participation in public (and especially Dissenting) religion peaked, a reaction to the relative freedom of religious performance that women had claimed during the Interregnum.[6] From the 1680s through the early eighteenth century, women like Savage came under intense criticism and scrutiny, both in their performance of religion and in their acts of female sociability. Savage in fact rejected most outward performances of sociability in deference to a cultivation of an inward society of the mind, as she attempted to reconcile her Nonconformist beliefs with traditional understandings of female alliances.

Prosopography of a Female Dissenter

Sarah Henry Savage was born on August 7, 1664, in a place called Broad Oak, in Flintshire, just outside of Chester. Broad Oak was located in the corner of England closest to the northern border with Wales and today lies on the Welsh side of that border. Her parents were Katherine Henry and Rev. Philip Henry. Philip Henry was a Christ Church, Oxford-educated minister who shunned Anglicanism and adopted the Dissenting faith. Philip Henry is now identified as a Presbyterian, but in the late seventeenth and early eighteenth centuries this religious categorization was much more fluid. Savage herself rarely used the word *Presbyterian* to describe her faith, instead calling herself a Dissenter, a Nonconformist, or even a member of the "Despised Religion."[7] Philip Henry was ejected from his Anglican living in the mid-seventeenth century, and he and his family participated actively in political debates about Nonconformist rights.[8] Sarah Savage thus was raised within a vigorous network of allied Dissenters in Wales and its bordering counties: her father ran one of the chief seventeenth-century Dissenting Academies out of his Broad Oak home, and Wales more largely was the site of much Nonconformist activity throughout this period.[9]

Like many seventeenth- and eighteenth-century women, Savage was educated at home. Her tutor was another divine, Rev. William Turner, who lived with the Henry family at Broad Oak; Turner was probably one of Philip Henry's Dissenting Academy students. Her father assisted in her education by teaching her Hebrew. Although foreign language training was not usually offered to women, Savage's knowledge of Hebrew probably reflected the religious priorities of her family and especially of her father.[10] She shared a close and enduring relationship with her parents and siblings and spent most of her life in and around Chester: first at her natal home of Broad Oak and then, after her marriage, about ten miles away at Wrenbury Wood near Nantwich. She was married on March 28, 1687, at the age of twenty-three, to a man named John Savage, a cousin who was a farmer and land agent. John had been previously married, and his first wife had died.[11] Sarah's and John's first child was born in 1688—not long after Sarah had survived her bout with smallpox—and she and her husband went on to have six more, four of whom ultimately survived their parents.[12] When John died in 1731, Sarah left their farm of Wrenbury Wood to live with each of her surviving children, rotating through their households in semi-itinerant fashion.[13] In 1736 she made her final move to live with her daughter Hannah at West Bromwich, just north of Birmingham. Savage lived to an extremely old age and died on February 27, 1752.

Sarah Savage and her family were not wealthy, but they had enough money to ensure their comfort and well-being.[14] Although her father and brother were teachers and ministers, none of the family were landed or titled. One of Savage's diary entries mentioned that her sister had been married to a "tradesman in Chester"; another sister was married to a physician.[15] In addition to farming, Savage's husband, John, worked as a steward or land agent for Lord and Lady Manwaring. Savage took great pride in her family's genteel status. She found it important to contrast her lifestyle with that of the wealthier Manwarings, whom she characterized as noble, "declining," and dissolute. Heaping scorn on Lady Manwaring's son, "Sir T.," Savage once noted that in the course of his work, her husband "went to Peover, [to] settle accounts with Lady M[anwaring]. Sir T her son lives a loose profane life sells his birth-right etc., so that my Husband serves a declining family." Reasserting her own family's thriftiness and her husband's hard work, Savage was careful to add that John did not take advantage of his employers or in "any way raise himself on their ruins, but deserv's double the salary for his care and pains."[16] The social status of the Savage family and their position within their local community were both flexible and a matter of constant performance by Sarah Savage.

Savage kept a daily diary for roughly sixty years, that is, through most of her adult life, from 1686 to 1745.[17] The diary comprised many volumes and represents a truly astounding and complete record of an early modern person's life. The first volume, which offers evidence of Savage's courtship and early married life (1686–88), survives and is kept at the Cheshire and Chester County Record Office. In the eighteenth century a volume of Savage's diary covering the years 1688–95 was copied out by hand; this copy is held at Dr. Williams's Library, London. Two further eighteenth-century copies recall Savage's middle age (1714–23 and 1724–45) and are held at the Bodleian Library, Oxford, and the Harris Manchester College Library, Oxford, respectively.[18] An original volume covering some of the same years (1714–38) is held in the Henry Papers at the British Library, London.[19] Two more copied volumes (1727–30 and 1739–43) are held at the Beinecke Library, Yale University, and another eighteenth-century copy (1724–51) resides at Syracuse University, in its Special Collections Research Center.[20] The final volume of the diary is original in Savage's hand and describes her old age (1743–48); this volume is also held at Dr. Williams's Library, London.[21] Despite the length and unusual detail of the Savage texts, few historians have made her an object of in-depth study, and the piece studied most by scholars has been the first volume of Savage's diary.[22] But my analysis of Savage's female friendships draws instead from three texts which are more representative of the full span of her life: the first volume of Savage's diary (1686–88); the volume of the diary held at the Bodleian (1714–23); the last volume (1743–48) from Dr. Williams's Library; and a nineteenth-century biography of Savage (1686–1748) written by J. B. Williams. In his biography Williams claimed he consulted all of the original manuscripts written by Savage, many of which are now lost, as well as some of her personal papers and her correspondence.[23]

Savage made entries in her diary nearly every day, each piece ranging in length from a few lines to whole pages. The average entry is five to six sentences long. The diary was intended as a spiritual exercise, and in her very first essay Savage wrote that she hoped keeping a diary would enable her "therby [to] bee furthered in a Godly life." Savage's diary therefore has some resonance with a text written by another seventeenth-century Puritan, Nehemiah Wallington. Paul Seaver's description of Wallington's diary applies equally well to Savage's, as Savage's texts are also products of "unremitting self-examination, as though constantly before the throne of judgment."[24] Savage's self-examination took two forms: she wrote in the diary, recording God's influence on her life, copying sermons and prayers, analyzing religious texts, and noting events in which she felt God had intervened. But she also continually read through her own entries, reminding herself of past resolutions, finding inspiration in spiritual excerpts, reexamining her life for evidence that she was counted among the Elect. The role that this type of spiritual diary keeping played in the creation of an inward, contemplative sense of authorial self has received much scholarly attention, particularly from literary critics. But Savage's diary, like the other genres of women's writing examined here, offers additional evidence of the importance of sociability to women's gendered identity creation, to the creation of a type of femininity which privileged self-in-community.[25]

Savage wrote her diary within and about her godly community, many of whose members were women. Her constant struggles to construct and maintain female alliances are evidenced on every page of her voluminous text. But her diary was also read and used by many other women. Savage did not address her diary to a specific person—in fact, on one occasion she wrote of "fear [of the diary's] coming to the view of others." But Savage herself took great pleasure in reading through and studying the spiritual diaries of her deceased female friends, and it is likely that she recognized that her own diary might be read similarly after she died.[26] Whatever Savage's ultimate wishes, there is conclusive proof that her manuscripts were admired and emulated by her female inheritors. One of the unique features of Savage's original diary was that she used a heart symbol to represent the written word *heart*. Two generations later this symbol was still being used by her female descendants. One of Savage's granddaughters, a namesake Sarah Savage, kept an eighteenth-century religious diary that employed a heart symbol in its text.[27] Such replication demonstrates that Savage's female progeny inherited her written legacy and that they consciously modeled their own religious diaries after those of their ancestor. Savage's identity was thus created in reference to the women who shared with her these important familial, religious, and authorial ties.

Religiously Inspired Friendships

Savage's Nonconformist beliefs structured both her life and her diary. I have shown here the many ways in which early modern women used gendered activities like cooking food, tending children, making medicines, and providing health care in order to create and maintain female alliances. But for Savage, gendered activities were best performed according to Nonconformist sensibilities. Shunning most social interactions and categorizing them as wasteful or decadent, Savage rejected typical practices of feminine sociability in favor of "godly" conversation with other female Dissenters, women whom she called "praying friends."[28] She visited select female neighbors to read or discuss godly books with them. She encouraged the lower-status women who worked in her household to adopt Nonconformist religious practices. She ensured that extensive prayer accompanied the childbirth rituals of her daughters and sisters, and she traveled with other Dissenting women to attend sermons and local religious events.

Even in performing the domestic labor and daily chores that marked most early modern British women's lives, Savage referenced her Nonconformist religious ideals. She used Nonconformism as a reference point for common household tasks. In one diary entry Savage wrote that she had been "employed in the garden"—which, as we have seen, was a traditional employ for elite women in this period—when she was reminded of her belief in the sinful nature of humankind. She noted that this garden task made her "affected to see how much the weeds come on faster than the plants and herbs. Just so do corruptions thrive and grow in my own soul."[29] At harvest time in August 1687, Savage witnessed ripe fruit dropping off of some of the trees in the family's orchard; examining the windfall, she noticed that many of these fruits had been damaged by insects. This too became an opportunity for spiritual reflection, this time on the sin of temptation: "[August 1687] Meditation by seeing how the Fruit which was blown of the trees had generally a worm at [heart], I was inabled to beg of god that I may bee sincere that I may bee able to indure winds of temptation or affliction and not be blown down by them. Tis through my God that I shall bee inabled to stand."[30] The care of children, typically ceded to early modern women and stereotypically assumed to offer them opportunities for pleasant sociability, was for Savage an unwelcome duty; in a letter to her sister she once remarked on the "tediousness of [the] nursery."[31] Watching over and caring for children did annoy Savage, but in the pages of her diary she managed to turn these experiences into the type of private, inward contemplation prized by Dissenters, writing that she was "this day at home all day yet profited little, Cos. Kirk's little Sam tedious, I would reflect on mine infant age how many years did I live and trouble others ere I was so much as sensible yet I was capable of serving and enjoying God."[32]

Almsgiving and charity were daily chores that acted as reference points for Savage's Nonconformist faith. Charitable giving was an activity that was expected of early modern women and was a task which was thought to afford elite women a chance to interact positively with their lower-status neighbors and servants. Certainly members of Savage's community expected her to give charitably, for Savage wrote frequently of "seeing poor beggars wait at the door for their alms."[33] But as an early Presbyterian, Savage would have believed that the performance of acts of charity had no bearing on her possible status among God's Elect. Reconciling social expectations about charity with her beliefs proved difficult. She wrote in December 1714 that she was "reading this week in Mr. Gouge concerning Alms-giving," which was probably an edition of William Gouge's popular *Domestical Duties* of 1622. Reading Gouge reminded Savage that giving food or clothing to the poor was a "duty press'd from a thankful sense of God's goodness—he [Gouge] sais 'ye true and right spring of mercy to our poor neighbor is a sense of God's mercy to us.'" Resolving to remember this sentiment the next time she offered alms to the poor, Savage wrote that she would "bless God if I am enabl'd to give Alms in any measure with a chearful thankful heart," but, she acknowledged, "I find the duty of giving, hard to manage *aright*."[34]

Other activities that were expected of or traditionally performed by early modern women also acted as channels for Savage's religious beliefs. In June 1714 Savage's "Daughter M" fell unexpectedly "ill one afternoon [with] much pain in her head, and vomiting," and Savage wrote that she "fear'd the beginning of a Feavor." During her daughter's illness Savage would have been expected to perform the traditional arduous female labor of caring for the sick: staying near the patient throughout the illness, keeping them clean, and administering medicines. But Savage wrote that the illness ultimately gave her an opportunity for prayer. Savage's religious beliefs helped her to "resign" her daughter's fate to God, and she recorded that she had "solemnly and perticularly resign[ed] her to the good pleasure of God." When "by the next morn: she was well," Savage saw her daughter's recovery as a fulfillment of God's blessings on her family and as probable proof of her daughter's status among the Elect: "Our good God is slow to afflict, but swift to shew mercy."[35] Similarly, when Savage's "Daughter Keay" was ill following a difficult childbirth in the autumn of 1714, Savage employed prayer to heal her.

She inscribed a written prayer, "Lord spare her in usefulness," into the diary alongside evidence of the sickness itself: "This day I sent to Whitchurch to see Daughter Keay who is stil very weak, but recovering—Lord spare her in usefulness."[36]

Savage relied on similar techniques when providing health care for her female friends and neighbors. In June 1717 Savage went "at noon . . . to see my friend Mrs. Braddock who has 5 children ill of smalpox—only one of 'em can sit up—4 in bed, and in very afflictive circumstances." In addition to whatever help Savage might have dispensed in personal skill and physical care, she offered aid to her friend Braddock in the form of prayer, recording the appeal directly into her diary: "I entreated for mercy for them." A few days later Savage again expressed sympathy for Braddock alongside a written plea. On "Wednesday I wrote to Mrs. Braddock—cannot choose but sympathize with em, I hear her daughter Betty is stil as she was." This entry was followed by the inscribed appeal, "Lord hear prayer."[37]

Prayer and religion structured Savage's understanding and use of medicine as well. Unlike most early modern women, who inscribed their medical knowledge and recipes directly into their diaries and account books, Savage framed her manufacture and use of medicines within spiritual contexts. When Savage's daughter Katherine was sick, she wrote that the use of a medicine which she merely called "means used" throughout her diary had helped her.[38] It was not Savage's personal expertise in concocting the medicine that helped Katherine but "God's blessing on means used [that the illness] soon went off."[39] Savage's account of her own use of medicines during illness followed the same pattern. On her fifty-third birthday on August 7, 1717, Savage found herself "not well with grips and vomiting— went to bed there full of tossings before the dawning of the day I arose but stil the same violent thorn in the flesh, most of Thursday ill." She eventually found "much relief" in a medicine given to her by a neighbor, Mrs. Voyce: "Towards evening better—blessed be God—I had much relief by somthing that my neighbor Mrs. Voyce sent me." Savage's gratitude for her recovery was devoted solely to God; even her recollection of the relief she received from the medicine was tied not to Voyce but to a prayer inscription Savage included: "Blessed be God."[40] And the healing of Savage's daughter Sarah Lawrence in January 1716 received similar treatment in the diary. When six months pregnant, Lawrence was "much afflicted with Collick, and in much peril being near 6 months gone with child." Savage observed that she had "sent a messenger to see Daughter Lawrance" and that "in the use of means is now better." Savage was grateful that the medicine had helped her daughter recover but gave credit for this healing solely to God. When Lawrence was "safely deliv'd of a Daughter" the following April, Savage stated, "God was gracious in strenthning both."[41]

Childbirth rituals such as these were, for Savage, particularly invested with spiritual meaning. In September 1688 Savage wrote that she had been composing a letter to her "Sister Hulton" when she "heard tidings of her not being well." Conjecturing that this illness was morning sickness—Savage "supposed [her] yong with Child"—she did not celebrate her sister's fertility or her success in perpetuating her husband's family but instead "commended her to God. . . . Lord preserve her or fit her for thy will."[42] When Katherine Savage "was near her time" in September 1714, Savage traveled to her home at Motehouse in order to aid in the birth. After her arrival Savage went to bed, only to be awakened that night with the news that her daughter's labor had begun: "I went to Motehouse my daughter I knew was near her time, but proved more neer than I expected, for she fell in travel that very night before she slept, tho did not wake me till 2 a clock in the morning." Although this news must have been a surprise and may have called for some haste, Savage paused to pray, spending time in what she called "reflection," before beginning the childbirth rituals. Savage wrote that, after waking, she "arose and to my comfort after in the reflection begun with prayer that God would be a present help, which indeed he was." This brief solitude allowed Savage herself some "comfort," but it also marked the rest of the birth, for although she wrote that her daughter's labor was lengthy and intense, marked by "constant pain all that day and night," Savage felt that God had "directed and help'd" the entire process: "She lingr'd with constant pain all that day and night, then her pains were more sharp, next morn: fell asleep and slept for an hour or more, which much discourag'd me lest her labour should not return, but it did and God so directed and help'd us that about 2 a clock on Thursd Afternoon she was safely deliv'd of a Daughter. . . . God heard our prayers prevented fears tho' flesh & heart began to fail, God was a present help. . . . it pleases God to make her a nursing mother, none but the dear child has suckt her breast."[43] Savage's reference to her daughter as a "nursing mother" probably indicated the means her daughter used to nourish her infant.[44] But it was also surely indicative of Savage's faith. The image of the nursing mother was one frequently employed by Nonconformists to describe a righteous woman who was a nurturing, supportive religious influence, and by invoking this reference Savage sought to position her daughter among the Elect.[45]

That Savage privileged the prayerful, Nonconformist birth rituals practiced by her family members was made clear when she described the labor of an Anglican woman in her village, her "neighbor Ann Lee." Savage considered her attendance at the event to be "a work of mercy," part of her duties as an elite woman living in a small, semirural community. The birth went smoothly, and Savage recorded that "about one at noon she was deliv'd of a son with a sharp but successful labour." But ultimately Savage was disappointed in Lee's behavior during her labor. She "observed [Lee] oft call'd on God for help in her extreamity" but expressed her displeasure that "when delivered [she gave] no mention of thanks." Savage considered this to be an insult to God and remarked, "It is to me a sad tho't that the most of our neighbors, tho' moraly civil, live with out any thing of the true life and power of Religion."[46]

Savage's writings about women like her neighbor Ann Lee emphasized both her close monitoring of other women's religiosity and the duty she felt to act as a moral example to them. Savage noted happily any exhibition of Nonconformist tendencies in her neighbors, servants, and friends. She commented in September 1714 that she had spent the "afternoon poor old Mrs. Robinson with me, I read to her Mr. Reynolds sermon for dear Brother."[47] Robinson was a neighbor who was an object of pity to Savage, and it is possible that Robinson did occasional domestic labor at Savage's home of Wrenbury Wood. Savage's apparent pity for Robinson was owing at least partially to the woman's advanced age, for in the diary Savage never failed to refer to Robinson as being both poor and old. Savage's compassion for Robinson could also have been the result of the woman's declining health. Savage wrote on one occasion that she "was at home all day. . . . in the afternoon poor old Mary Robinson come to be with me, we read and pray'd as we could I see her much declin'd."[48] Savage's feelings of sympathy for Robinson were again made manifest one Sunday, when she found herself "at home in the afternoon poor old Mary Robinson was with me, whom I always pity— under some domestick troubles but I am pleased to day she tels me she is more easy than usual—which I take as the fulfilling of that Psalm 25, *His soul shal dwell at Ease*."[49] Savage was referring to the portion of the psalm that reads, "His soule shall dwell at ease, and his seede shall inherite the land. The secrete of the Lorde is reveiled to them, that feare him: and his covenant to give them understanding."[50] Savage found herself bound to Robinson out of compassion for the woman's "domestick troubles," but she also found in Robinson an affirmation of her faith and of the pleasure she took in God's "covenant to give her understanding." Savage regarded her fulfillment of her duties to care and provide aid to vulnerable women in her neighborhood as being entwined with Nonconformist religious practice.

Talking, praying, and sharing news with women whom she considered to be of lower status was a practice which brought Savage additional pleasure. She conveyed that she was on easy, friendly terms with her mother's servants, as demonstrated in a diary entry from 1694 in which she wrote, "My Mother's maid from Broad Oak came to see us. She brought me a comfortable letter from my dear father."[51] In this example, Savage remembered the female servant's visit not only for the company it provided but also for the message it brought: a letter from her father the minister, whom Savage much admired and whose spiritual example she tried to follow. And Savage worked to cultivate a relationship with her own servants which was both pious and patronizing. She recorded in her diary that a female servant complained of overwork and exhaustion, writing, "Overhearing a servant, being weary, wishing earnestly for night, that she might rest, I could not but be affected." But Savage was not "affected" with sympathy. Rather this remark reminded her that she, too, "was thoroughly weary of this world, which is so full of toil, labour, and sorrow, I should long for the rest of death, when my body shall sleep in the grave, and my spirit return to God who gave it."[52] In Savage's eyes, care for those in her employ was better expressed through spiritual discipline than through succor or compassion.

One of the most revealing examples of Savage's desire to employ Nonconformist practices in relations with her servants occurs in the example of her relationship with a woman named Mary Bate. Bate had a long association with Savage and her relations (see the introduction), being allied with the family for at least eight years. In September 1714, by which time Bate had been working at Wrenbury Wood for some years, Savage averred that "my maid Mary Bate [is] I hope a religious servant." Bate shared Savage's Dissenting sympathies, and Savage wrote that she appreciated Bate's religious "knowledge and piety." These were qualities which encouraged Savage to continue Bate's employment. But Savage also felt that the woman lacked "other qualifications" which she considered to be necessary in a good servant:

"I have some careful tho'ts about the servants for another year, my maid Mary Bate I hope a religious servant but of a perverse temper, Lord make my way plain concerning her I love her for her knoledge and piety and could wish she were adorn'd with other qualifications as I should desire."[53]

Despite these misgivings and Savage's open dislike of Bate's supposedly "perverse temper," Bate shared a privileged relationship with Savage and her daughters, and Savage felt a continuing responsibility for her physical and spiritual well-being, even after the woman had left Savage's employ. In the spring of 1716, when Bate fell dangerously ill with "a violent inflammation, great pain all over, sore throat," Savage rushed to her bedside to care for her. She kept track of Bate's illness in the diary over the course of several days, writing that on "Satt[urday] I was sent for to my old servant Mary Bate ill at Marbury" and that by "Sabb[ath]d[ay] I hear Mary is stil ill, yet rested and is a little more easy—Lord do for her as the matter requires, if it please thee reprieve, succor, spare." By Monday Savage was relieved to hear that Bate continued to recover and offered further prayers and gratitude for her salvation: "Monday I hear M. Bate begins to recover—how merciful is God."[54]

But Bate's and Savage's relationship was difficult for Savage to manage. Savage's lasting reservations about her servant came through quite clearly in the pages of her diary, despite the fact that Bate shared many social and religious ties with the Savage family. In March 1719, when Bate was chosen for the special task of carrying one of Savage's infant grandchildren to its baptism, Savage wrote, "Mary Bate is over from Chester, was at Motehouse & carried the child to be baptized."[55] Despite the weighty role Bate played in the life of Savage's family, Savage continued to complain of her defects. Alongside this entry about the baptism, Savage reflected on her aversion to Bate, attempting to bury her dislike beneath her preference for Nonconformist female companions: "I do love those who I have reason to hope God loves, notwithstanding their faults."[56] More than four years later Bate and Savage were still socializing. In a diary entry sometime after 1723 Savage noted that the former servant had come to visit her: "Mary Bate (that was) our old servant, came to see us; staid two nights: has much affliction by a froward husband and his carnal relations."[57] It is difficult to determine the layers of obligation, solicitation, or even unwelcome responsibility that may have either colored or motivated this stopover, but Savage's record of Bate's visit includes evidence that the women socialized for at least two days and talked of both personal family matters and religious ones. Savage's observation that

Bate suffered from "much affliction" as a result of her husband's "carnal relations" indicates Savage's sympathy toward Bate's domestic problems and perhaps even the offering of advice and religious consolation.

Savage relied on her Dissenting beliefs to mitigate and interpret awkward or unpleasant interactions with women in her employ and in her neighborhood, and we have seen that in some cases these beliefs necessitated the maintenance of ties with women whom Savage personally disliked. But the impact of Savage's Nonconformist ideals on her female alliances was made particularly clear when she socialized with women who she felt shared her Dissenting faith and her social status. In the diary Savage twinned comments about this type of sociability with remarks on spiritual matters. She wrote on one occasion that her son-in-law's sisters "Mrs. Dean and Mrs. Barns" had "come down from London" for a visit. Savage and the two sisters traveled "to Broad-Oak to meet my Brother Henry who preach'd there to a full congregation," and Savage wrote that she had "found welcome and comfort" in these spiritual activities.[58] Savage's religious perspective also colored her meeting with "Cos Kirk from Chester." When Kirk "came to us and her two youngest children," Savage expressed her thanks to God for Kirk's friendship and for fellowship with Jesus, whom she imagined as their mutual best friend: "Blessed be God for friends especially blessed be God for Jesus Christ our best friend."[59] When her friend Mrs. Kelsal visited Broad Oak in February 1715, Savage expressed pity that the woman was "unequaly yoak'd" with her husband, indicating that Kelsal's husband did not share the religious beliefs treasured by both Savage and Kelsal: "This evening Mrs. Kelsal came home with me, a good Christian under great Affliction and trouble, unequaly yoak'd yet turn'd by God to her great good, to turn her from youthful vanity."[60] Savage used this experience of her "good Christian" friend's marital trouble to see the "great good" in the situation, as it had apparently brought Kelsal closer to the Dissenting faith and removed her further from the "youthful vanity" that both women shunned.

Sociable religiosity with other women was practiced in addition by Savage with her immediate female family members. She recorded that two of her daughters, Lawrance and Molly, had planned to walk to a sermon in nearby Nantwich with female friends; but when the day arrived it was "very wett, [so] we discourag'd them because of incessant rain." And although Savage was disappointed that the weather prevented their trip, she wrote that she and her daughters still had found particular "comfort within doors—Daughter L[awrance]'s company, our friends about us, Cos Eddows's children, Miss Jenny Hunt, etc."[61] On January 5, 1698, Savage wrote of visiting her "dear sister Tylston" at their natal home of Broad Oak. This triggered in Savage bittersweet memories of the society she used to share with her siblings as a child and young woman: "I went to dear Broad Oak. I found dear sister Tylston there. She and I are all that are left of four. A joyful, sorrowful meeting."[62] Savage's records of sociability with the women in her family almost always referenced the way they combined social exercises, like visiting, talking, walking, and reading aloud, with religious ones, like expressions of gratitude, communal prayer, and the righteous contemplation of earthly sorrows.

Savage undoubtedly valued spiritual and familial company, and she believed that this kind of sociability could even grant succor and healing in times of illness. In June 1694 Savage took her husband and three daughters to Broad Oak when she went to care for her ailing mother. Upon arrival they met a crowd of family, for various siblings, nieces, and nephews had also gathered at the home farm. She wrote that the presence of this collective, religiously minded family helped to revive her mother's spirits as well as her physical body: "My husband and I went to Broad Oak with our three little daughters. My dear aged mother hath been for some weeks much indisposed. Now blessed be God, better. She cannot but be revived with eight of her grand-children about her." Working to further intertwine physical presence and bodily intimacy with spiritual growth, Savage went on to note that on this visit to Broad Oak she shared an especially "comfortable time with my dear mother" because the two women "slept together, and often prayed together, with comfort, at our bedside."[63]

Savage's social relationships with her female relatives even offered positive inspiration for her private spiritual life. On one occasion Savage wrote that although she "was at home all day" alone, the memory of a conversation she had shared with her mother spurred her to pray. Savage wrote that she began this private spiritual conversation by "call[ing] to mind some discourse I had with my dear mother lately . . . [on] an excellent minister." Savage's prayers were motivated by information her mother had gleaned from this "excellent minister," but also especially by the "discourse" Savage had shared with her mother. Savage often structured her interior spiritual life around verbal conversations she remembered from the past. She wrote on one occasion that she had felt "comfort in the society of my dear mother, especially when we prayed together in that which was, once, my dear father's closet, and which he, so solemnly, dedicated to the service of God." For Savage, the "comfort" she experienced by being with her mother was "especially" enhanced as they prayed together and as they conducted this prayer in her father's "closet," his personal space of study and religious contemplation. The space that her father had occupied in life was, to Savage, a conduit both for his posthumous religious messages and for a heightened awareness of her own relationship with her widowed mother.

Struggles with Normative Female Sociability

In the pages of her diary Savage demonstrated her commitment to the spiritual and physical care of those few women with whom she shared alliances. Her clear preference for Nonconformist society was made visible in her notations of daily family chores, her interactions with neighbors, and her conversations with religiously minded female companions. But how and to what degree Savage expected she should concern herself with her Anglican family, neighbors, and friends was a constant source of worry. Like many other early Presbyterians, Savage and her family practiced "occasional conformity" by attending some masses at their local Anglican church, while also traveling to hear Nonconformist ministers, including Savage's father and brother, preach.[64] But Savage expressed anxieties over how often to conform to Anglicanism. On September 25, 1715, she recorded that "my Husband and Children and Cos. M. Hulton etc. all attended" the Anglican mass at Nantwich. But when the family arrived in Nantwich, Savage and her sister Tylston balked when it came time to enter the church; Savage wrote that, instead of going inside to listen, "Sister Tylston and I, staid by the stuff," sitting in the family's cart with the baggage and supplies while everyone else attended the service. This caused Savage some worry: "I am oft in doubt in the matter," for she was afraid of insulting Nantwich's Anglican priest, Mr. Newnam: "[I am] sorry to discourage Mr. Newnam who I believe intends well." Savage recognized that insulting Newnam was a bad idea and also that her practice of occasional conformity made her an enemy of two groups simultaneously, as the Anglicans disliked her occasional refusal to attend church and the Nonconformists criticized her for being disloyal: "[I] cannot but think it my duty to own the Dissenters & their cause, tho' we lye under the reproach of halting between two."[65] That Savage felt her spiritual beliefs

forced her to "[halt] between two" groups of people is indicative of the difficulties she faced when socializing with the women in her neighborhood. The
ongoing resolution of tensions between religion and community was therefore present in each act of sociability Savage performed.

Uncomfortable with traditional female sociability and alliance building,
Savage's most frequent recourse was simple avoidance. She took great pleasure in spending time alone, reading and praying quietly by herself. A vora-
cious reader, Savage often specified in her diary what books and sermons she
was studying. Her attitude toward reading, religion, and learning undoubtedly structured her approach to the writing of her diary, but her reading
practices were especially illustrative of her view of female alliances.[66] Savage
considered books to be her friends. Savage prided herself on her love of
"good books," by which she meant pamphlets, books, and sermons of a religious nature—this feeling may have been a reflection of her rigorous education. And Savage fostered what she considered to be an almost sociable
relationship with books and pamphlets. She believed that her reasoned, scholarly activities were gifts from God, and she felt no guilt at using these talents:
"I have the use of reason, and peace in my own conscience, those unspeak-
able blessings. How much am I indebted!"[67] And while she expressed discomfort with many of the social rituals undertaken by elite British women, she
found solace and a higher purpose in reading and literary study. These
bookish, contemplative activities never clashed with her religious ideals.[68]

Savage believed that books gave her the comfort and company typically offered to an early modern woman by her female friends. Most early
modern women relied on their female friends for advice when struck by
medical or financial disaster, just as they were taught to reach out to companions when they felt isolated or lonely. Most early modern women looked to
those in their alliance groups for solace in times of emotional distress or loss.
In chapter 1 I demonstrated that most women of the time observed closely
and critically the experiences and trials of their friends in order to learn how
to model their lives. But Savage was different. She wrote that she was aided
by literary companions rather than by personal, bodily ones. These fictional
friends filled many, if not all, of the roles typically played by real women in
the early modern period. Savage believed that books taught her how to live
an exemplary life, writing that spiritual works supplied her with "excellent
helps" because they offered paradigms for living religiously: "I had excellent
helps by good books—the lives of holy persons of both sexes."[69] Religious

books and printed sermons could even be "company," as Savage wrote that "among my sweetest enjoyments" she counted "good books, which I have found very profitable, and good company, often, in my solitude."[70]

Standard practices of female sociability—visits, conversations, gift exchange, correspondence, and travel—were for Savage an acute burden, especially when they necessitated spending time with Anglicans. While performing an act of neighborly charity, sitting up with "a neighbor that was not well" in the early spring of 1687, Savage expressed her distraction and annoyance, writing that the ill woman was "new married pining in a consumption in appearance near the gates of death," but Savage was discomfited at the woman's lack of religiosity, noting, "Alas [I] could perceive [what] little sence shee has of what is before her."[71] Even women whom Savage regularly visited, such as her neighbors the Robinsons, were sometimes an annoyance to her. She wrote testily of an "afternoon which I intended to spend wholy in retirement," which she was "robb'd of unavoidably by the visit of a neighbor (Martha Robinson)."[72] Categorizing the rituals of visiting, conversing, and exchanging news as a component of dissolute elite life, Savage distanced herself in January 1717 from some of her high-ranking neighbors, for after a "splendid Entertainment" at a neighbor's home she avowed in her diary that "I envy not the great man's state." Ruing the wasted hours she had spent eating and talking with these impious Anglicans, Savage acknowledged that although someone of her status had a basic "duty to be friendly and respectful to those who are so to us," she quickly affirmed that she received "more inward satisfaction with a good Book in my own Closet than with all the visit, modes and forms, etc."[73]

Shunning elite sociability and embracing solitude allowed Savage to avoid activities and conversations she considered to be immoral, but although she was often physically alone, she believed that religious literature supplied all of the aid, support, and encouragement she required. In June 1714 she wrote in her diary that she was "at home, I praise God not alone, good books and especially a good God are my good companions."[74] On another occasion she spent "all day at home" with only her namesake granddaughter "little S[arah] L[awrence] [for] my companion." Yet Savage was not left uninspired. Despite the fact that the day had been spent entirely in the company of a preverbal infant—a duty which was usually onerous to Savage—she wrote that she had "yet met with quickning and comfort from good Books."[75] Books were a source of solace even in times of sickness. When Savage found herself "troubled with a cold and sore throat and kept home all day," she confided to her diary that, even in midst of this illness, when most early modern women sought the company, advice, and aid of their female friends, Savage felt herself to be "alone but blessed be God not lonely had good Books, [and] read much."[76] Books could also fill the role of a religious advisor. Savage wrote that although she did find occasional "satisfaction in going to [Anglican] Church and owning publick Assemblys" in the company of neighborhood women, she felt a far "more present advantage by being in my closet with good Books."[77]

The only times Savage reported feeling truly alone were on those occasions when she lost, loaned, or misplaced a particularly beloved text. On these instances, Savage wrote of experiencing the isolation and melancholy typically expressed by early modern women who lived apart from their family and friends. And when beloved books were returned to her, she became ecstatic over the joy of reunion. Comparing herself to a biblical shepherd who had lost his sheep, Savage noted that, upon finding a book that had once belonged to her father, she felt "much elevated and delighted tonight with the return of one of my good old books dear Fathers legacy of his notes wrote with his dear hand—I had lost it I believe 6 years, I tho't of the good shepherds joy over one lost sheep."[78] Seeing her father's scrawl inside of the book, reading the words he had written "with his dear hand" connected Savage to someone long dead but still revered. Looking over the rediscovered book, Savage found herself emotionally and spiritually renewed.

Savage's preference for reading, private contemplation, and solitary prayer was no doubt reinforced by her sense of being an "outsider," an outcast from Anglican society. As Patricia Crawford has demonstrated in her study of Katherine and Philip Henry, Sarah Savage's mother and father, early modern Dissenters often found it difficult to integrate themselves into their Anglican communities: "[Philip Henry] became an outcast. . . . After 1689 the Dissenters were tolerated . . . [but] they still lived in a community in which their separation was criticized and their scruples of conscience mocked."[79] Sarah Savage certainly saw herself as a member of a persecuted religious minority. This was at times expressed with stubborn pride. In April 1716 Savage compared herself to a biblical pilgrim when writing about her separation from Anglican "natives," saying that she envisioned herself as "a stranger and a Pilgrim, this is not my home if so then I should walk circumspectly giving no offence to the natives, I should ask the way to Zion and walk in it." And yet Savage expressed some uneasiness at this godly distance. Unwilling to conform to her neighbors, Savage was nonetheless "sometimes a little concern'd to see neighbors look shy, and cold, on us (as we are Dissenters)."[80]

From Savage's earliest days at her home Wrenbury Wood, to which she moved when she was married, she discerned that most of her Anglican neighbors treated her with suspicion and scorn. Used to the more concordant community at her natal Broad Oak, Savage was surprised and disappointed by the harsh treatment offered by her new neighbors. Her neighbors had initially expressed curiosity about her Nonconformity, and shortly after moving to Wrenbury Wood Savage mentioned that "some Neighbors came in to us to joyn in singing Acts and in Prayer." Despite this early attempt at friendliness, it soon became clear to Savage that the religious practices of her new neighbors were very different from her own. During her very first visit to the Anglican church near Wrenbury Wood in April 1687, she noted reservedly that there was a "great diff[erence] betw[een] this and such Sabbaths as I have seen." Two months later the situation had deteriorated. By June 1687 the local Anglican preacher was attacking Nonconformists in his sermons: "Sab[bathday] Mr. Brown preached at Wrenb[ury] . . . yet had some flings at Dissenters Father forgive the bitternes that is in the spirits of men." And by October 1687 the criticisms had spread, as Savage wrote sadly that "wee dayly hear of the scoffs and scorns of our neighbors." Such contempt ran both ways. Scornful in her own right of the Anglicans who surrounded her, Savage, when invited to a nearby home, decried "the Profanetion of the Sab[bath] that I saw there." And when invited to visit a female neighbor, Savage acknowledged grudgingly that she had been "kindly entertained" but was more "concerned to see how little regard most of our neighbors have to the best things, most live as if they had only bodyes and no souls."[81]

Two examples bring into high relief Savage's struggles with the performance of traditional female sociability. In the winter of 1717 Savage felt compelled to attend Anglican church, and she paired this act of community obedience with one of feminine charity. Savage wrote that on "Sab[bathday] Jan 13 I went to Church, [and] called at Wil: Golbourns whose wife is begun of the smallpox, likely to be very thick." This visit, in which Savage offered support to an ill woman, was designed to show Savage's care and compassion, as it represented an exhibition of gendered sympathy as well as an expression of Savage's willingness to be a good neighbor. Savage left the

Golbourns' home "satisfied with my charitable visit" but was disappointed soon thereafter. Arriving at church, she found that the Anglican minister's "sermon . . . was uncharitable, the text 'lean not to thine own understanding,' from whence he took occasion to reflect severly on them that differ from the establish'd church as guilty of great pride." Feeling as if she had been personally attacked—which may indeed have been the case—Savage was infuriated and defended herself angrily in her diary: "If my heart deceive me not, I am not a Dissenter thro' Pride or Arrogancy," and she insisted that she actively sought reconciliation with those Anglicans around her: "[I am] ready to say, the lord the judge be judge between them and us, we do not revile or censure them, but come frequently to hear 'em, tho they hate and fear us, as we cannot in every thing be of their mind." Reflecting on the defeat of her attempts at integration that day, Savage wondered sadly, "Lord when shal it be that our unhappy divisions shal be heal'd."[82]

Savage's dealings with her Anglican neighbors may have been troubled, but her interactions with relatives who were Anglican were perhaps even more challenging. In these instances Savage struggled to balance her duty to be friendly and loving to her female relations with the demands of her Nonconformist conscience. When Savage's "Daughter K[atherine]" was married to her "Coz. Savages eldest son," Savage anticipated a potential source of conflict, for the man's "Father and Mother [are] sober people but much for the Church of England." This caused Savage and her other Nonconformist relations to have "many discouraging tho'ts" about the match.[83] Nonetheless, the two were married, and just as Savage had feared she soon faced discord with these new Anglican relatives. Savage felt acutely pressured by her female in-laws. Savage wrote that one "Tuesday our new relation, son Savages mother come to see us," and this woman "urg'd me to encourage my daughter to join with them at Church." Savage was torn. She understood that her daughter would have to accommodate her Anglican relations, neighbors, and friends. But she also privately supported her daughter in her Nonconformist preferences and practices. Savage eventually relented to the Anglican woman and "said I would not hinder her [from attending Church of England services]—we left it much to God and their consciences." But the encounter bothered her, mainly because she felt it was unfair that she was "expected [to] put her upon what I am not free to do myself."[84]

Savage learned that removing herself too far from Anglican society was dangerous, for it could have violent consequences for her family, servants, and friends. In the summer of 1715 the ongoing Sacheverell Riots exposed tensions between Anglicans and Nonconformists in both England and Wales.[85] Over several weeks Savage fearfully cited a "Jacobite mob" that was tearing down Dissenting meetinghouses and setting fire to them. The violence began in June, when, Savage reported, "great outrages" had been committed "in London—Oxford, York, Manchester, Fire kindled in some meetinghouses, etc."[86] A few weeks later Savage wrote that she had heard "more tydings of the rudeness of the mob in many places" and that "the meeting house in Manchester [was] quite demolished."[87] By July 10, the riots had reached the north of Wales. Savage had heard "great talk of violence & spoil, meetinghouses at Salop & Wem said to be pull'd down or near it." Saddened by this destruction and terrified of the effect it might have on her family, Savage hid inside her home and prayed desperately to "hear O our God for we are despised. . . . I [stayed] at home in the morning, could not but have a true concern for the places of our solemnitys."[88]

Five days later Savage confirmed that her own local, Dissenting community had been attacked. Attempting to resign the matter to God, she lamented the destruction of two chapels she had frequented, in Wem and in Whitchurch: "This week it pleas'd the Al-wise God to permit it, that on Tuesd[ay] Wem Chappel was pull'd down, and on Frid[ay] Whitchurch of the latter I was an ear-witness July 15 in the Afternoon (we going to Whitchurch that day) at 5 or 6 o'clock the rabble crowded to the Chappel and with great heat & violence broke all to pieces, thay triumph & rejoice." Savage was furious at the divisions this revealed in her town: she "could not but be affected to see so many good people with their eyes & hearts failing, while others triumph & rejoice making the town ring with their Acclamations."[89] The destruction of the chapels represented a personal loss to Savage, loss of a place to gather and worship with members of her faith. With the riots ongoing, Savage wrote that only "2 or 3 [Nonconformists] (in an upper chamber) met to . . . pray & sing" that week, fearing retribution.[90] But their demolition also represented the loss of her father's hard work. Rev. Philip Henry had founded the chapel at Whitchurch, and Savage felt the loss of this meetinghouse the most keenly: "[I was] much affected with the state of poor Wem & especially Whitchurch a society of my Dear Fathers planting & watering."[91] The destruction of Nonconformist ministries continued, and Savage recorded over the next few days that meetinghouses had been pulled down in the nearby towns of Uttoxeter and Stoke.

The demolition of Dissenting chapels was tragic for Savage personally and spiritually, but the Sacheverell riots caused lasting community rifts between the Savage family and their neighbors. Shortly after the destruction of the Whitchurch chapel, Savage wrote anxiously that at "the beginning of this week my Husband had some trouble with one of the villains that help'd to pull down Whitchurch meeting." One night the man had approached the Savage's farm, Wrenbury Wood, and "behaved Insolently." Savage, her family, and some neighboring Dissenters, terrified that this was a sign that a mob was coming to attack them, huddled inside the house and prayed: "All night on Tuesday we had fears of a mob coming upon us in the night who were gather'd at Wrenbury—but our good God who is a witness to the innocency & integrity of his poor Servants did watch about & protect us from all Evil." A few days later their fears were renewed, for "it being Wrenbury Wakes there was a great concourse of people so that many fear'd it might occasion some disturbance."[92] But the crowds dispersed, and eventually Savage and her family felt safe enough to begin taking legal action against the assailants. John Savage traveled to Chester, where he formally accused the man who had trespassed at Wrenbury Wood. Savage wrote exultantly that the case was "proved against him, [and] he was on Wednesday committed to Chester Castle."[93]

Savage believed these legal actions were "act[s] of necessary justice," defenses of the hard-won rights Dissenters had achieved in the Act of Toleration of 1689. John and Sarah Savage worked repeatedly to bring legal action against any local women and men whom they felt had broken the act, but frequently they were disappointed, as they found that their city government officials were reluctant to enforce the law. In July Savage wrote, "The H[igh] Sheriff & Justice came to examine the riots lately committed, in pulling down the Chappel—the mob insolent, & justices not zealous, so little done, but they were found guilty of a riot."[94] By September John Savage was still "employ'd in the Prosecution of one of the Rioters, taken in July at Nantwych—and now found guilty of Treasonable words he is fined & sentenc'd to stand in the Pillory in Chester, Nantwych & Middlwich etc."[95] But even in this apparent victory Savage was disappointed. She noted angrily that when it came time for the man to be punished, her Anglican neighbors were sympathetic to the guilty party: "[Oct 1715] This day the forementioned Prisoner stood on the Pillory at Nantw[ich]: an hour at noon—had some affronts, but much foolish Pity."[96] Four years later the Savages again found themselves seeking legal restitution after Sarah Savage's sister, nieces, son, and cousins were harassed and assaulted by drunken locals: "In the Evening . . . sister T and daughter's and Cous[in] M.R. etc. had a fright by some drunken Fellows that follow'd them out of town—and were abusive to my son Phil . . . my son had some hurt on his face and one arm, but God (who protects the innocent) suffer'd 'em not to do the mischief they easily might, being two against one, and he having not so much as a staff." But when Savage and her family attempted to press charges, they were convinced by local authorities to let the matter drop. Savage wrote bitterly that she and her husband were "advised to take their acknowledgements and 30lb for the poor etc. and the charges rather than let 'em be sent to jayl as they well deserved."[97]

Savage and her family were regarded as rank outsiders, and their unwillingness to conform to Anglicanism was considered by most of their neighbors to be strange and even dangerous. Savage's personal struggles with neighborliness and sociability were therefore of the utmost importance. If she could integrate herself into her neighborhood, if she could form positive connections with Anglican women who lived nearby, she and her family might cease to seem so perplexing and suspicious. A final example offers evidence of Savage's efforts to transcend differences in her community through acts of female sociability. Sarah and John Savage faced intense criticism from one neighbor in particular, a man named Mr. Starkey. Savage wrote in her diary that "this Gentelman was a great enemy to us as Dissenters," a matter made worse by the fact that Starkey was also the Savages' landlord.[98] Savage clearly disliked Starkey, believing he was profligate and untrustworthy. On several occasions she criticized his "lusts" and "intemperance," and she carefully registered those instances in which Starkey harassed her family. In October 1687 Savage wrote that "Mr. Starkey next day gave my Husband a severe cheek," which John Savage defused by "answer[ing] him mildly that hee was sorry any shoulde take offence for hee intended to give none." A few months later Savage wrote that John had "received an angry caviling letter from his landlord Mr. Starkey—tis plain hee waits for occasion against us."[99]

But although Savage was convinced that Starkey "hated and despised" her, she worked hard to overcome his animosity. And in order to do this Savage cultivated a friendship with Starkey's wife. In July 1714 Savage wrote that she had gone "to day to see good old Mrs. Starky."[100] The visit paid off. By that winter, in December 1714, Savage reported her distress at learning that "our good old friend Mrs. Starky is weak and ill." This sickness became an occasion for more visits, and Savage wrote happily that on "Wednesday [when] I was seeing her, they tho't her beter."[101]

Conducting sociable visits and offering companionship and health care during periods of illness were traditional methods of creating female alliances, and Savage was able to use them to good effect. By July of the next year, 1715, Starkey and Savage were fast friends. And what was more, they were beginning to share the kinds of homosocial activities that Savage so valued: religious discussion, communal prayer, and the exchange of spiritual books. Savage attended some Anglican church services with Starkey and even shared meals with her between the morning and afternoon services. On one of these occasions Savage wrote that while eating lunch with Starkey during the Anglican intermission, Mrs. Starkey offered her the gift of a book: "I dined this day at old Mrs. Starkys, and staid the intermission, she gave me a good Book to read in, Bishop Halls Contemplations—which edify'd me more than what I heard at Church."[102] Savage's confession that Hall's *Contemplations* were more edifying than what she had "heard at Church" is certainly striking, for although Hall himself possessed certain sympathies for Presbyterianism, many of his writings defended the Anglican policies of Archbishop of Canterbury William Laud.[103] That this spiritual discovery was facilitated by Mrs. Starkey attests to the success of Savage's efforts at forming a friendship. Through the use of female sociability, Savage was able to overcome some of the neighborhood conflict her Nonconformist religious beliefs had caused.

Savage's diaries act as an especially useful conclusion and counterpoint to this book's study of seventeenth- and early eighteenth-century female alliances. Savage rejected most of the practices and performances of traditional female sociability. She did not enjoy idle or "profane" talk, and she refused to exchange gossip. Although she attended the childbirth rituals of her neighbors, she was made uncomfortable by birthing-room customs which were not strictly religious. She was disapproving of large banquets and disliked frivolity. She was reluctant to attend the social and spiritual events sponsored by her local Anglican church. Happier alone in a corner reading her book and shutting out the temporal world, Sarah Savage would not have been considered an easy companion by most of her contemporaries. We have seen that her self-isolation made Savage a pariah, disliked and even abused by her neighbors. But this discussion has shown also that she was not an unsocial person. Savage valued her unique female interactions, ones which centered on the Nonconformist spirituality she favored. Reading and praying in groups, traveling to sermons, and discussing godly literature enriched Savage's personal and spiritual life and tied her tightly to the women who shared her beliefs. Savage's diary offers conclusive proof of the existence and meaningfulness of female sociability, for while it contains examples of special, Nonconformist alliances, it reveals as well the pervasiveness of conventional ones in seventeenth- and early eighteenth-century Britain. As Savage criticized the behaviors of others, she reinforced the normativity of these practices as they were experienced by most early modern British women.

Epilogue

At the end of the seventeenth century Mary Parker composed a series of long and affectionate letters to her friend Sarah Jennings.[1] Written in France, Parker's letters related the things she had seen and experienced on her journey and updated Jennings on her health, activities, and general well-being. Parker was traveling abroad, and she was homesick for the friends and family she had left behind in Britain. She felt she had been gone for a long time and noted wryly, "A month or 6 weeks absance in another contry would worck a greater change in the hart of the most heroicke man of our age." Parker claimed to have some similarity to these heroic men, for while "you know there is few will alow our sex perfections above theres," she too felt distant, lonely, heartsick, and changed, all owing to the absence of her good friends. Craving the friendship to which she was accustomed at home, Parker wrote longingly to Jennings that she wanted to hear from her friend more often, for "I love you so well I cannot help wishing a letter from you every week."

Correspondence helped to repair what Parker perceived as a break in the friendship she normally shared with Jennings, but Parker's desire to maintain her connections with her female friend led her to write an extensive, brightly playful, and fictional story about their alliance, emphasizing the value she placed on the bonds she had with women back home. In a letter dated October 8, Parker created an elaborate story for Jennings: she said she had climbed to the roof of a famous French château, where she encountered an old man sitting in front of a large picture frame.[2] The man was not painting but was holding the framed canvas in front of him at arm's length, turning from side to side and pointing the canvas in different directions. When Parker asked the man what he was holding, he told her "twas a prospective [picture] was left him by an inchantress and which had formerly belong'd to one of the Sybills." That the work of art originally had been owned by an alliance of powerful classical priestesses influenced its magical powers, for through the frame the man was able to view groups of talented, beautiful ladies.[3] By turning the picture in various directions, the man could see preeminent women in any foreign country he wished. Parker wrote that she urged the man to point the painting to Britain, where he "told with amasment that he saw hundreds of wemen or Angels for he could not distinguish which of the tow they were . . . for of all hee had seen in this world hee never found any thing soe beutyfull as what hee saw there."

Parker's elaborate fiction of the power and beauty of female alliances then turned toward a description of her own circle of intimates. Parker wrote that she told the man to focus his painting upon St. James's Park in London, where "there hapen'd to bee a great deale of Company," but that nonetheless, "hee made an exact discription of 50 I believe of my aquaintance, which were all there." Parker then refocused her imagination again. Paring down the large alliance network of the fifty women with whom she was acquainted, Parker concentrated her story on her ten closest, most valuable, and accomplished friends, of whom Jennings was one. Describing Jennings in flattering detail, Parker wrote that the old man described "a yong beuty coming downe the great walk . . . she is in a crowd that followes her wher ever she goes, but there is 9 people that never quitts her one minnet." Explaining the characteristics of this loyal and devoted group of friends, Parker offered attributes which were typical of seventeenth- and early eighteenth-century idealizations of female alliances. The women were not reproachful, envious, or jealous, for "of these 9 adorers thers not one that reproches her of any kindness to one more then another . . . theres not one of them that is ether jealous or envyes the hapyness of one another a thing unheard of before amongst rivalls." Instead, Parker explained, the women were not "rivalls" at all. They were women who exhibited a supportive, loving, even egalitarian style of friendship, personified in the actions of Jennings herself, for "she carrys her self with such an equality that she obliges all [who] admires her." Claiming to recognize her own companions in this image of perfected female friendship, Parker exclaimed, "I found by this description it cold bee none but you."

This book has shown how women like Parker created and maintained female alliances in early modern Britain. We have seen that, in this period, elite women were expected to make enduring and emotionally significant friendships with other women. Part of the modernization of gender identity, seventeenth- and eighteenth-century prescriptive texts offered idealized models of female friendship to women readers whom they depicted as self-monitoring. Prescriptive authors privileged women's alliances as harmonious, mutually supportive, generous, and kind, and they encouraged early modern women to create such positive relationships by structuring their friendships around feminized displays of emotion. Considered to be more impassioned in their feelings than men, women were told to use their "natural" feminine ardor to bind themselves more tightly to other women; by expressing heartfelt, sincere, and fervent sentiments, women could find much in common, could take pity on one another, could be moved to assistance, and could offer one another sororal love.

From evidence in women's own writings—in correspondence, diaries and autobiographies, recipe collections, spiritual journals, travel logs, household accounts and receipts—we have seen that many women attempted to live up to the examples presented to them in prescriptive literature. Early modern women's writings illustrate that they sought to tie themselves to other women through displays of emotion, love, and feeling. Whether conveyed in correspondence, in the exchange of gifts and services, in the shared burden of labor, or through acts of extensive travel, these sentiments bound women together. And alliances were cultivated by elite women alongside behaviors, speech, and gestures considered to be polite, refined, genteel, and tasteful. Appealing to the heightened emotions and behaviors of their female friends, these women strove to create happy friendships and simultaneously worked to avoid the negative qualities that Parker shunned in her letter, as envy, resentment, bitterness, and greed were all considered to be anathema to elite femininity as well as to female alliances.

Although women tried hard to circumvent antagonism, they were not always successful. Misunderstandings and disagreements did sometimes arise among women who were separated by strict and enduring distinctions of social status, age, education, religious belief, and wealth. These differences were essential components of seventeenth- and early eighteenth-century life, and they often made it difficult for elite women to live up to the tranquil and accommodating ideal of female friendship. Nonetheless, and despite their many divisions, some early modern women did share important moments or aspects of alliance with disparate friends, family members, employers, and servants.

Women's writings offer evidence of the internalization of these positive constructions of homosociability. Conveying a sense of gender identity predicated on homosocial bonds and communal activities, women cared for children, distilled medicines, embroidered, gardened, read, slept, and prayed in the company of other women. This enabled elite British women to construct identities which were communal, not individualized; collective, not bounded; feminized, not masculinized. These gendered identities were formed and informed by elite women's female friendships and alliances. As women wrote letters to distant companions, soaked and rehabilitated in hot spring spas, created elaborate gifts and presented them to their friends, walked in groups to religious services, and even as they endured prison sentences and traveled together across oceans, they understood themselves to be people who lived within homosocial communities and who shared important homosocial bonds.

When Parker composed the creative fantasy about the Sibylline painting for her friend Jennings, she did so in order to indicate the enormous value and emotional power that she placed on female alliances. To Parker, the intimate relationships she shared with other women were the most important in her life. Contrasting herself with male "learn'd phelosophe[rs]," Parker claimed that the heightened emotions rendered in her female friendships were constitutive of her own feminine identity and priorities. While men might coolly and indifferently analyze the classical attributes of friendship, Parker was "of an opinion there never was any woman learn'd in that kind of phelosiphy." Instead, Parker valued the emotional intensity of her homosocial relationships, "for," she concluded, "there is nothing in the world I intrest my self in with [as much] heat or impatience as the concerns of my frinds."[4]

Notes

Introduction

1. Mary Evelyn's letter to Ralph Bohun, Add. 78530, British Library (hereafter cited as BL), from Gillian Darley, *John Evelyn: Living for Ingenuity* (New Haven: Yale University Press, 2006), 245. Emphasis added.

2. Joan Kelly, *Women, History and Theory: The Essays of Joan Kelly* (Chicago: University of Chicago Press, 1986); Barbara Hanawalt, *Women and Work in Preindustrial Europe* (Bloomington: Indiana University Press, 1986); Betty Travitsky, *The Paradise of Women: Writings by Englishwomen of the Renaissance* (Westport, Conn.: Greenwood Press, 1981).

3. These studies include, but certainly are not limited to, Olwen Hufton, "Women in the French Revolution," *Past and Present* 53 (Nov. 1971), 90–108; Natalie Zemon Davis, "Women on Top," "Women," and "City Women and Religious Change," in *Society and Culture in Early Modern France* (Stanford: Stanford University Press, 1975); Carolyn Lougée, *Le Paradis des Femmes: Women, Salons, and Social Stratification in Seventeenth-Century France* (Princeton: Princeton University Press, 1976); Joan Landes, *Women in the Public Sphere in the Age of the French Revolution* (Ithaca: Cornell University Press, 1988); Suzanne Desan, "The Role of Women in Religious Riots during the French Revolution," *Eighteenth-Century Studies* 22, no. 3 (Spring 1989), 451–68; Dena Goodman, "Enlightenment Salons: The Convergence of Female and Philosophic Ambitions," *Eighteenth-Century Studies* 22, no. 3 (Spring 1989), 329–50; Carla Hesse, "Reading Signatures: Female Authorship and Revolutionary Law in France, 1750–1850," *Eighteenth-Century Studies* 22, no. 3 (Spring 1989), 469–87.

4. Kelly, *Women, History and Theory*, xiii–xiv, 66.

5. Joy Wiltenburg, *Disorderly Women and Female Power in the Street Literature of Early Modern England and Germany* (Charlottesville: University Press of Virginia, 1992); Linda Pollock, "Childbearing and Female Bonding in Early Modern England," *Social History* 22, no. 3 (October 1997), 286–306; Laura Gowing, *Domestic Dangers: Women, Words, and Sex in Early Modern London* (Oxford: Clarendon, 1998).

6. Laura Gowing, *Common Bodies: Women, Touch and Power in Seventeenth-Century England* (New Haven: Yale University Press, 2003), 150.

7. Brian Cowan, *The Social Life of Coffee: The Emergence of the British Coffeehouse* (New Haven: Yale University Press, 2005); Alexandra Shepard, " 'Swil-bols and Tos-pots': Drink Culture and Male Bonding in England, c. 1560–1640," in *Love, Friendship and Faith in Europe, 1300–1800*, ed. Laura Gowing, Michael Hunter, and Miri Rubin, 110–30 (New York: Palgrave Macmillan, 2005); David S. Shields, *Civil Tongues and Polite Letters in British America* (Chapel Hill: University of North Carolina Press, 1997); and Lawrence E. Klein, *Shaftesbury and the Culture of Politeness: Moral Discourse and Cultural Politics in Early Eighteenth-Century England* (Cambridge: Cambridge University Press, 1994).

8. Amy M. Froide, *Never Married: Singlewomen in Early Modern England* (New York: Oxford University Press, 2005); Naomi Tadmor, *Family and Friends in Eighteenth-Century England: Household, Kinship, and Patronage* (Cambridge: Cambridge University Press, 2001); Karin Wulf, *Not All Wives: Women of Colonial Philadelphia* (Ithaca: Cornell University Press, 2000).

9. Thomas A. Foster, *Long Before Stonewall: Histories of Same-Sex Sexuality in Early America* (New York: New York University Press, 2007); Alan Bray, *The Friend* (Chicago: University of Chicago Press, 2003); Valerie Traub, *The Renaissance of Lesbianism in Early Modern England* (New York: Cambridge University Press, 2002); Harriette Andreadis, *Sappho in Early Modern England: Female Same-Sex Literary Erotics, 1550–1714* (Chicago: University of Chicago Press, 2001).

10. Stephanie Tarbin and Susan Broomhall, eds., *Women, Identities and Communities in Early Modern Europe* (Burlington, Vt.: Ashgate, 2008); Susan Frye and Karen Robertson, *Maids and Mistresses, Cousins and Queens: Women's Alliances in Early Modern England* (New York: Oxford University Press, 1999).

11. Such study of female alliances does not necessitate false homogenization or collectivization. Joan Wallach Scott, *Gender and the Politics of History* (New York: Columbia University Press, 1999), 4–6.

12. Amanda Vickery, *The Gentleman's Daughter: Women's Lives in Georgian England* (New Haven: Yale University Press, 1998), 13–14.

13. Margaret Hunt, *The Middling Sort: Commerce, Gender and the Family in England, 1680–1780* (Berkeley: University of California Press, 1996), 15.

14. Hunt, *The Middling Sort*, 9.

15. Ingrid Tague, *Women of Quality: Accepting and Contesting Ideals of Femininity in England, 1690–1760* (Rochester: Boydell, 2002), 11.

16. James Horn, for example, argues that colonial British America "was emphatically a male society." James Horn, "Tobacco Colonies: The Shaping of English

Society in the Seventeenth-Century Chesapeake," in Nicholas Canny, *The Oxford History of the British Empire*, Volume I: *The Origins of Empire, British Overseas Enterprise to the Close of the Seventeenth Century* (New York: Oxford University Press, 1998), 182; David Hancock, *Citizens of the World: London Merchants and the Integration of the British Atlantic Community, 1735–1785* (Cambridge: Harvard University Press, 1995); David Hancock, *Oceans of Wine: Madeira and the Emergence of American Trade and Taste* (New Haven: Yale University Press, 2009), 40–141, 147, 148, 200–209.

17. The important exception is Ellen Hartigan-O'Connor's *The Ties that Buy: Women and Commerce in Revolutionary America* (Philadelphia: University of Pennsylvania Press, 2009).

18. Thomas Laqueur, *Making Sex: Body and Gender from the Greeks to Freud* (Cambridge: Harvard University Press, 1992).

19. Jerrold Seigel, *The Idea of the Self: Thought and Experience in Western Europe since the Seventeenth Century* (New York: Cambridge University Press, 2005); Dror Wahrman, *Making of the Modern Self: Identity and Culture in Eighteenth-Century England* (New Haven: Yale University Press, 2004); Charles Taylor, *Sources of the Self: The Making of the Modern Identity* (Cambridge: Harvard University Press, 1989).

20. Michael McKeon, "Historicizing Patriarchy: The Emergence of Gender Difference in England, 1660–1760," *Eighteenth-Century Studies* 28, no. 3 (Spring 1995), 295–322; Anthony Fletcher, *Gender, Sex, and Subordination in England 1500–1800* (New Haven: Yale University Press, 1995), 376–400; Tague, *Women of Quality*; Wahrman, *Making of the Modern Self*.

21. Tague, *Women of Quality*, 22–23. See also Jonathan Sawday, "Self and Selfhood in the Seventeenth Century," and Roger Smith, "Self-Reflection and the Self," both in *Rewriting the Self: Histories from the Renaissance to the Present*, ed. Roy Porter (New York: Routledge, 1997); Fletcher, *Gender, Sex, and Subordination*, 376–400; Wahrman, *Making of the Modern Self*, 77–82.

22. Many scholarly works on constructions of femininity connect modern constructions of women's identity with gender-specific "separate spheres" and proto-capitalist reforms of women's labor. One of the most influential works of this kind was the literary critic Nancy Armstrong's *Desire and Domestic Fiction*. Historians who have employed models similar to Armstrong's include Anthony Fletcher, *Gender, Sex, and Subordination*, 296. For work that criticizes Armstrong's scholarship, see McKeon, "Gender Difference in England"; and Vickery, *The Gentleman's Daughter*. Ingrid Tague's book *Women of Quality* is "informed by the recent criticisms of the idea of separate spheres" and argues convincingly for a fresh examination of this topic, "a subtler interpretation that

resists replicating the separate spheres dichotomy in an equally strict dichotomy between ideology and practice." Tague, *Women of Quality*, 6.

23. Wahrman, *Making of the Modern Self*, 44; Goodman, *Becoming a Woman in the Age of Letters*, 84–99.

24. Hannah Woolley, *The Gentlewomans Companion or, a Guide to the Female Sex: The Complete Text of 1675*, ed. Caterina Albano (Blackawton, UK: Prospect, 2001), 67, 88.

25. Hannah Woolley, *Gentlewomans Companion* (London, 1673), dedication; William Hill, *A New-Years-Gift for Women* (London, 1660), title page.

26. John Shirley, *The Accomplished Ladies Rich Closet . . .* (London, 1691), preface.

27. Quentin Skinner shows that early prescriptive guides had intellectual origins in *Ars dictaminis*, treatises which helped educated men to learn skills of rhetoric by copying from, or "modeling," sample letters and speeches composed originally by classical philosophers. By studying and then imitating exemplars, late medieval Italian rulers were told that they could become *vir virtutis*, perfectly masculine and virtuous men. The purpose of this prescriptive tradition also means, however, that early modern women probably gained little from early prescriptive texts. And Skinner himself acknowledges that early Italian guidebooks advocated "specifically masculine" behaviors, with the result that "women [were] excluded almost by definition from taking part" in these long-standing literary forms or the experiences that they promoted. Amanda Vickery has quite correctly shown that for centuries western Europeans had been describing women as emotional, passionate, and ruled by their feelings; Vickery argues that as early as the sixteenth century elite women were offered biographies of exemplary classical and biblical women, which were thought to provide them with models for imitation. Scholars such as Anthony Fletcher have counterargued that sixteenth century "moralizing and didactic" texts for women differed fundamentally from seventeenth- and eighteenth-century prescriptive literature, which focused on the internalization of prescription rather than on the imitation of exemplars: it was this impulse toward self-monitoring and self-criticism which was essential to constructions of "modern" identity. Quentin Skinner, *Visions of Politics*. Volume II: *Renaissance Virtues* (Cambridge: Cambridge University Press, 2002), 10–21, 125–126, 134–138; Vickery, *The Gentleman's Daughter*, 5–6; Fletcher, *Gender, Sex, and Subordination*, 378. On the use of exemplary women as models for female behavior in early modern British literature, see Margaret Sommerville, *Sex and Subjection: Attitudes to Women in Early-Modern Society* (New York: Arnold, 1995), 40–78. On the lasting importance of classical modeling throughout the early modern period,

see Jamie Gianoutsos, "Reading a Gendered Rome: Classical History and Republican Thought in Early Modern England" (Ph.D. diss., Johns Hopkins University, in progress).

28. Dror Wahrman argues that "the fluidity and versatility of [early modern] culture," or what he calls the "space for play," was destroyed by the process of western European identity creation. Anthony Fletcher interprets the late seventeenth-century impetus toward self-monitoring and the surveillance of others as constraining, limiting, and even damaging to women, where increased prohibitions on independent female behavior served to "remove the immediacy of the threat" of women's agency and to "reconstruct patriarchy on more effective foundations." Wahrman, *Making of the Modern Self*, 43; Fletcher, *Gender, Sex, and Subordination*, 392, 396.

29. Goodman, *Becoming a Woman*, 3.

30. Sarah Lucia Hoagland, *Lesbian Ethics: Toward New Value* (Palo Alto: Institute of Lesbian Studies, 1988), 145.

31. Jennifer Baumgardner and Amy Richards, *Manifesta: Young Women, Feminism, and the Future* (New York: Farrar, Straus and Giroux, 2010), 218–19; Jessica Valenti, *Full Frontal Feminism: A Young Woman's Guide to Why Feminism Matters* (Berkeley: Seal Press, 2007); Astrid Henry, *Not My Mother's Sister: Generational Conflict and Third-Wave Feminism* (Bloomington: Indiana University Press, 2004); Rebecca Walker, *To Be Real: Telling the Truth and Changing the Face of Feminism* (New York: Anchor Books, 1995).

32. Nancy Chodorow, *Feminism and Psychoanalytic Theory* (New Haven: Yale University Press, 1989), 57; Nancy Chodorow, *The Power of Feelings: Personal Meaning in Psychoanalysis, Gender, and Culture* (New Haven: Yale University Press, 1999).

33. Michael Mascuch, *Origins of the Individualist Self: Autobiography and Self-Identity in England, 1591–1791* (Stanford: Stanford University Press, 1996), 8.

34. Elspeth Graham, Hilary Hinds, Elaine Hobby, and Helen Wilcox, eds., *Her Own Life: Autobiographical Writings by Seventeenth-Century Englishwomen* (London: Routledge, 1989), 19.

35. Anna Bryson, *From Courtesy to Civility: Changing Codes of Conduct in Early Modern England* (Oxford: Oxford University Press, 1998), 2–3; Norbert Elias, *The History of Manners: The Civilizing Process*, vol. 1 (New York: Pantheon, 1978); Norbert Elias, *Power and Civility: The Civilizing Process*, vol. 2 (New York: Pantheon, 1983); Norbert Elias, *The Court Society* (New York: Pantheon, 1983).

36. Cowan, *The Social Life of Coffee*, 225–56; Klein, *Shaftesbury and the Culture of Politeness*, 6.

37. Klein, *Shaftesbury and the Culture of Politeness*, 7–9; Hunt, *The Middling Sort*, 102.

38. Tague, *Women of Quality*, 14, 21.

39. Ibid.

40. Jonathan Goldberg, *Writing Matter: From the Hands of the English Renaissance* (Stanford: Stanford University Press, 1990), 254–55; Anne Kugler, *Errant Plagiary: The Life and Writing of Lady Sarah Cowper, 1664–1720* (Stanford: Stanford University Press, 2002), 3.

41. The letter is signed "E Lindsey," but it is listed in the catalogue under "Elizabeth Bertie," a sister or sister-in-law of Danby's. Elizabeth Bertie, Letter to Lady Danby, 1674, Leeds Papers, Egerton Manuscripts, EG 3338, f. 52, BL. Susan Frye and Karen Robertson point out that the word *alliance* was often used to describe "the marriage alliance." Frye and Robertson, *Maids and Mistresses*, 4.

42. Alice Thornton, *The Autobiography of Mrs. Alice Thornton, of East Newton, Co. York* (Durham, 1875).

43. Mary Caithnes, Lady Sinclair, Letter to Lady Lauderdale, 1673 and 1678, Lauderdale Papers, Add. 23135 ff. 255, 259, 265, 268, BL.

44. Bernard Capp, *When Gossips Meet: Women, Family, and Neighbourhood in Early Modern England* (Oxford: Oxford University Press, 2003); Vickery, *Gentlewoman's Daughter*, table 1; Magdalena S. Sánchez, *The Empress, the Queen, and the Nun: Women and Power at the Court of Philip III of Spain* (Baltimore: Johns Hopkins University Press, 1998), 38.

45. Mrs. S. Savage, Diary, entitled "Mrs. S. Savage's diary from May 31st 1714 to Decem 25th 1723," MS. Engl.misc.e.331, Bodleian Library (hereafter cited as BOD).

46. Susan Whyman, *Sociability and Power in Late-Stuart England: The Cultural Worlds of the Verneys 1660–1720* (Oxford: Oxford University Press, 2002); Vickery, *The Gentleman's Daughter*.

47. Naomi R. Lamoreaux, "Rethinking Microhistory: A Comment," *Journal of the Early Republic* 26, no. 4 (Winter 2006), 555–61; Richard D. Brown, "Microhistory and the Post-Modern Challenge," *Journal of the Early Republic* 23, no. 1 (Spring 2003), 1–20; David A. Bell, "Total History and Microhistory: The French and Italian Paradigms," in *A Companion to Western Historical Thought* (Malden, Mass.: Blackwell, 2002), ed. Lloyd Kramer and Sarah Maza, 262–76; Jill Lepore, "Historians Who Love Too Much: Reflections on Microhistory and Biography," *Journal of American History* 88, no. 1 (June, 2001), 129–44.

48. Bell, "Total History and Microhistory," 263.

Chapter 1. "Small Expressions of My Passionate Love and Friendship to Thee"

1. Anne Cottrell Dormer, Letters to her sister Elizabeth Cottrell Trumbull, 1685–91, Add. MS 72516, f.156–243, British Library (hereafter cited as BL).

2. Laura Gowing, Michael Hunter, and Miri Rubin, eds., *Love, Friendship and Faith in Europe, 1300–1800* (New York: Palgrave Macmillan, 2005), 4–8.

3. Susan Whyman, *The Pen and the People: English Letter Writers 1660–1800* (New York: Oxford University Press, 2009); Dena Goodman, *Becoming a Woman in the Age of Letters* (Ithaca: Cornell University Press, 2009); James Daybell, *Women Letter-Writers in Tudor England* (New York: Oxford University Press, 2006); Gary Schneider, *The Culture of Epistolarity: Vernacular Letters and Letter Writing in Early Modern England, 1500–1700* (Newark: University of Delaware Press, 2005); Susan Whyman, *Sociability and Power in Late-Stuart England: The Cultural World of the Verneys 1660–1720* (New York: Oxford University Press, 1999); Victoria E. Burke, "Medium and Meaning in the Manuscripts of Anne, Lady Southwell," in *Women's Writing and the Circulation of Ideas: Manuscript Publication in England, 1550–1800*, ed. George L. Justice and Nathan Tinker, 94–120 (New York: Cambridge University Press, 2002). Some studies of transatlantic correspondence among men include David S. Shields, *Civil Tongues and Polite Letters in British America* (Chapel Hill: University of North Carolina Press, 1997); Toby L. Ditz, "Shipwrecked; or, Masculinity Imperiled: Mercantile Representations of Failure and the Gendered Self in Eighteenth-Century Philadelphia," *Journal of American History* 81, no. 1 (June, 1994), 51–80.

4. This chapter draws heavily from a few large, particularly detailed sets of female correspondence: letters written to Anna Livingston, c. 1620–30, from the Papers of the Montgomerie Family at the National Archives of Scotland in Edinburgh; letters from Bridget Croft to her friend and cousin Lucy Hastings, c. 1650, from the Hastings Collection at the Huntington Library in San Marino, California; letters from Mary Lewis Leke to her sister Elizabeth Lewis Hastings, c. 1670–80, also from the Hastings Collection; and letters from Anne Dormer to her sister Elizabeth Trumbull, c. 1685–90, held at the British Library, London. These four chronologically consecutive collections, unusual in their breadth and detail, allow for a detailed examination of the personal relationships that structured these early modern women's alliances. The collections also act as an important foundation for examination of many smaller, more fragmentary pieces of correspondence, which provide further important examples of women's alliances. Use of these letter fragments allows for a much broader and more comprehensive examination of women's alliances across early modern Britain, but it does mean that it is not always possible—or practical—to elucidate and describe the personal relationships of each of the women quoted in this chapter.

5. Daniel T. Lochman, Maritere López, and Lorna Hutson, eds., *Discourses and Representations of Friendship in Early Modern Europe, 1500–1700* (Burlington, Vt.: Ashgate, 2011), 3.

6. Alan Bray, *The Friend* (Chicago: University of Chicago Press, 2003), 257; John Marshall, *John Locke: Resistance, Religion and Responsibility* (New York: Cambridge University Press, 1994), 300; Lorraine Smith Prangle, *Aristotle and the Philosophy of Friendship* (New York: Cambridge University Press, 2003), 67.

7. Aristotle, *Nicomachean Ethics*, trans. Terence Irwin (Indianapolis: Hackett, 1999), 120; Cicero, *On Duties*, trans. Walter Miller (Cambridge: Harvard University Press, 1997), 49–59; Prangle, *Aristotle and the Philosophy of Friendship*, 152–54; Lochman, López, and Hutson, *Discourses and Representations of Friendship*, 3.

8. Michel de Montaigne, "On Friendship," in *The Complete Works: Essays, Travel Journal, Letters*, trans. Donald M. Frame (New York, 2003), 169.

9. David Konstan, *Friendship in the Classical World* (New York: Cambridge University Press, 1997), 90–91.

10. Montaigne, "On Friendship," 167.

11. Caroline Winterer, "The Female World of Classical Reading in Eighteenth-Century America," in *Reading Women: Literacy, Authorship, and Culture in the Atlantic World, 1500–1800*, ed. Heidi Brayman Hackel and Catherine Kelly, 105–23 (Philadelphia: University of Pennsylvania Press, 2008). For two examples of early modern English women reading classical works in translation as well as reading the works of Montaigne, see Katherine Acheson's and D. J. H. Clifford's analyses of Anne Clifford's library, and Allison Coudert and Taylor Corse's analysis of Anne Conway's writings. Katherine O. Acheson, ed., *The Diary of Anne Clifford 1616–1619* (New York: Garland, 1995), 6; D. J. H. Clifford, *The Diaries of Lady Anne Clifford* (Wolfeboro Falls, N.H.: Alan Sutton, 1990), 41; Anne Conway, *The Principles of the Most Ancient and Modern Philosophy*, ed. Allison Coudert and Taylor Corse (New York: Cambridge University Press, 2006).

12. Augustine, Aquinas, and Donne are quoted in Margaret Sommerville, *Sex and Subjection: Attitudes to Women in Early-Modern Society* (New York: Arnold, 1995), 45.

13. Laura Gowing, "Politics of Women's Friendship in Early Modern England," *Love, Friendship and Faith in Europe, 1300–1800*, ed. Laura Gowing, Michael Hunter, and Miri Rubin (New York: Palgrave Macmillan, 2005); Mary Beale, "A Discourse of Friendship," in Charles Crompton's Commonplace Book, 1667, V.A. 220, Folger Shakespeare Library (hereafter cited as FL).

14. Lucy Hutchinson, *Memoirs of the Life of Colonel Huchinson*, ed. N. H. Keeble (London: Everyman's Library, 1995), 11.

15. G. C. Moore Smith, *The Letters of Dorothy Osborne to William Temple* (Oxford: Clarendon, 1928), 60, 66.

16. Mary Eliot, Correspondence with mother Johana Barrington, Egerton Collection, EG 2650, f. 227–30, BL.

17. Arthur Clifford, *Tixall Letters; Or the Correspondence of the Aston Family, and Their Friends*, vol. 1 (London: Longman, Hurst, Rees, Orme, and Brown, 1816), 131.

18. Mary Lewis Leke (Countess Scarsdale), Letter to Elizabeth Lewis Hastings (Countess Huntingdon), c. 1671–81, Hastings Collection, box 31 HA 8202, Huntington Library (hereafter cited as HL).

19. Anne Cottrell Dormer, Letters to her sister Elizabeth Cottrell Trumbull, 1685–91, Add. MS 72516, f.156–243, BL.

20. Gowing, Hunter, and Rubin, *Love, Friendship and Faith in Europe, 1300–1800*, 5.

21. Konstan, *Friendship in the Classical World*, 160–61.

22. Klaus Oschema, "Sacred or Profane? Reflections on Love and Friendship in the Middle Ages," in *Love, Friendship and Faith in Europe, 1300–1800*, ed. Gowing, Hunter, and Rubin, 43–65; Lochman, López, and Hutson, *Discourses and Representations of Friendship*, 8; Konstan, *Friendship in the Classical World*, 157, 165.

23. Konstan, *Friendship in the Classical World*, 156–57.

24. Claire Walker, *Gender and Politics in Early Modern Europe: English Convents in France and the Low Countries* (New York: Palgrave Macmillan, 2003).

25. Constance M. Furey, "Bound by Likeness: Vives and Erasmus on Marriage and Friendship," in *Discourses and Representations of Friendship in Early Modern Europe, 1500–1700*, ed. Daniel Lochman, Maritere López, and Lorna Hutson, 29–43 (Burlington, Vt.: Ashgate, 2011).

26. Bray, *The Friend*, 142–44.

27. Jeremy Taylor, *The Whole Works of the Right Rev. Jeremy Taylor, D.D. . . . with an Essay Biographical and Critical* (London, 1835), 3:43–44.

28. Ibid., 3:43.

29. Ibid.

30. Ibid., 3:41.

31. Crawford and Gowing, eds., *Women's Worlds in Seventeenth Century England*, 238; Laura Gowing, "Politics of Women's Friendship in Early Modern England," 142–47; Rachel Weil, *Political Passions: Gender, the Family, and Political Argument in England 1680–1714* (New York: Manchester University Press, 1999); Mary E. Fissell, *Vernacular Bodies: The Politics of Reproduction in Early Modern England* (Oxford: Oxford University Press, 2004).

32. Isabella Seton (Countess Perth), Letter to her sister Anna Livingston (Countess Eglinton), c. 1617, Papers of the Montgomerie Family, GD3/5/133, National Archives of Scotland (hereafter cited as NAS).

33. This example comes from Amy Froide, *Never Married: Singlewomen in Early Modern England* (New York: Oxford University Press, 2005), 55.

34. Elizabeth Oxenden, Letters to her Mother in Law, Lady Katherine Oxenden, 1658–1669, Family of Oxenden Correspondence, Add MS 28004, ff. 59, 60, 338, 363, 386, 391, BL.

35. "Considering remarriage: Katherine Austen, 1665," in *Women's Worlds in Seventeenth Century England*, ed. Crawford and Gowing, 184.

36. "Wabrege" refers to Weybridge, southeast of London.

37. Mary Lewis Leke (Countess Scarsdale), Letter to her sister Elizabeth Lewis Hastings (Countess Huntingdon), c. 1682, Hastings Collection, box 43 HA 8218, HL.

38. Arthur Clifford, *Tixall Letters*, 87–88, 122.

39. Gowing, "Politics of Women's Friendship in Early Modern England," 140–42.

40. Jane Barker, volume of verse titled "Poems on Several Occasions, in three parts: the first referring to the times, the second, are poems writ since the author was in France, or at least most of them. The third, are taken out of a miscellany heretofore printed and writ by the same author," c. 1680–1700, Magdalen College Archives, MS 343, Oxford University.

41. Rebecca Sherbrook, Letters to her granddaughter Dorothea Crisp, and one to her daughter Mrs. Crisp, 1680–95, B. A. Taylor Papers, Add MS 37682, f. 141–43, BL. Address on the back of one of the letters reads, "For Mrs. Dorethea Crisp at Mr. Sherbrooks Marchant behind St. Patchers church."

42. Bridget Croft, Letter to Theophilus Hastings (7th Earl Huntingdon), 17 November 1690, Hastings Collection, box 56 HA 1796, HL.

43. Elizabeth Masham, Correspondence with her mother, Johana Barrington, Egerton Collection, EG 2650, f. 285–309, BL.

44. Elizabeth DeGrey, Letters to her daughter Anne DeGrey, Lady Gawdy, c.1670, Correspondence of the Family of Gawdy, ADD 36989, ff. 533, 535, BL.

45. Elizabeth Fanshawe, Letter to Cecilia Tufton, Lady Hatton, 1665, Hatton-Finch Papers, ADD 29551, f. 144, BL.

46. Lucy Hastings (Countess Huntingdon), Letter to her son Theophilus Hastings (7th Earl Huntingdon), 1664, Hastings Collection, box 24 HA 5760, HL.

47. Phyllis Mack, *Visionary Women: Ecstatic Prophecy in Seventeenth-Century England* (Berkeley: University of California Press, 1992), 150.

48. Ibid., 158.

49. Christine Trevett, *Quaker Women Prophets in England and Wales, 1650–1700.* Vol. 41 of *Studies in Women in Religion* (Lewiston, N.Y.: Edwin Mellen, 2000).

50. *A short journal of the labours and travels in the work of the ministry of that faithful servant of Christ, Deborah Bell* (London, 1762).

51. Rebecca Sherbrook, Letters to her granddaughter Dorothea Crisp, and one to her daughter Mrs. Crisp, 1680–95, B. A. Taylor Papers, Add MS 37682, f. 141–43, BL.

52. I owe many thanks to Olivia Weisser for her excellent insights into this material and for her helpful suggestions on the chapter as a whole. Olivia Weisser, *Ill Composed: Patients, Gender, and Belief in Early Modern England* (New Haven: Yale University Press, forthcoming); Olivia Weisser, "Gender and Illness in Seventeenth-Century England" (Ph.D. diss., Johns Hopkins University, 2010). See also Nicole Eustace, *Passion Is the Gale: Emotion, Power, and the Coming of the American Revolution* (Chapel Hill: University of North Carolina Press, 2008); Susan Broomhall, ed., *Emotions in the Household, 1200–1900* (New York: Palgrave Macmillan, 2007); Linda A. Pollock, "Anger and the Negotiation of Relationships in Early Modern England," *Historical Journal* 47, no. 3 (2004), 567–90; G. J. Barker-Benfield, *The Culture of Sensibility: Sex and Society in Eighteenth-Century Britain* (Chicago: University of Chicago Press, 1992).

53. Fissell, *Vernacular Bodies.*

54. Anthony Fletcher, *Gender, Sex, and Subordination in England 1500–1800* (New Haven: Yale University Press, 1995), 67–82; Fissell, *Vernacular Bodies,* 61–63.

55. Weisser, *Gender and Illness.*

56. Cavendish is quoted in Anthony Fletcher, *Gender, Sex, and Subordination in England,* 69.

57. Fissell, *Vernacular Bodies,* 224; Fletcher, *Gender, Sex and Subordination,* 60–82; Sommerville, *Sex and Subjection*; and Weisser, *Gender and Illness.*

58. Thomas Heywood, *Generall History of Women* (London, 1657), 453.

59. William Hill, *A New Years Gift for Women . . .* (London, 1660), 31–32.

60. Anon., *The Whole Duty of a Woman . . .* (London, 1696), 21.

61. John Pechey, *A General Treatise of the Diseases of Maids, Bigbellied Women, Childbed Women and Widows* (London, 1696), preface. Pechy is quoted in Fletcher, *Gender, Sex, and Subordination,* 62.

62. Woolley, *Gentlewomans Companion,* 217.

63. Mary Sinclair, Lady Caithnes, Letter to Elizabeth Maitland, Lady Lauderdale, 1673, 1678, Lauderdale Papers, Add. 23135 ff. 255, 259, 265, 268, BL.

64. H[enrietta] Borlase, Letter to her friend Lady Alltom, August 1, c. 1660–80, X.c.66, FSL.

65. Priscilla Rolle, Letter to her niece Elizabeth Lewis Hastings (Countess of Huntingdon), 1672, Hastings Collection, box 32 HA 10563, HL.

66. Beatrix Clerke, Letter to Theophilus Hastings (7th Earl Huntingdon), 18 March 1661, Hastings Collection, box 22 HA 1751, HL.

67. Bridget Croft, Letter to Lucy Hastings (Countess of Huntingdon), 1656, Hastings Collection, box 20 HA 1741, HL.

68. Sarah Brookes, Letter to Theophilus Hastings (7th Earl of Huntingdon), 1672, Hastings Collection, box 32 HA 1037, HL.

69. Dorothy Harvey, Letter to Theophilus Hastings (7th Earl of Huntingdon), 1671, Hastings Collection, box 31 HA 4619, HL.

70. Weisser, *Gender and Illness*; Sommerville, *Sex and Subjection*; Fletcher, *Gender, Sex, and Subordination*, 73–74.

71. Beata Poole Pope, Letter to her daughter Frances Pope North, 1671–1679, North Collection, HM 52410, HL.

72. Arthur Clifford, *Tixall Letters*, 125.

73. Anne Cottrell Dormer, Letters to her sister Elizabeth Cottrell Trumbull, 1685–1691, Add. MS 72516, f. 156–243, BL.

74. Ibid.

75. Amanda Vickery, *The Gentleman's Daughter: Women's Lives in Georgian England* (New Haven: Yale University Press, 1998), 145.

76. Hill, *Young Secretarys Guide* (1696).

77. [Jean Puget] de la Serre, *The Secretary in Fashion, An Elegant and Compendious way of Writing all manner of Letters* (London, 1668).

78. Anne Jacques, Letter to Mary Hastings, 1669, Hastings Collection, box 27 HA 7636, HL.

79. Gervase Jacques, Letter to Mary Hastings, 1669, Hastings Collection, box 27 HA 7667, HL.

80. Vickery, *Gentleman's Daughter*, 89, 124–25.

81. This guide has three surviving editions, from 1673, 1675, and 1682; pieces of this work were excerpted in many more books, including (but surely not limited to) the *Accomplished Ladies Delight* (1675), the *Accomplished Ladies Rich Closet* (1691), the *Ladies Dictionary* (1694), and the *Compleat Servant-Maid* (1677, 1683, 1685, 1691, and 1700). Hobby, *Virtue of Necessity*, 165–89, 244–47.

82. Woolley, *Gentlewomans Companion*, 212–13.

83. Ibid., 212.

84. Woolley, *Supplement to the Queen-Like Closet*, 104.

85. Bridget Croft, Letter to Lucy Hastings (Countess of Huntingdon), 1656, Hastings Collection, box 20 HA 1741, HL.

86. Sarah Savage, Diary, 1686–88, Z-D/Basten/8, Cheshire and Chester Archives and Local Studies (hereafter cited as CCAL).

87. Henrietta Stuart, Letter to Anna Livingston (Countess Eglinton), 1611–16, Papers of the Montgomerie Family, GD3/5/29, NAS. My translation.

88. The quote has biblical origins; in Genesis 42:38 Jacob worries that the loss of his son Benjamin would "bring downe my gray haires with sorrow to the grave." Authorized [King James] Bible (London, 1611). Mary Pease, Letter to her daughter Baynes, 1651/2, Baynes Correspondence, Add. 21421, f. 36, BL.

89. Eliza Blennerhassett, Letter to Lady Eleanor Hastings, 30 October 1656, Hastings Collection, box 20 HA 840, HL.

90. Julie Campbell and Anne Larsen, eds., *Early Modern Women and Transnational Communities of Letters* (Burlington Vt.: Ashgate, 2009); Konstantin Dierks, *In My Power: Letter Writing and Communications in Early America* (Philadelphia: University of Pennsylvania Press, 2009); Ellen Hartigan-O'Connor, *The Ties that Buy: Women and Commerce in Revolutionary America* (Philadelphia: University of Pennsylvania Press, 2009); Sarah Pearsall, *Atlantic Families: Lives and Letters in the Later Eighteenth Century* (New York: Oxford University Press, 2008); Natalie Zacek, "Searching for the Invisible Woman: The Evolution of White Women's Experience in Britain's West Indian Colonies," *History Compass* 7 (2008); Trevor Burnard, " 'Gay and Agreeable Ladies'; White Women in Mid-Eighteenth-Century Kingston, Jamaica," *Wadabagei, A Journal of the Caribbean and Its Diaspora* (2006); Lucille Mair, *A Historical Study of Women in Jamaica 1655–1844* (Jamaica: University of the West Indies Press, 2006); Sarah Yeh, " 'A Sink of All Filthiness': Gender, Family, and Identity in the British Atlantic, 1688–1763," *The Historian* 68 (2006); Kathleen Wilson, *The Island Race: Englishness, Empire and Gender in the Eighteenth Century* (New York: Routledge, 2003); Toby L. Ditz, "Formative Ventures: Eighteenth-Century Commercial Letters and the Articulation of Experience," in *Epistolary Selves: Letters and Letter-writers, 1600–1945*, ed. Rebecca Earle, 59–78 (Burlington, Vt.: Ashgate, 1999); Alison Games, *Migration and the Origins of the English Atlantic World* (Cambridge: Harvard University Press, 1999); Karen Ordahl Kupperman, *Providence Island, 1630–1641: The Other Puritan Colony* (New York: Cambridge University Press, 1993). Manuscript correspondence from women living in Britain's West Indian colonies is practically impossible to find; although seventeenth- and early eighteenth-century white, literate women who emigrated to the West Indies surely exchanged letters with family and friends in metropolitan Britain, archival mismanagement, disorganization, deliberate destruction, and climatic disasters have caused nearly all of these manuscripts to be lost. Zacek, "Invisible Woman," 333. Some evidence of British women's correspondence from the West Indies can be found in chapter

5 of this book, where the writings of Quaker women who traveled to the West Indies on missions are examined in detail.

91. Games, *Migration and the Origins of the English Atlantic World*, 84.

92. Katheryne Hunlocke, Letter to her daughter, August 15, 1649. This letter is quoted in Krystyna Puc, "Leaving England Behind: The Experience of Women in Northampton County, Virginia, 1650–1699" (Ph.D. diss., George Washington University, 1994).

93. Stafford's letter is part of the Sloane Papers at the British Library (MSS 338 f. 33) but was transcribed and edited in 1980 by St. Julien R. Childs. St. Julien R. Childs, "A Letter Written in 1711 by Mary Stafford to Her Kinswoman in England," *South Carolina Historical Magazine* 81, no. 1 (January 1980), 1–7.

94. John and Elizabeth Clarke, Letter to their Aunt Lemmon, August 12, 1729, Salisbury Family Papers, 1674–1758, MSS box "S," box 1, folder 1, American Antiquarian Society (hereafter cited as AAS).

95. Sueanna Perry, Letter to her Aunt Lemmon, June 17, 1729, Salisbury Family Papers, 1674–1758, MSS box "S," box 1, folder 1, AAS.

96. Jane Bradley, Letter to her Aunt Lemmon, July 12, 1729, Salisbury Family Papers, 1674–1758, MSS box "S," box 1, folder 1, AAS.

97. Ibid.

98. John and Elizabeth Clarke, Letter to their Aunt Lemmon, August 12, 1729, Salisbury Family Papers, 1674–1758, MSS box "S," box 1, folder 1, AAS.

99. Sueanna Perry, Letter to her Aunt Lemmon, June 17, 1729, Salisbury Family Papers, 1674–1758, MSS box "S," box 1, folder 1, AAS.

100. Tague, *Women of Quality*, 23.

101. Crawford and Gowing, *Women's Worlds in Seventeenth-Century England*, 6; Suzanne Hull, *Chaste, Silent and Obedient: English Books for Women 1475–1640* (San Marino, Calif.: Huntington Library, 1982), 1; Elaine Hobby, *Virtue of Necessity: English Women's Writing, 1649–88* (Ann Arbor: University of Michigan Press, 1989), 5.

102. Dror Wahrman, *Making of the Modern Self: Identity and Culture in Eighteenth-Century England* (New Haven: Yale University Press, 2004), 44; Dena Goodman, *Becoming a Woman in the Age of Letters* (Cornell: Cornell University Press, 2009), 84–99.

103. Mary Ellen Lamb, "The Agency of the Split Subject: Lady Anne Clifford and the Uses of Reading," *English Literary Renaissance* 22 (Autumn 1992), 347–68.

104. Joanna Moody, ed., *The Private Life of an Elizabethan Lady: The Diary of Lady Margaret Hoby 1599–1605* (Gloucestershire, UK: Sutton, 1998).

105. Three hand-copied recipes, for "damson wine with raisins," "stepony," and "treacle wine," match exactly those found in one of Hannah Woolley's texts,

entitled *The New Closet or Rather Rich Cabinet* (1670). Woolley's *The New Closet or Rather Rich Cabinet* (entitled on each page, *Ladies Cabinet*) was sometimes bound together with *The Queen-Like Closet or, Rich Cabinet* (1670). References to Digby and Salmon probably come from Kenelm Digby, *The closet of the eminently learned Sir Kenelme Digbie Kt. opened whereby is discovered several ways for making of metheglin, sider, cherry-wine, &c.* (1669); and William Salmon, *Polygraphice or the Arts of Drawing Limning Painting &c.* (London, 1675 or 1681). The manuscript recipe book also mentions Phylotheus Physiologus, *Monthly Observations For the preserving of health, with a Long and Comfortable Life, In this our Pilgrimage on Earth; But more particularly for the Spring and Summer Seasons* (London, 1688), and John Worlidge, *Vinetum Britannicum, or, A treatise of cider, and other wines and drinks extracted from fruits growing in this kingdom with the method of propagating all sorts of vinous fruit-trees* (1678). There is also mention of a "Verulams Nat. Hist." which is probably Francis Bacon (Lord Verulam), *Historie naturall and experimentall, of life and death* (1638), or *The natural and experimental history of winds &c.* (1671). Charles Brigham, Anna Cromwell, Sarah Prentice and others, Account Book, 1650–1730, MSS Dept., Folio Vols. "B," AAS.

106. Hobby, *Virtue of Necessity*, 166.
107. Ibid.; Paula McDowell, *The Women of Grub Street: Press, Politics and Gender in the London Literary Marketplace, 1678–1730* (New York: Oxford University Press, 1998), 51–52; Wendy Wall, *The Imprint of Gender: Authorship and Publication in the English Renaissance* (Ithaca: Cornell University Press, 1993); *The London Book Trade: Topographies of Print in the Metropolis from the Sixteenth Century*, ed. Robin Myers, Michael Harris, and Giles Mandelbrote (London: British Library, 2003); James Raven, *The Business of Books: Booksellers and the English Book Trade, 1450–1850* (New Haven: Yale University Press, 2007); Joseph Loëwenstein, *The Author's Due: Printing and the Prehistory of Copyright* (Chicago: University of Chicago Press, 2002); and Roméo Arbour, *Les Femmes et Les Métiers du Livre en France, de 1600 à 1650* (Paris: Didier Érudition, 1997). Elaine Hobby argues that several of the guides claiming to be written by Woolley were not composed by the original author. The multiple editions of Woolley's works—whether original or invented—attest to significant demand, high profits for her publishers, and a loyal following of readers. I have followed Hobby's model, treating the *Gentlewomans Companion, Compleat Servant-Maid*, and *Accomplished Ladies Delight* as false attributions; throughout the book, all of these texts are marked with explanatory footnotes. Hobby, *Virtue of Necessity*, 165–89.

108. Hannah Woolley, *The Gentlewomans Companion or, a Guide to the Female Sex: The Complete Text of 1675*, ed. Caterina Albano, 77 (Blackawton, UK: Prospect Books, 2001).

109. N.H., *The Ladies Dictionary* (London, 1694), 223–25.

110. Anon., *The Lady's New-years Gift* . . . (London, 1688), 119–20.

111. Arthur Clifford, *Tixall Letters*, 101, 108.

112. Ibid., 111.

113. N.H., *The Ladies Dictionary* (London, 1694), 223.

114. Mary Sibbald, Letter to Lady Hastings, August 26, 1672, Hastings Collection, box 33 HA 446, HL.

115. Elizabeth Lindsey, Letter to Lady Danby, 1674, Leeds Papers, Egerton Manuscripts, EG 3338, f. 52, BL.

116. Bridget Croft, Letter to Lucy Hastings (Countess Huntingdon), 9 September 1671, Hastings Collection, box 31 HA 1761, HL.

117. Catherine Caryll, Letter to Mrs. Bowman, c. 1680, Family of Caryll Correspondence, Add. 28227 f.3, BL.

118. Anon., *The Lady's New-years Gift* . . . (London, 1688), 125–26.

119. Anne Montagu, Letters to her niece Lady Hatton, 1676–90, Hatton-Finch Papers, Add. 29569, f.247–256, BL.

120. "Jeld" comes from *jelouse*—suspected, guessed, conjectured. Alexander Warrack, ed., *Chambers Scots Dictionary* (Edinburgh: W. and R. Chambers, 1979), 290–92.

121. Margaret Seton, Countess of Winton, Letter to daughter-in-law Anna Livingston, Countess of Eglinton, 1618, Papers of the Montgomerie Family, GD3/5/136, NAS.

122. Mary Man, Letter to Lucy Hastings, Countess of Huntingdon or Lady Mary Hastings, 1674, Hastings Collection, box 38 HA 9123, HL.

123. Anne Dormer, Letters to her sister Elizabeth Trumbull, 1685–1691, Add. MS 72516, f. 156–243, BL.

Chapter 2. Noble Presents

1. An early version of this chapter was presented at the Omohundro Institute of Early American History and Culture's Colloquium, and many thanks go to the members of this group for their insightful comments and helpful criticisms. On how women conceived of their property before and after marriage as well as in widowhood, see Amy Louise Erickson, *Women and Property in Early Modern England* (New York: Routledge, 1993).

2. "Coors," or "corse," (n. 5), *Oxford English Dictionary Online* 2d ed. (1989).

3. Margaret Seyliard, Accoumpts of Sir T. Seyliard, 1687–92, Add. 34784, British Library (hereafter cited as BL).

4. Amanda Vickery, "Women and the World of Goods: A Lancashire Consumer and Her Possessions," in *Consumption and the World of Goods*, ed. John Brewer and Roy Porter, 281–82 (New York: Routledge, 1993); Amanda Vickery, *Behind Closed Doors: At Home in Georgian England* (New Haven: Yale University Press, 2010).

5. Vickery, "Women and the World of Goods," 274–301.

6. Marcel Mauss, *The Gift: Forms and Functions of Exchange in Archaic Societies*, trans. Ian Cunnison (New York: Norton, 1967), 1, 58–59; Lewis Hyde, *The Gift: Imagination and the Erotic Life of Property* (New York: Vintage Books, 1983), xv; Alan D. Schrift, ed., *The Logic of the Gift: Toward an Ethic of Generosity* (New York: Routledge, 1997); David Cheal, *The Gift Economy* (New York: Routledge, 1988); Jacques Derrida, *Given Time: I. Counterfeit Money*, trans. Peggy Kamuf (Chicago: University of Chicago Press, 1992); Natalie Zemon Davis, *The Gift in Sixteenth-Century France* (Madison: University of Wisconsin Press, 2000), 9.

7. Peter Charles Hoffer, *Sensory Worlds in Early America* (Baltimore: Johns Hopkins University Press, 2003), 8; Richard Cullen Rath, *How Early America Sounded* (Ithaca: Cornell University Press, 2003); Emily Cockayne, *Hubbub: Filth, Noise and Stench in England* (New Haven: Yale University Press, 2007), 16.

8. Ilana Krausman Ben-Amos, *The Culture of Giving: Informal Support and Gift-Exchange in Early Modern England* (New York: Cambridge University Press, 2008); Felicity Heal, "Food Gifts, the Household, and the Politics of Exchange in Early Modern England," *Past and Present* 199 (May 2008); Jessica R. S. Spivey, "Red Rat and the Maker: British American and Native American Exchange in the Colonial Southeast" (Ph.D. diss., Johns Hopkins University, 2007); Jason Scott-Warren, *Sir John Harington and the Book as Gift* (New York: Oxford University Press, 2001); Davis, *The Gift*; Mary Hill Cole, *The Portable Queen: Elizabeth I and the Politics of Ceremony* (Amherst: University of Massachusetts Press, 1999); Craig Muldrew, *The Economy of Obligation: The Culture of Credit and Social Relations in Early Modern England* (New York: St. Martin's, 1998); Lisa M. Klein, "Your Humble Handmaid: Elizabethan Gifts of Needlework," *Renaissance Quarterly* 50 (1997), 459–93; Alan Hunt, *Governance of the Consuming Passions: A History of Sumptuary Law* (New York: St. Martin's Press, 1996); Martha Howell, "Fixing Movables: Gifts by Testament in Late Medieval Douai," *Past & Present*, no. 150 (February 1996), 3–45; Erickson, *Women and Property*; Diana O'Hara, "The Language of Tokens and the Making of Marriage," *Rural History* 3, no. 1 (1992); Paula Findlen, "The Economy of

Scientific Exchange in Early Modern Italy," in *Patronage and Institutions: Science, Technology, and Medicine at the European Court, 1500–1750,* ed. Bruce T. Moran, 5–24 (Rochester: Boydell Press, 1991); Sharon Kettering, "Gift-Giving and Patronage in Early Modern France," *French History* 2, no. 2. (1988), 131–51; Marion Kaplan, *The Marriage Bargain: Women and Dowries in European History* (New York: Harrington Park Press, 1985); Alisha Rankin, *Panacea's Daughters: Noblewomen as Healers in Early Modern Germany* (Chicago: University of Chicago Press, 2013). Many thanks to Alisha Rankin for allowing me to consult her manuscript prior to its publication.

9. Natalie Zemon Davis admits that "gender and gift obligation, too, could be considered further. . . . women were active givers and recipients of presents of all kinds." Alana Krausman Ben-Amos also wrote that she explicitly chose not to "systematically address gendered forms of gift giving and support." Davis, *The Gift,* 125; Ben-Amos, *The Culture of Giving,* 9.

10. Linda Levy Peck, *Consuming Splendor: Society and Culture in Seventeenth-Century England* (New York: Cambridge University Press, 2005), 6.

11. John Brewer and Roy Porter, "Introduction," in *Consumption and the World of Goods,* 3; Hunt, *Governance of the Consuming Passions,* 225.

12. D. R. Woolf, *Reading History in Early Modern England* (New York: Cambridge University Press, 2000), 228; William Sherman, *Used Books: Marking Readers in Renaissance England* (Philadelphia: University of Pennsylvania Press, 2008); Mary Fissell, "The Marketplace of Print," in *Medicine and the Market in England and Its Colonies, c. 1450–1850* (New York: Palgrave Macmillan, 2007); Carole Shammas, *The Pre-Industrial Consumer in England and America* (Oxford: Clarendon Press, 1990); Hoh-cheung Mui and Lorna Mui, *Shops and Shopkeeping in Eighteenth-Century England* (Montreal: McGill-Queen's University Press, 1989). See also J. A. Chartres, *Internal Trade in England, 1500–1700* (London: Macmillan, 1977). On the early modern dismembering and misuse of older, medieval books, see Jennifer Summit, *Memory's Library: Medieval Books in Early Modern England* (Chicago: University of Chicago Press, 2008), 102.

13. Peck, *Consuming Splendor,* 8.

14. This is similar to what James Jaffe and Avner Offer have identified as the "economy of regard" in nineteenth-century England. Avner is quoted in James Jaffe, *Striking a Bargain: Work and Industrial Relations in England, 1815–1865* (Manchester: Manchester University Press, 2000), 156–57.

15. Hyde, *The Gift,* 62; see also an article about Hyde's work by Daniel B. Smith, "What Is Art For?" *New York Times Magazine* (November 16, 2008), 39–43.

16. Hyde's definitions of "modern, capitalist" societies are not historically grounded and should be treated with some caution; but his claim that gift

exchange is often gendered as well as his philosophy of valuing the labor that goes into the creation of a gift are very useful. Hyde, *The Gift*, 106–8; Vickery, "Women and the World of Goods," 282, 284.

17. Anne Clifford Herbert, *The Diary of Anne Clifford, 1616–1619: A Critical Edition*, ed. Katherine O. Acheson (New York: Garland, 1995), 92.

18. Sidney W. Mintz, "Changing Roles of Food in the Study of Consumption," in *Consumption and the World of Goods*, ed. John Brewer and Roy Porter, 262 (New York: Routledge, 1993).

19. Heal, "Food Gifts," 44.

20. Allestree, *The Ladies Calling in Two Parts* (London, 1696).

21. See Allestree's *Ladies Calling* in comparison to his *Gentleman's Calling* (London, 1696).

22. Anne Dormer, Letters to her sister Elizabeth Trumbull, 1685–91, Add. 72516, ff. 156–243, BL.

23. Hannah Woolley, *The Gentlewomans Companion or, a Guide to the Female Sex: The Complete Text of 1675*, ed. Caterina Albano (Devon, UK: Prospect Books, 2001), 189–211.

24. Woolley, *Gentlewomans Companion*, 189–91.

25. Stephen Mennell, *All Manners of Food: Eating and Taste in England and France from the Middle Ages to the Present* (Chicago: University of Illinois Press, 1996), 75.

26. Jean-Louis Flandrin, "Introduction: The Early Modern Period," in *Food: A Culinary History from Antiquity to the Present*, ed. Jean-Louis Flandrin and Massimo Montanari, 271 (New York: Columbia University Press, 1999).

27. Bridget Croft, Letter to Lady Mary Hastings, 1670, Hastings Collection, box 29 HA 1759, HL.

28. Katherine Oxenden, Letters to her Mother, Lady Katherine Oxenden, 17th c., Family of Oxenden Correspondence, Add. 28004 ff. 9–13, BL.

29. Anne North, Letters to her daughter Lady Foley, 1676–1681, Family of North Correspondence, Add. 32500, ff. 15–56, BL.

30. Elizabeth Wood, Letters to her Mother (or Mother in Law), Lady Katherine Oxenden, 1660, Family of Oxenden Correspondence, Add. 28004 ff. 111–115, 309, 343, BL.

31. Wilson, *Food and Drink*, 282.

32. Ibid., 298. On the forced and exploitative labor of enslaved women, a practice inextricable from seventeenth-century sugar production in the West Indies, see Jennifer L. Morgan, *Laboring Women: Reproduction and Gender in New World Slavery* (Philadelphia: University of Pennsylvania Press, 2004); see also Mintz, *Sweetness and Power*.

33. Wilson, *Food and Drink*, 299.

34. Kim F. Hall, "The Gendering of Sugar in the Seventeenth Century," in *Feminist Readings of Early Modern Culture: Emerging Subjects*, ed. Traub, Kaplan, and Callaghan, 176 (New York: Cambridge University Press, 1996).

35. Mintz, *Sweetness and Power*, 3–7.

36. Gervase Markham, *The English Housewife: Containing the Inward and Outward Virtues Which Ought to Be in a Complete Woman*, ed. Michael R. Best (Montreal: McGill-Queen's University Press 1986), 112.

37. Woolley, *Gentlewomans Companion*, 194.

38. Thanks to Martin Crawford for permission to quote from his article. Martin Crawford, "Quince," *Agroforestry News* 6, no. 2 (January 1998), 16.

39. Lady Hewytt, Letter to sister Dorothy Barrington, 1675–76, Egerton Collection, EG 2650, ff. 1, 170, 346, BL.

40. Elizabeth Freke, Second Commonplace Book, Add. 45719, 29A, BL.

41. Elizabeth Ker, Letter to her niece Margaret Scott (Countess of Eglinton), 1647, Papers of the Montgomerie Family, GD3/5/406, National Archive of Scotland (NAS).

42. Elizabeth Wood, Letters to her Mother (or Mother in Law), Lady Katherine Oxenden, 1660, Family of Oxenden Correspondence, Add. 28004 ff. 111–115, 309, 343, BL.

43. Mary Lewis Leke (Countess of Scarsdale), Letter to her sister Elizabeth Lewis Hastings (Countess of Huntingdon), c. 1682, Hastings Collection, box 43, HA 8212, HL.

44. "Chairwomen," or "charwomen" were low-status individuals; see Hannah Woolley, *Compleat Servant-Maid* (London, 1700), and Eleanor Hubbard, *City Women: Money, Sex, and the Social Order in Early Modern London* (New York: Oxford University Press, 2012), 196–97. Michael MacDonald, *Witchcraft and Hysteria in Elizabethan London: Edward Jorden and the Mary Glover Case* (New York: Routledge, 1991); Mary Fissell, *Vernacular Bodies: The Politics of Reproduction in Early Modern England* (New York: Oxford University Press, 2004), 54–61.

45. Anon., *Adducismus Debellatus: or, a True Narrative of the sorceries and witchcrafts exercis'd by the devil and his Instruments upon Mrs. Christian Shaw* (1698).

46. Fissell, *Vernacular Bodies*, 53–89.

47. Clifford, *Diaries of Lady Anne Clifford*, 1–18, 60.

48. Acheson, *Diary of Anne Clifford*, 92.

49. Loftis, *Memoirs of Halkett and Fanshawe*, 145.

50. Holly Dugan, *The Ephemeral History of Perfume: Scent and Sense in Early Modern England* (Baltimore: Johns Hopkins University Press, 2011), 1–3;

Sophia Dicks, "Perfume for a Lady's Chamber: A Seventeenth-Century Perfume Burner," *Silver Studies: The Journal of the Silver Society* 23 (London 2004), 141–45.

51. Perfumes were also made in cake form, by mixing herbs and spices with oil, forming them into tablets, and letting them dry. Woolley, *The Queen-like Closet or, Rich Cabinet* (London, 1672).

52. Woolley, *The Ladies Directory, in Choice Experiments and Curiosities* (London, 1662).

53. Heironymous Brunschwig, *The Vertuose Boke of Distyllacyon of the Waters of all Maner of Herbes* . . . (1527).

54. Thomas Dawson, *The Good Huswifes Jewell* (London, 1596); and Thomas Dawson, *The Second Part of the Good Hus-wives Jewell* (London, 1606).

55. Woolley, *Gentlewomans Companion* . . . (London, 1673), 199.

56. Helena Dering and Katherine Moore, Accounts, 1678–79, Egmont Papers, Add. 46956B, f. 137; see also: Add. 46955B, f. 94, BL; this might also have been because urban areas were widely acknowledged by early modern Britons to smell worse than country ones; see Cockayne, *Hubbub*.

57. Markham, *English Housewife*, 125.

58. Ibid., 136.

59. "Candle-wood" (n. 2), and "Benjamin," (n. 1), *Oxford English Dictionary Online*, 2d ed. (1989). *Candle-wood* sometimes also refers to *Fouquiera splendens*, *Sciadophyllum capitatum*, or *Amyris balsamifera*, all of which originated in the new world.

60. Woolley, *Queen-Like Closet* (London, 1672).

61. Markham, *English Housewife*, 132. Emphasis added.

62. Alain Corbin, *The Foul and the Fragrant: Odor and the French Social Imagination* (Cambridge: Harvard University Press, 1986), 59–60, 78; Holly Dugan, "Scent of a Woman: Performing the Politics of Smell in Late Medieval and Early Modern England," *Journal of Medieval and Early Modern Studies* 38, no. 2 (Spring 2008), 229–52.

63. Corbin, *Foul and the Fragrant*, 40, 69.

64. Woolley, *Gentlewomans Companion*, 77.

65. Allestree, *Ladies Calling*, 62.

66. Although this book is recorded under the name Barrett, the portion I referenced was labeled as belonging to a woman named Ann Egerton; it is unclear whether Egerton was also Barrett. Lady Barrett, Recipe Book, 17th c., MS 1071, WL.

67. Anne Lovelace, Medical and Culinary Recipe Book, 1659–63, Add. 34722, BL.

68. Loftis, *Memoirs of Halkett and Fanshawe*, 96–99.

69. Ibid., 145.

70. Jane Hooke, Correspondence with Johana Barrington, Egerton Collection, EG 2650, f. 282, BL.

71. I speak here not of any single sumptuary law but of criticism and monitoring of dress and clothing more broadly. England's last sumptuary law was repealed in 1604, but, as Linda Levy Peck has written, "Moralists continued to rail against luxury, effeminacy, and the commodification of honor" through the seventeenth century, and "sumptuary bills continued to be introduced [if not passed] in Parliament up to 1640." Alan Hunt argues even for the persistence of "projects of governance of personal appearance and of private consumption" into the present day. Peck, *Consuming Splendor*, 10; Hunt, *Governance of the Consuming Passions*, xviii.

72. Hunt, *Governance of the Consuming Passions*, 216.

73. Klein, "Your Humble Handmaid," 471, 477; Susan Frye, "Sewing Connections: Elizabeth Tudor, Mary Stuart, Elizabeth Talbot, and Seventeenth-Century Anonymous Needleworkers," in *Maids and Mistresses, Cousins and Queens: Women's Alliances in Early Modern England*, ed. Susan Frye and Karen Robertson, 165–66 (New York: Oxford University Press, 1999); Susan Frye, *Pens and Needles: Women's Textualities in Early Modern England* (Philadelphia: University of Pennsylvania Press, 2010).

74. Bridget Cadogan, Correspondence with Mrs. Hays, 1684, William Petty's Papers, Lady Petty's Correspondence with her Children, Add. 72857, BL.

75. Elizabeth Montague and A. Montague, Letters to Lady Hatton, c. 1680, Hatton-Finch Papers, Add. 29558, ff. 187–199, BL.

76. Peter Stallybrass and Ann Rosalind Jones, "Fetishizing the Glove in Renaissance Europe," *Critical Inquiry* 28, no. 1, "Things" (Autumn 2001), 114–32; Davis, *The Gift*, 31.

77. Katherine Perceval, Ledger Books Pertaining to her Husband's Accounts After his Death, 1686, Egmont Papers, Add. 47038 & 47039, BL; Margaret Seyliard, Accoumpts of Sir T. Seyliard, 1687–92, Add. 34784, BL.

78. Elizabeth Freke, First Commonplace Book, entitled "Elizabeth Frek her book Given mee by my Cosen Sep. 1684," Add. 45718, 90B, BL.

79. Jane Hooke, Correspondence with Johana Barrington, Egerton Collection, EG 2650, F282, BL.

80. Raymond A. Anselment, ed., *The Remembrances of Eliʒabeth Freke 1671–1714*, Camden Fifth Series (Cambridge: Cambridge University Press, 2001), 18:1–36.

81. Woolley, *Supplement to the Queen-Like Closet* (1684).

82. Lisa Jardine, *Worldly Goods: A New History of the Renaissance* (London: Macmillan, 1997), 21.

83. Woolley, *Supplement to the Queen-Like Closet* (1684).

84. Amy Butler Greenfield, *A Perfect Red: Empire, Espionage, and the Quest for the Color of Desire* (New York: HarperCollins, 2005) 35–36, 76, 103.

85. Woolley, *Gentlewomans Companion*, 194.

86. Markham, *English Housewife*, 168–70.

87. Woolley, *A Supplement to the Queen-Like Closet, or a Little of Every Thing* (London, 1684).

88. Woolley, *Gentlewomans Companion*, 52, 57.

89. Woolley, *Supplement to the Queen-Like Closet*, 51–52.

90. Ibid., 135.

91. *A Collection of above Three Hundred Receipts in Cookery, Physick and Surgery . . .* (1719). Closed stores EPB / B 31072/B/1, WL.

92. Woolley, *Supplement to the Queen-Like Closet*, 60–61.

93. Katherine Oxenden, Letters to her Mother, Lady Katherine Oxenden, 17th c., Family of Oxenden Correspondence, Add. 28004 ff. 9–13, BL.

94. Jane Barker, Volume of verse entitled "Poems on Several Occasions . . ." c. 1680–1700, MS 343, 46, Magdalen College Archives, Oxford University (hereafter cited as MCA).

95. Frances Dillon (Lady Roscomon), Letter to Mary Dering, 1662–1674, Dering Correspondence, Stowe Collection, Stowe 744, f. 84, BL.

96. Anselment, *The Remembrances of Elizabeth Freke*, 1–36.

97. Jennifer Fletcher, "The Renaissance Portrait: Functions, Uses and Display," in *Renaissance Faces: Van Eyck to Titian*, ed. Lorne Campbell, Miguel Falomir, Jennifer Fletcher, and Luke Syson, 46–65 (London: National Gallery, 2008); Jennifer L. Hallam, "All the Queen's Women: Female Double Portraits at the Caroline Court," in *Women and Portraits in Early Modern Europe: Gender, Agency, Identity*, ed. Andrea Pearson, 137–60 (Burlington, Vt.: Ashgate, 2008).

98. Jardine, *Worldly Goods*, 17.

Chapter 3. Cooperative Labor

1. My intention in this chapter is not to engage explicitly in the historiography of labor and artisanal craftsmanship in early modern Europe but to suggest that production in elite homes constitutes an important and largely unexplored topic in labor history. Among the many histories of material working conditions in early modern Europe are E. P. Thompson, *The Making of the English Working Class* (New York: Vintage Books, 1966); William H. Sewell Jr., *Work and Revolution in France: The Language of Labor from the Old Regime to 1848* (New York: Cambridge University Press, 1980); Michael Sonenscher, *Work and*

Wages: Natural Law, Politics and the Eighteenth-Century French Trades (New York: Cambridge University Press, 1989); James Farr, *Artisans in Europe, 1300–1914* (New York: Cambridge University Press, 2000), 96.

2. These include, but certainly are not limited to, Alice Clark, *Working Life of Women in the Seventeenth Century* (Boston: Routledge and Kegan Paul, 1982); Barbara Hanawalt, ed., *Women and Work in Preindustrial Europe* (Bloomington: Indiana University Press, 1986); Olwen Hufton, *The Prospect Before Her: A History of Women in Western Europe* (London: Harper Collins, 1995); Judith Bennett, *Ale, Beer and Brewsters in England: Women's Work in a Changing World 1300–1600* (New York: Oxford University Press, 1996); Deborah Simonton, *A History of European Women's Work, 1700 to the Present* (New York: Routledge, 1998).

3. Amanda Vickery, *Behind Closed Doors: At Home in Georgian England* (New Haven: Yale University Press, 2010), 2–3.

4. Amanda Flather, *Gender and Space in Early Modern England* (Rochester: Boydell Press, 2007), 77, 93.

5. This term is respectfully modeled on Amanda Vickery's work on the "domestic interior." Vickery, *Behind Closed Doors*.

6. Eleanor Hubbard, *City Women: Money, Sex, and the Social Order in Early Modern London* (New York: Oxford University Press, 2012); Paula Humfrey, ed., *The Experience of Domestic Service for Women in Early Modern London* (Burlington, Vt.: Ashgate, 2011); Sarah Hand Meacham, *Every Home a Distillery: Alcohol, Gender, and Technology in the Colonial Chesapeake* (Baltimore: Johns Hopkins University Press, 2009); Carolyn Steedman, *Labours Lost: Domestic Service and the Making of Modern England* (New York: Cambridge University Press, 2009); Ann Rosalind Jones, "Maidservants of London: Sisterhoods of Kinship and Labor," in *Maids and Mistresses, Cousins and Queens: Women's Alliances in Early Modern Europe*, ed. Susan Frye and Karen Robertson, 21–32 (New York: Oxford University Press, 1999); Sara Mendelson and Patricia Crawford, *Women in Early Modern England* (Oxford: Clarendon, 1998), 303–13; Carol Loats, "Gender, Guilds, and Work Identity: Perspectives from Sixteenth-Century Paris," *French Historical Studies* 20, no. 1 (Winter 1997), 15–30; Linda Pollock, *With Faith and Physic: The Life of a Tudor Gentlewoman, Lady Grace Mildmay 1552–1620* (London: Collins and Brown, 1993). Kathleen Brown's "P[ar]cell of Murdereing Bitches" serves as an important reminder that women's cooperative work in colonial British American elite households was marked by, and often marred by, critical and distinctive differences in race as well as rank. Kathleen Brown, " 'A P[ar]cell of Murdereing Bitches': Female Relationships in an Eighteenth-Century Slaveholding Household," in *Maids*

and Mistresses, Cousins and Queens: Women's Alliances in Early Modern Europe, ed. Susan Frye and Karen Robertson, 87–96 (New York: Oxford University Press, 1999).

7.   Elizabeth Freke, "Kitchen Inventory," October 18, 1711, Freke Papers, MS 45718, British Library (hereafter cited as BL); Katherine Perceval, Ledger Books pertaining to her husband's accounts after his death, 1686, Egmont Papers, ADD 47038 & 47039, f. 22B-23, BL; Anne Southwell, Miscellany of Lady Anne Southwell, 1587–1636, V.b.198, Folger Shakespeare Library (hereafter cited as FSL). Elaine Leong, "Making Medicines in the Early Modern Household," *Bulletin of the History of Medicine* 82 (2008), 145–68.

8.   Southwell's inventory was compiled by a man named John Bowker. Bowker was assisted by two women who were probably servants, as the inventory was "witnessed by Margaret Mitton & Mary Musgrave." Anne Southwell, Miscellany of Lady Anne Southwell, FSL.

9.   Victoria Burke, "Women and Early Seventeenth-Century Manuscript Culture: Four Miscellanies," *Seventeenth Century* 12, no. 2 (1997), 135–50; Jean Klene, " 'Monument of an Endless Affection': Folger MS V.b.198 and Lady Anne Southwell," *English Manuscript Studies* 9 (1989), 165–86.

10. Anne Southwell, Miscellany of Lady Anne Southwell, FSL.

11. The Perceval inventory is in two pieces: the first piece was recorded in 1665 and was written by one of Perceval's children. This inventory included goods and furniture from two Perceval homes, one called Burton House, an estate thirty-four miles north of the city of Cork, and the other located in the town of Kinsale, seventeen miles south of the city of Cork. Although the two houses were some distance apart, their furniture and goods mingled and were probably transported between locations depending on need. For example, the Perceval inventory of 1665 has a separate subsection devoted entirely to "goods either att Kisale or Burton." The second piece of the Perceval inventory relates only to the Burton House residence and was created twenty years later, on May 31, 1686, after the death of Perceval's husband, John. The Burton House inventory was "made and appraised by" four local men: three "gentlemen," named "William Taylor of Baley, Richard Conzon of Walehestown, [and] Edward Bradston of Churchtown all within the Parish of Bruhinny," also in County Cork, and a tradesman named "Arthur Virgin of the City of Cork, upholsterer." Katherine Perceval, Household Inventory, fols. 167–169, BL; Katherine Perceval, Ledger Books pertaining to her husband's accounts after his death, fols. 22B-23, BL.

12. Elizabeth Freke, "Kitchen Inventory," October 18, 1711, Freke Papers, MS 45718, BL. Stephanie Tarbin and Susan Broomhall, eds., *Women, Identities and*

Communities in Early Modern Europe (Burlington, Vt.: Ashgate, 2008); and Amy Erickson, "Review of *The Remembrances of Elizabeth Freke, 1671–1714*" (review no. 393), Reviews in History, accessed October 20, 2011, http://www.history.ac.uk/reviews/review/393.

13. John E. Crowley, *The Invention of Comfort: Sensibilities and Design in Early Modern Britain and Early America* (Baltimore: Johns Hopkins University Press, 2003); James Deetz, *In Small Things Forgotten: An Archeology of Early American Life* (New York: Anchor Books, 1996).

14. Anne Southwell, Miscellany of Lady Anne Southwell, 1587–1636, V.b.198, f.60B, FSL.

15. A hack was a small metal rack used either over a fire or to hold pans when they were not in use. "Hack," (n. 2), *Oxford English Dictionary Online*, 2d ed. (1989).

16. Elizabeth Freke, "Kitchen Inventory," October 18, 1711, Freke Papers, BL.

17. Joanna Moody, *The Private Life of an Elizabethan Lady: The Diary of Lady Margaret Hoby 1599–1605* (Phoenix Mill, UK: Sutton Publishing, 1998), 48.

18. Susanna and Mungo Karnes, Letters to Theophilus Hastings (7th Earl Huntingdon), 1693, Hastings Collection, box 59 HA 8000 and 8003, Huntington Library (hereafter cited as HL).

19. D. J. H. Clifford, *The Diaries of Lady Anne Clifford* (Wolfeboro Falls, N.H.: Alan Sutton, 1991), 25; Alan Bray, *The Friend* (Chicago: University of Chicago Press, 2006), 153.

20. Katherine Perceval, Household Inventory, 1665, Egmont Papers, ADD 46942, f.167–169, British Library (BL). BL.

21. Elite families often hired lower-status women to care for and monitor their children. But the rules for doing so were not hard and fast, and child-care routines differed widely according to household, some elite women choosing to take active roles in the care and feeding of their children. This means that bedchambers would have been employed by both elite and lower-status women, who would have engaged in similar, sometimes competing, tasks. Gowing, *Common Bodies*, 149–76; Ilana Krausman Ben-Amos, *Adolescence and Youth in Early Modern England* (New Haven: Yale University Press, 1994); Linda A. Pollock, "Childbearing and Female Bonding in Early Modern England," *Social History* 22, no. 3 (October 1997), 286–306; Woolley, *The Compleat Servant-Maid . . .* (London, 1683), 105.

22. Sarah Savage to her daughter Hannah Witton, 2 April 1734, in Mrs. S. Savage's Letters to her Father, Brother, Sister, Son, Daughters, etc., 1687, 1712, 1714, 1734, Henry MSS 90 (4), f. 25, Dr. Williams's Library (hereafter cited as DWL).

23. Katherine Perceval, Ledger Books pertaining to her husband's accounts after his death, 1686, Egmont Papers, ADD 47038 & 47039, f. 22B-23, BL.

24. *"Movent"* (adj. and n.), *Oxford English Dictionary Online*, 3d ed. (2003). An entry for this word was included in the *New English Dictionary* (1908).

25. Elizabeth Freke, "Kitchen Inventory," October 18, 1711, Freke Papers, MS 45718, BL.

26. Clifford, *Diaries of Lady Anne Clifford*, 55, 68.

27. Anne Southwell, Miscellany of Lady Anne Southwell, 1587–1636, V.b.198, f.60B-61, FSL.

28. Alice Thornton, *The Autobiography of Mrs. Alice Thornton, of East Newton, Co. York* (Durham, UK: Andrews, 1875), 122–23.

29. Clifford, *Diaries of Anne Clifford*, 25.

30. Olivia Weisser, "Gender and Illness in Seventeenth-Century England" (Ph.D. diss., Johns Hopkins University, 2010). Thornton, *The Autobiography of Mrs. Alice Thornton*, 222–23.

31. Anne Southwell, Miscellany of Lady Anne Southwell, 1587–1636, V.b.198, FSL.

32. Ju: Barrington, Correspondence with her daughter, 17th c., Egerton Collection, EG 2650, f. 158–165, BL.

33. Elizabeth Oxenden, Letters to her mother-in-law Katherine Oxenden, 28 October 1664, Family of Oxenden Correspondence, ADD 28004 ff. 59, 60, 338, 363, 386, 391, BL. A *slip* was an early modern word for a plant cutting, used in horticultural grafting. *"Slip"* (n. 2), *Oxford English Dictionary Online*, 2d ed. (1989).

34. Elizabeth Boyle, Letter to her daughter, 24 June 1683, Hyde Papers, ADD 15892, f. 152, BL. *Blast* was a horticultural term that referred to a destructive plant disease. "Blast" (n.), *Oxford English Dictionary Online*, 2d ed. (1989).

35. Anne Southwell, Miscellany of Lady Anne Southwell, 1587–1636, V.b.198, f.60B, FSL.

36. Elizabeth Freke, "Kitchen Inventory," October 18, 1711, Freke Papers, MS 45718, BL.

37. Audrey Horning argues that in the seventeenth century "within England, beer and ale were primarily brewed and consumed in individual households." Audrey Horning, " 'The Root of All Vice and Bestiality': Exploring the Cultural Role of the Alehouse in the Ulster Plantation," in *Plantation in Ireland: Settlement and Material Culture, c.1 550-c.1700*, ed. James Lyttleton and Colin Rynne, 113–31 (Portland, Ore: Four Courts Press, 2009).

38. Gervase Markham, *The English Housewife* . . . (London, 1637), 207.

39. Ibid.

40. A *keeler* was a "vessel for cooling liquids." "Keeler" (n. 2), *Oxford English Dictionary Online*, 2d ed. (1989).

41. Elizabeth Freke, "Kitchen Inventory," October 18, 1711, Freke Papers, MS 45718, BL.

42. Anne Southwell, Miscellany of Lady Anne Southwell, 1587–1636, V.b.198, f.59–61, FSL.

43. Flather, *Gender and Space in Early Modern England*, 88; Joan M. Jensen, *Loosening the Bonds: Mid-Atlantic Farm Women, 1750–1850* (New Haven: Yale University Press, 1986), 97–98.

44. Information on the mechanics of seventeenth-, eighteenth-, and nineteenth-century churning can be found in Jensen, *Loosening the Bonds*, 99–108.

45. Moody, *The Private Life of an Elizabethan Lady*, 142, 157.

46. Ibid., 145.

47. Elizabeth Petty (Lady Shelburne), Correspondence with her children, specifically notes to her daughter Ann Petty, 14 February 1684/5, William Petty's Papers, Lady Petty's Correspondence with her Children, ADD 72857, ff. 3–56, BL.

48. Elizabeth Petty (Lady Shelburne), Correspondence with her children, specifically notes to her daughter Ann Petty, 10 March 1684, William Petty's Papers; Lady Petty's Correspondence with her Children, ADD 72857, ff. 3–56, BL.

49. Ingrid Tague, *Women of Quality: Accepting and Contesting Ideals of Femininity in England, 1690–1760* (Rochester: Boydell and Brewer, 2002), 112.

50. Bailey, *Dictionarium Domesticum . . .* (London, 1736).

51. Julia Abramson, "Vegetable Carving: For Your Eyes Only," in *Vegetables: Proceedings of the Oxford Symposium on Food and Cookery 2008*, ed. Susan Friedland, 9–18 (Blackawton, UK: Prospect Books, 2009); Julia Abramson, "Deciphering *La vraye mettode de bien trencher les viands* (1926)," in *Authenticity in the Kitchen: Proceedings of the Oxford Symposium on Food and Cookery 2005*, ed. Richard Hosking, 11–26 (Blackawton, UK: Prospect Books, 2006); Julia Abramson, "Legitimacy and Nationalism in the *Almanach des Gourmands* (1803–1812)," *Journal for Early Modern Cultural Studies* 3, no. 2 (Fall/Winter 2003), 101–35. I would like to thank Julia Abramson for her generosity and help with these references.

52. William Henderson, *The Housekeeper's Instructor . . .* (London, 1780), frontispiece.

53. Woolley, *The Queen-Like Closet, or Rich Cabinet . . .* (London, 1681), 333–34.

54. Ibid.

55. Woolley, *The Compleat Servant-Maid . . .* (London, 1683).

56. Hannah Woolley, *The Accomplish'd Ladies Delight . . .* (London, 1685).

57. Woolley, *The Compleat Servant-Maid . . .* (London, 1700).

58. James Raven, *The Business of Books: Booksellers and the English Book Trade, 1450–1850* (New Haven: Yale University Press, 2007); *The London Book Trade:*

Topographies of Print in the Metropolis from the Sixteenth Century, ed. Robin Myers, Michael Harris, and Giles Mandelbrote (London: Oak Knoll Press and the British Library, 2003).

59. Woolley, *The Compleat Servant-Maid* . . . (London, 1685), 10–11.

60. Woolley, *The Compleat Servant-Maid* . . . (London, 1683), 105.

61. John Shirley, *The accomplished ladies rich closet of rarities. Or, the ingenious gentlewoman and servant-maids delightful companion* . . . (London, 1691), 84–85.

62. Richard Brathwaite, *The English Gentlewoman, drawne out to the full Body* . . . (London, 1631).

63. Woolley, *The Compleat Servant-Maid* . . . (London, 1683).

64. Shirley, *The accomplished ladies rich closet* . . . (London, 1691), frontispiece.

65. W. S., *Aristotle's Compleat and Experience'd Midwife: In Two Parts* . . . (London, 1700).

66. Jane Sharp, *The Compleat Midwife's Companion: Or, the Art of Midwifry Improv'd* . . . (London, 1725).

67. Brathwaite, *The English Gentlewoman*, frontispiece.

68. Ibid., front ephemera.

69. In his landmark book *Revel, Riot, and Rebellion*, David Underdown showed that the popular ritual known as the "skimmington" was used as a method of social control over early modern people—particularly early modern women— who did not adhere to early modern mores. Sex outside of marriage, spousal abuse, and other "female challenges to patriarchal authority" were actions that triggered skimmingtons. Even the ritual itself was named after a dairy tool, the skimming ladle, used by female dairy workers to lift cream off of the surface of milk in preparation for churning butter. In these forms of popular protest, the dairy was so ritualized as a space for feminine productivity and obedience that it was used, quite literally, as a tool of punishment against those who trans-gressed early modern sexual norms: women and men subjected to a "skimmity" were often physically beaten with skimming ladles. David Underdown, *Revel, Riot, and Rebellion: Popular Politics and Culture in England 1603–1660* (New York: Oxford University Press, 1987), 99–105; see also David Underdown, "The Taming of the Scold: The Enforcement of Patriarchal Authority in Early Modern England," *Order and Disorder in Early Modern England*, ed. Anthony Fletcher and John Stevenson, 116–36 (New York: Cambridge University Press, 1985). E. P. Thompson discussed the skimmington ritual, also mentioning, briefly but fascinatingly, that legendary rebels and folk heroes were sometimes called Lady Skimmington. E. P. Thompson, *Customs in Common: Studies in Traditional Popular Culture* (New York: New Press, 1991), 516. The use of the phrase *Lady Skimmington* to describe riot leaders is also explored by Buchanan

Sharp, *In Contempt of All Authority: Rural Artisans and Riot in the West of England, 1586–1660* (Berkeley: University of California Press, 1980), 98.

70. Markham, *The English Housewife* . . . (London, 1637), 194.

71. Woolley, *The Compleat Servant-Maid* . . . (London, 1683).

72. Shirley, *The accomplished ladies rich closet of rarities* . . . (London, 1691).

73. Woolley, *The Compleat Servant-Maid* . . . (London, 1700).

74. R. Bradley, *The Country Housewife and Lady's Director, in the Management of a House, and the Delights and Profits of a Farm* . . . (London, 1727).

75. This last vignette draws on twenty-five to thirty manuscript recipe books, all of which were composed by a woman or groups of women and all of which were written or compiled primarily in the late seventeenth century. Most of the books were created in Great Britain, but some made their way across the Atlantic and were added to, edited, and amended in colonial British America.

76. Deborah Harkness, *The Jewel House: Elizabethan London and the Scientific Revolution* (New Haven: Yale University Press, 2007); Fissell, *Vernacular Bodies*; Pamela Long, *Openness, Secrecy, Authorship: Technical Arts and the Culture of Knowledge from Antiquity to the Renaissance* (Baltimore: Johns Hopkins University Press, 2001); Lorna Weatherill, *Consumer Behaviour and Material Culture in Britain 1660–1760* (London: Routledge, 1988); and Margaret Spufford, *Small Books and Pleasant Histories: Popular Fiction and Its Readership in Seventeenth-Century England* (Athens: University of Georgia Press, 1982).

77. Alisha Rankin, *Panacea's Daughters: Noblewomen as Healers in Early Modern Germany* (Chicago: University of Chicago Press, 2013); Elaine Leong and Alisha Rankin, eds., *Secrets and Knowledge in Medicine and Science, 1500–1800* (Burlington, Vt.: Ashgate, 2011); Rebecca LaRoche, *Medical Authority and Englishwomen's Herbal Texts, 1550–1650* (Burlington, Vt.: Ashgate, 2009); Edith Snook, "The Beautifying Part of Physic: Women's Cosmetic Practices in Early Modern England," *Journal of Women's History* 20 (2008), 10–33; Alisha Rankin, "Becoming an Expert Practitioner: Court Experimentalism and the Medical Skills of Anna of Saxony (1532–1585)," *Isis* 98 (2007), 23–53; Elaine Leong and Sara Pennell, "Recipe Collections and the Currency of Medical Knowledge in the Early Modern 'Medical Marketplace,' " in *Medicine and the Market in England and Its Colonies, c. 1450–c. 1850*, ed. Mark Jenner and Patrick Wallis, 133–52 (New York: Palgrave Macmillan, 2007); Wendy Wall, *Staging Domesticity: Household Work and English Identity in Early Modern Drama* (New York: Cambridge University Press, 2007); Elaine Leong, "Medical Recipe Collections in Seventeenth-Century England: Knowledge, Text and Gender" (D. Phil. thesis, University of Oxford, 2006); Sara Pennell, "Perfecting Practice? Women, Manuscript Recipes and Knowledge in Early Modern

England," in *Early Modern Women's Manuscript Writing: Selected Papers from the Trinity/Trent Colloquium* (Burlington Vt.: Ashgate, 2004), 237–55; Monica Green, "The Possibilities of Literacy and the Limits of Reading: Women and the Gendering of Medical Literacy," in *Women's Healthcare in the Medieval West* (Burlington, Vt.: Ashgate, 2000); Sara Pennell, " 'Great Quantities of Gooseberry Pie and Baked Clod of Beef': Victualling and Eating Out in Early Modern London," in *Londinopolis: Essays in the Cultural and Social History of Early Modern London*, ed. Paul Griffiths and Mark Jenner, 228–49 (New York: Manchester University Press, 2000); Linda Pollock, *With Faith and Physic: The Life of a Tudor Gentlewoman, Lady Grace Mildmay, 1552–1620* (London: Collins and Brown, 1992).

78. Men also kept recipe books, and many women's recipe books contain recipes from men as well as from women. On women sharing recipes with friends, see for example Rankin, *Panacea's Daughters*; Leong, "Making Medicines," 153; Fissell, *Vernacular Bodies*, 108; and Monica Green, "Books as a Source of Medical Education for Women in the Middle Ages," *Dynamis: Acta Hispanica ad Medicinae Scientiarumque Historian Illustrandam* 20 (2000), 331–69.

79. Leong and Pennell find that as many as one-third of manuscript recipes were transmitted through exchange. Leong and Pennell, "Recipe Collections and the Currency of Medical Knowledge," 138–43.

80. Jane Baber, Recipe Book, 1625, MS 108, f. 18, 22, Wellcome Library (herefter cited as WL).

81. Mrs. Carr, Recipe Book, 1682, MS 1511, f. 42B, WL; and Mary Dacre, Lady Mary Dacres Book of Receipts, 1666–1696, ADD 56248, f. 49, 56–57, BL.

82. Eliza Blennerhassett, Letter to Elizabeth Hastings, c. 1658, Hastings Collection, box 20 HA 843, HL.

83. Anne Lany, Letter to Anne De Gray, c. 1670, Correspondence of the Family of Gawdy, ADD 36989, F540, BL.

84. Beatrix Clerke, Letter to Lucy Hastings, Countess Huntingdon, 1665, Hastings Collection, box 25 HA 1466, HL.

85. Anonymous Woman [Possibly Mrs. M. Baesh], Recipe Book, 1640, MS 8086, f. 14, 19, 35B, 54, 81, 94–94B, and 102, WL.

86. Amy and Mary Eyton, Recipe Book, 1691, MS 2323, f. 23, 61–68, WL.

87. Elizabeth Freke, First Commonplace Book, MS 45718, BL.

88. Lady Barrett, Recipe Book, 17th c., MS 1071, f. 32, WL.

89. Amy Louise Erickson, *Women and Property in Early Modern England* (New York: Routledge, 1995), 190–91, 202, 222.

90. Anne Lovelace, Medical and Culinary Recipe Book, 1659–63, ADD 34722, f. 2, BL.

91. Elizabeth Okeover, Recipe Book, 1675, MS 3712, f. 2, WL.

92. Sara Pennell, ed., *Women and Medicine: Remedy Books, 1533–1865* (Detroit: Primary Source Media, 2004).

93. Amy and Mary Eyton, Recipe Book, 1691, MS 2323, WL.

94. Elizabeth Digby, Recipe Book, 1650, Egerton Manuscripts, EG 2197, BL.

95. Lady Frances Catchmay, Recipe Book, 1625, MS 184A, f. 2B, WL.

96. Mary Bent, Recipe Book, 1664, MS 1127, f. 2, WL.

97. Theresa Herbert and Mary Preston, Recipe Book, early 1700s, MS 3995, ff. 114, 139, WL.

98. Elizabeth Okeover, Recipe Book, 1675, MS 3712, f.113, WL.

99. Lady Ayscough, Medical Recipe Book, 1692, MS 1026, f. 58B, WL.

100. Anne Brumwich and Others, 1625–1700, MS 160, f. 94, WL.

101. Elizabeth Godfrey and Others, Recipe Book, 1686, MS 2535, f. 106, WL.

102. Pennell, "Perfecting Practice?," 237–55.

103. Mary Dacre, Lady Mary Dacres Book of Receipts, 1666–96, ADD 56248, f. 72, 89, 90–91B, BL.

104. Amy and Mary Eyton, Recipe Book, 1691, MS 2323, f. 109B, WL.

105. Lady Barrett, Recipe Book, 17th c., MS 1071, f. 58, WL.

106. Alisha Rankin discusses the tradition of medical "orality," sharing recipes by word of mouth, in her book *Panacea's Daughters*.

107. Mary Chantrell and Others, Recipe Book, 1690, MS 1548, f. 84, WL.

108. Mrs. Carr, Recipe Book, 1682, MS 1511, f. 59B-60, WL.

109. Anonymous, Recipe Book, mid-17th c., MS 7391, f. 121, WL.

110. Mary Chantrell and Others, Recipe Book, 1690, MS 1548, f. 84, WL.

111. Leong, "Making Medicines," 153.

112. Anonymous Woman [possibly Mrs. M. Baesh], Recipe Book, 1640, MS 8086, f. 100, WL.

113. Anonymous [possibly "EG"], Recipe Book, 17th c., MS 7391, WL; Elizabeth Okeover, Recipe Book, 17th c., MS 3712, WL; Richard Aspin, "Who Was Elizabeth Okeover?," *Medical History* 44, no. 4 (October 2000), 531–40.

114. Mary Chantrell and Others, Recipe Book, 1690, MS 1548, f. 32B, Recipe Book, WL.

115. Anne Lovelace, Medical and Culinary Recipe Book, 1659–63, ADD 34722, f. 95B, BL.

116. Anne Brumwich and Others, 1625–1700, MS 160, WL.

117. Anonymous Woman [possibly Mrs. M. Baesh], Recipe Book, 1640, MS 8086, f. 25b and f. 88, WL.

118. Elizabeth Digby, Recipe Book, 1650, Egerton Manuscripts, EG 2197, BL.

119. Mary Dacre, Lady Mary Dacres Book of Receipts, 1666–1696, ADD 56248, ff. 90–91, BL.
120. Elizabeth Freke, First Commonplace Book, MS 45718, ff. 141B, 242B, BL.
121. Jane (Whyte) Newton, Recipe Book, 1675, MS 1325, f. 91B, WL.
122. Anna Cromwell started the book in 1650. Later owners included Mary Parks, Mary Brigham-Clark, and Sarah Prentice, whose ownership marks all appear in the book's pages. Although nothing is known about several of these contributors, Mary Brigham-Clark was related to Charles Brigham (1700–1781) an early resident of Grafton, Massachusetts, and Sarah Prentice (1716–92) was married to Solomon Prentice (1705–73), who was the first minister of Grafton. Anon., "Brigham, Charles Account Book, 1650-c. 1730s," Manuscript Collections Finding Aids, 13 January 1999, American Antiquarian Society (hereafter cited as AAS).
123. Charles Brigham, Anna Cromwell, Sarah Prentice and Others, Account Book, 1650–1730, MSS. Dept., Folio Vols. "B," AAS. On the pearl trade in Great Britain and the West Indian and British American colonies, see Molly Warsh, "Adorning Empire: A History of the Early Modern Pearl Trade, 1492–1688" (Ph.D. diss., Johns Hopkins University, 2009).
124. Leong and Pennell, "Recipe Collections and the Currency of Medical Knowledge," 144.
125. Lady Barrett, Recipe Book, 17th c., MS 1071, WL, 22B–23. Despite the fact that this book is attributed to Lady Barrett, most of it was written by a husband and wife, Mr. and Mrs. F. Head. Mrs. Head was the daughter of a doctor named Sir George Ent, and many of his recipes were included by both his daughter and his son-in-law. A few excerpts in the book were written by Ann Egerton, whose name appears on f. 1B.
126. Anonymous [possibly "EG"], Recipe Book, 17th c., MS 7391, WL.
127. Anne Brumwich and Others, 1625–1700, MS 160, f. 108, WL.
128. Amy and Mary Eyton, Recipe Book, 1691, MS 2323, f. 35B, WL.
129. Anne Lovelace, Medical and Culinary Recipe Book, 1659–63, ADD 34722, f.45B, BL.
130. Sarah Palmer, Recipe Book, early 18th c., MS 3740, WL.
131. Lady Barrett, Recipe Book, 17th c., MS 1071, f. 47B, WL.
132. Ibid.
133. Theresa Herbert and Mary Preston, Recipe Book, early 18th c., MS 3995, f. 99B, WL.
134. Elizabeth Okeover, Recipe Book, 1675, MS 3712, f. 58, WL.
135. Anne Brumwich and Others, 1625–1700, MS 160, f. 16, WL.
136. Elizabeth Digby, Recipe Book, 1650, Egerton Manuscripts, EG 2197, f. 11B, BL.

137. Mary Chantrell and Others, Recipe Book, 1690, MS 1548, ff. 60, 66B, WL.

138. Seth Stein LeJacq, "The Bounds of Domestic Healing: Medical Recipes, Storytelling and Surgery in Early Modern England," forthcoming, *Social History of Medicine*, 2013; Seth Stein LeJacq, " 'Butcher-Like and Hatefull': Domestic Medicine and Resistance to Surgery in Early Modern England," manuscript (March 2011). I would like to thank Seth LeJacq for allowing me to consult both of these manuscripts, the first of which was the winner of the Roy Porter Student Essay Prize.

139. Elizabeth Freke, First Commonplace Book, MS 45718, f. 158B, BL.

140. Lady Ayscough, Medical Recipe Book, 1692, MS 1026, f. 112B, WL.

141. Various Women, Recipe Book, early 18th c., MS 7124, f. 4B, WL.

142. Jane Newton, Recipe Book, 1675, MS 1325, ff. 29–30, WL.

143. See also Pennell, "Perfecting Practice?", 248.

144. Mary Bent and Others, Recipe Book, 1664, MS 1127, f. 37, WL.

145. Ibid., f. 106.

146. Ibid., ff. 5, 9, 25.

147. Elizabeth Okeover, Recipe Book, 1675, MS 3712, f. 137, WL.

148. Anne Brumwich and Others, 1625–1700, MS 160, f. 70B, WL.

149. Charles Brigham, Anna Cromwell, Sarah Prentice and Others, Account Book, 1650–1730, MSS. Dept., Folio Vols. "B," AAS.

150. Elizabeth Freke, First Commonplace Book, MS 45718, f. 122, BL.

Chapter 4. Hot Spring Sociability

1. David Gadd, *Georgian Summer: Bath in the Eighteenth Century* (Bath, UK: Adams and Dart, 1971); R. S. Neale, *Bath 1680–1850: A Social History, or, A Valley of Pleasure, Yet a Sink of Iniquity* (London: Routledge and Kegan Paul, 1981); Roy Porter, ed., *The Medical History of Waters and Spas* (London: Wellcome Institute for the History of Medicine, 1990); Phyllis Hembry, *The English Spa, 1560–1815: A Social History* (Rutherford, N.J.: Fairleigh Dickinson University Press, 1990); David S. Shields, *Civil Tongues and Polite Letters in British America* (Chapel Hill: University of North Carolina Press, 1997); Amanda Vickery; *The Gentleman's Daughter: Women's Lives in Georgian England* (New Haven: Yale University Press, 1998), 225–84; Anne Borsay, *Medicine and Charity in Georgian Bath: A Social History of the General Infirmary, c. 1739–1830* (Burlington, Vt.: Ashgate, 1999); Peter Borsay, "Health and Leisure Resorts 1700–1840," in *The Cambridge Urban History of Britain.* Volume 2: *1540–1840*, ed. Peter Clark, 775–803 (New York: Cambridge University Press, 2000); Peter Borsay, *The Image of Georgian Bath, 1700–2000: Towns, Heritage, and History* (New York: Oxford University Press, 2000); Annick Cossic and Patrick Galliou,

eds., *Spas in Britain and in France in the Eighteenth and Nineteenth Centuries* (Newcastle, UK: Cambridge Scholars Press, 2006); Alison Hurley, "A Conversation of Their Own: Watering Place Correspondence Among the Bluestockings," *Eighteenth-Century Studies* 40, n. 1 (Fall 2006), 1–21.

2. Katherine Perceval, letters to her mother, Helena Southwell, 1676–78, Egmont Papers, Add. 46953 f. 220; Add. 46954 B ff. 95, 164, 189, 207; Add. 46955 A ff. 48, 125, 164, 179, 205; Add. 46955 B ff. 5, 17, 112, 121, British Library (hereafter cited as BL).

3. Anne Dormer, letters to her sister Elizabeth Trumbull, 1685–91, Add. 72516, ff. 156–243, BL.

4. Mary Lewis Leke, letter to her sister Elizabeth Lewis Hastings, c. 1682, Hastings Collection, box 42 HA 8209, Huntington Library (hereafter cited as HL).

5. See, for example, the anonymous *Tunbridge and Bath Miscellany* (1714), in which a fictional male correspondent confessed that "the chief Virtue ascrib'd to the Waters are the following two: They very often cure the Greensickness in Maids, and cause Fruitfulness in marry'd Women, provided they are but properly administered by a young vigorous Physician." And John Wilmot, Earl of Rochester's "Tunbridge Wells," declared that it was "brawny back and legs and potent prick / Who more substantially will cure thy wife / And on her half-dead womb bestow new life / From these the waters got the reputation / Of good assistants unto generation." Anon., *The Tunbridge and Bath Miscellany for the Year 1714* (London, 1714) Harding C 85 (2), Bodleian Library (hereafter cited as BOD); David M. Vieth, ed., *The Complete Poems of John Wilmot, Earl of Rochester* (New Haven: Yale University Press, 1968), 79. The few historians who have studied early modern spas have followed primary sources like these in characterizing them as places of sexual exploit. Neale, *Bath 1680–1850*, 17, 171; David Wheeler, "Jane Austen and 18th-Century English Spa Culture," *English Studies* 2 (2004), 120–33; Daniel Cottom, "In the Bowels of the Novel: The Exchange of Fluids in the Beau Monde," *NOVEL: A Forum on Fiction* 32, n. 2 (Spring 1999), 157–86.

6. Amanda Vickery, *The Gentleman's Daughter: Women's Lives in Georgian England* (New Haven: Yale University Press, 1998), 263; David E. Shuttleton, "Mary Chandler's Description of Bath (1733): A Tradeswoman Poet of the Georgian Urban Renaissance," in *Women and Urban Life in Eighteenth-Century England, "On the Town,"* ed. Rosemary Sweet and Penelope Lane, 173–94 (Burlington, Vt.: Routledge, 2003). On the size of spa towns, see Sylvia McIntyre, "Bath: The Rise of a Resort Town, 1660–1800," in *Country Towns in Pre-Industrial England*, ed. Peter Clark, 198–249 (New York: Palgrave Macmillan, 1981); Peter Clark and Jean Hosking, eds., *Population Estimates of English Small Towns, 1550–1851* (Leicester, UK: University of Leicester Centre for Urban History, 1993).

7. Miles Ogborn, *Spaces of Modernity: London's Geographies 1680-1780* (New York: Guilford Press, 1998), 42.

8. *The Household Book of Lady Grisell Baillie, 1692-1733*, ed. Robert Scott-Moncrieff (Edinburgh, UK: Edinburgh University Press, 1911), 108, 307.

9. Celia Fiennes, *The Journeys of Celia Fiennes*, ed. Christopher Morris (London: Cresset Press, 1949), 18.

10. Ibid., 19.

11. Ibid., 20.

12. Ibid., 133.

13. Mary Parker, letters to Sarah Churchill, 1677-89, Blenheim Papers, Add. 61474, ff. 1-5b, 10, BL.

14. Anne Dormer, letters to her sister Elizabeth Trumbull, 1685-91, Add. 72516, ff. 156-243, BL.

15. *The Household Book of Lady Grisell Baillie*, 107.

16. Jordan and Harrison are quoted in this context by John Wroughton, *Stuart Bath: Life in the Forgotten City, 1603-1714* (Bath, UK: Lansdown Press, 2004), 110.

17. Morris, *Journeys of Celia Fiennes*, xix. My use of the term *singlewoman* is deliberate and follows Amy Froide, *Never Married: Singlewomen in Early Modern England* (Oxford: Oxford University Press, 2005).

18. Daniel Defoe's descriptions of Bath are a useful counterpoint to Fiennes's; Defoe insisted that in the Cross-Bath pool "the Ladies and Gentlemen pretend to keep some distance, and each to their proper Side, but frequently mingle." However, even Defoe acknowledged that this practice was undertaken "not so often" in larger pools such as the King's or Queen's. He also described bathing practices similar to Fiennes', in which any "young Lady" was accompanied by "the Women that tend [her]." Daniel Defoe, *A Tour Thro' the Whole Island of Great Britain . . .*, ed. G. D. H. Cole (London: Peter Davies, 1927), 433; Morris, *Journeys of Celia Fiennes*, 18.

19. Eleanor Davies Douglas, known for her apocalyptic and experiential poetry, mentioned in her poem "Bath, Daughter of BabyLondon," that bathers were "by guides supported." Eleanor Touchet Davies Douglas, "Bath, Daughter of BabyLondon," 1670, Hastings Papers, HA Religious box 1, folder 28, HL.

20. Morris, *Journeys of Celia Fiennes*, 18-20.

21. *The Household Book of Lady Grisell Baillie,* 307.

22. Morris, *Journeys of Celia Fiennes*, 181.

23. Ibid., 18-20.

24. Ibid., 135.

25. Ibid., 350.

26. Katherine Moore, letter to grandmother Helena Southwell, 1678, Egmont Papers, Add. 46855B, BL.

27. Mary Dering, letter to her daughter, Lady Elizabeth (Betty) Southwell, 1680, Egmont Papers, Add. 46856C, f. 82, BL.

28. Katherine Manwaring [Maynwaring], letter to Frances Fowler Needham Hastings, 1695, Hastings Collection, box 61 HA 9227, HL.

29. Henry B. Wheatley, ed., *The Diary of Samuel Pepys* (New York: Heritage Press, 1942), 176.

30. Ibid., 204.

31. Ibid., 296–99.

32. Ibid., 194.

33. Ibid., 198–200.

34. Ibid., 213–21.

35. Elizabeth Harley, Account of Mrs. Elizabeth Harley 1687–88 and Mrs. Martha Hutchins 1692–1703–1785, MS 70348, BL. While Harley and Hutchins shared the account book, the early entries relating to London, Tunbridge Wells, and Brampton Bryan are widely acknowledged to be Harley's.

36. At Tunbridge, Harley gave money to fourteen women of lower status and six men of lower status, to one woman of high status and no men of high status, to four individuals of indeterminate gender. At London, she gave money to one woman of low status and one man of low status, no disbursements to those of high status, and two were given to those of indeterminate gender.

37. Elizabeth Harley, Account of Mrs. Elizabeth Harley 1687–88 and Mrs. Martha Hutchins 1692–1703–1785, MS 70348, BL.

38. Borsay, "Health and Leisure Resorts," 795.

39. Wheatley, *Diary of Samuel Pepys*, 195.

40. David Souden, "'East, West—Home's Best'? Regional Patterns in Migration in Early Modern England," in *Migration and Society in Early Modern England*, ed. Peter Clark and David Souden, 72 (London: Rowman and Littlefield, 1987).

41. Elizabeth Holland, "Occupations in Bath in the Reign of James I," and Marta Inskip, "City Plans," in *Citizens of Bath* (Bath, 1988), PP9G3, Bath Guildhall Archives (hereafter cited as BGA).

42. Bath Corporation Deeds, c. 1640–1740, BC152/196–785, Bath Guildhall Record Office (hereafter cited as BGRO). On women in brewing trades, see Judith Bennett, *Ale, Beer and Brewsters in England: Women's Work in a Changing World* (New York: Oxford University Press, 1999).

43. Mary Hatton Helsby, Letter to Lady Smythe, June 4, 1651, MS X.d.493 (8), FSL.

44. Joseph Gilmore, *The City of Bath*, c. 1694–1717, Russell Maps Vol. 1, p. 15, Gilmore IOB 308, Bath Central Library (hereafter cited as BCL).

45. Bath Corporation Deeds, c. 1640–1740, BC152/196–785, BGRO.

46. Mrs. Bruce, Letter to her anonymous female friend, 2 July 1707, Hastings Collection, box 69 HA 13823, HL.

47. Anne Cottrell Dormer, Letters to her sister Elizabeth Cottrell Trumbull, 1685–91, Add. MS 72516, f. 235, BL.

48. Katherine Moore, Letter to her maternal grandmother Helena Southwell, 1678, Egmont Papers, ADD 46855 B, ff. 34, 193, BL.

49. H[enrietta] Borlase, Letter to her friend Lady Alltom, August 1, c. 1660–80, X.c.66, Folger Shakespeare Library (hereafter cited as FSL).

50. Elizabeth Washington Shirley, Baroness Ferrers, Letter to her niece Lady Norse [Norris], c.1694, Hastings Collection, box 60 HA 10811, HL.

51. Theophilus Hastings, 7th Earl Huntingdon, Letter to his mother-in-law Anne Leveson, Lady Venables, 1692, Hastings Collection, box 58 HA 6089, HL.

52. Borsay, "Health and Leisure Resorts," 781.

53. Christiane Klapisch-Zuber, *Women, Family and Ritual in Renaissance Italy*, trans. Lydia G. Cochrane (Chicago: University of Chicago Press, 1985), 310–30.

54. *The Household Book of Lady Grisell Baillie*, 45–46.

55. Morris, *Journeys of Celia Fiennes*, 350.

56. George Hastings (8th Earl Huntingdon), Letter to his father Theophilus Hastings (7th Earl Huntingdon), 1690, Hastings Collection, box 55 HA 5293, HL.

57. Thomas Guidott, *The Register of Bath or, Two hundred observations* . . . (London, 1694).

58. Wroughton, *Stuart Bath*, 110–11.

59. Elizabeth Harley, correspondence with Robert Harley, 1685–91, MS 70238, folder 2, BL.

60. *The Household Book of Lady Grisell Baillie*, 45–46.

61. It is unclear from the reference whether Rachel Baillie was undergoing "dry cupping" (in which heated cups are applied to the body in order to draw blood to the surface of the skin), or "wet cupping" (in which small cuts are made in the patient's skin before heated cups are applied to the body in order to draw blood out of the body). Both treatments were common in early modern Britain and were thought to restore balance to a patient's humors. "Cupping," (n. 1), Oxford English Dictionary Online, 2d ed. (1989).

62. William Simpson, *The history of Scarbrough-spaw* . . . (London, 1679).

63. Guidott, *The Register of Bath*.

64. Elizabeth Petty, correspondence with her children, specifically notes to her daughter Ann Petty, William Petty's Papers; Lady Petty's Correspondence with her Children, Add. 72857, ff. 3–56, BL.

65. Ibid.

66. Joanna Gibson, John Gibson, and Joan Gibson, Recipe Book, 1632–1717, MS 311, Wellcome Library (hereafter cited as WL). Although John Gibson recorded some recipes in the volume, this particular entry was recorded in the section of the book kept by either Joan or Joanna.

67. Elizabeth Freke, Commonplace Book, 1684–1714, Freke Papers vol. 1, Add. 45,718, BL.

68. Morris, *Journeys of Celia Fiennes*, 23.

69. Ibid., 350.

70. Ibid., 338.

71. Ned Ward, *A Step to the Bath* (London, 1700). Ward's fictional account of his travels to Bath was a satire. But while he mocked the women who carried sweets in the Bath, he did not treat the practice as anything but typical and widespread. Daniel Defoe also mentioned women who swam with "a little floating Wooden Dish, like a Bason; in which the Lady puts a Handkerchief, and a Nosegay, of late the Snuff-box is added, and some Patches." Defoe, *Tour*, 433.

72. Reference to Samuel Gale's quote comes from Wroughton, *Stuart Bath*, 112–14.

73. Morris, *Journeys of Celia Fiennes*, 19.

74. Natalie Zemon Davis, "Boundaries and the Sense of Self in Sixteenth-Century France," in *Reconstructing Individualism: Autonomy, Individuality, and the Self in Western Thought*, ed. Thomas Heller, Morton Sosna, and David Wellbery, 61 (Stanford: Stanford University Press, 1986).

75. *The Household Book of Lady Grisell Baillie*, 108–9.

76. Elizabeth Harley, Account of Mrs. Elizabeth Harley 1687–88, and Mrs. Martha Hutchins 1692–1703–1785, MS 70348, BL.

77. Elizabeth Freke, Commonplace Book, c. 1684, Freke Papers vol. 1, Add. 45,718, BL.

78. Susan Frye, "Sewing Connections: Elizabeth Tudor, Mary Stuart, Elizabeth Talbot and Seventeenth-Century Anonymous Needleworkers," in *Maids and Mistresses, Cousins and Queens: Women's Alliances in Early Modern England*, ed. Susan Frye and Karen Robertson, 165–82 (New York: Oxford University Press, 1999).

79. McIntyre, *Bath: The Rise of a Resort Town, 1660–1800*, 202.

Chapter 5. Yokemates

1. For convenience I use the terms *missionaries, preachers, Public Friends,* and *ministers* interchangeably. But while many Quaker women "preached" in public from 1650 to 1670, it was not until the creation of the Monday (Second Day)

Morning Meeting in 1672 that a bureaucratic body oversaw and sanctioned the activities of certain Friends and that Quakers decried the proselytizing practices usually associated with missionary work. I also use the terms *Friends* and *Quakers* interchangeably, although these often were not used by seventeenth-century members of the faith. Phyllis Mack, *Visionary Women: Ecstatic Prophecy in Seventeenth-Century England* (Berkeley: University of California Press, 1992), 283–84.

2. On this particular journey Morris traveled from Pennsylvania to Ireland, from Ireland to Wales, and Wales to London; from London she went to Amsterdam, then back to England and Wales, and then to Durham, England, before embarking a second time for Holland, where she was shipwrecked. Margaret Hope Bacon, *Wilt Thou Go on My Errand? Journals of Three 18th Century Quaker Women Ministers, Susanna Morris 1682–1755, Elizabeth Hudson 1722–1783, Ann Moore 1710–1783* (Wallingford, Penn.: Pendle Hill, 1994), 56–58, 72; see also Susanna Morris, Travel Diary, 1682–1755, 1000/Gulielma M. Howland Collection, Haverford College Quaker Collection (hereafter cited as HCQC).

3. Sarah Crabtree, "A Holy Nation: The Quaker Itinerant Ministry in an Age of Revolution, 1750–1820" (Ph.D. diss., University of Minnesota, 2007); Rebecca Larson, *Daughters of Light: Quaker Women Preaching and Prophesying in the Colonies and Abroad, 1700–1775* (New York: Knopf, 1999).

4. All of the places listed here were visited by just three Quaker women: Joan Vokins, Elizabeth Whartnaby, and Susanna Morris. On Vokins, see Joan Vokins, *God's Mighty Power Magnified: as manifested and revealed in his faithful hand-maid Joan Vokins* . . . (London, 1691), Jenks Collection, BX 7742 V89 G5, HCQC; on Whartnaby, see Larson, *Daughters of Light*, 93; on Morris, see Margaret Hope Bacon, *Mothers of Feminism: The Story of Quaker Women in America* (San Francisco: Harper and Row, 1986), 37.

5. Anne G. Myles, "Border Crossings: The Queer Erotics of Quakerism in Seventeenth-Century New England," in *Long Before Stonewall: Histories of Same-Sex Sexuality in Early America*, ed. Thomas A Foster (New York: New York University Press, 2007); Elaine Forman Crane, *Ebb Tide in New England: Women, Seaports, and Social Change, 1630–1800* (Boston: Northeastern University Press, 1998).

6. Phyllis Mack very briefly but very importantly argues that "women traveling companions . . . often remained together for years, sustained by mutual encouragement." Mack, *Visionary Women*, 209.

7. Catie Gill, *Women in the Seventeenth-Century Quaker Community: A Literary Study of Political Identities, 1650–1700* (Burlington, Vt.: Ashgate, 2005), 1–2.

8. Kate Peters, *Print Culture and the Early Quakers* (Cambridge: Cambridge University Press, 2005), abstract; Ezell, *Writing Women's Literary History* (Baltimore: Johns Hopkins University Press, 1993), 137.

9. Catie Gill argues that Quakers published "discourses maintaining women's bodily inferiority" in order to silence their voices and that "those narratives that focus on the female sufferer's body often minimize their right to speak in the text, suggesting that women are more likely to be perceived as innocent when they are mute." Gill, *Women in the Seventeenth-Century Quaker Community*, 52–53; Peters, *Print Culture and the Early Quakers*, 124–25; Hilary Hinds, *God's Englishwomen: Seventeenth-Century Radical Sectarian Writing and Feminist Criticism* (New York: St. Martin's, 1996); Bernadette Andrea, *Women and Islam in Early Modern English Literature* (New York: Cambridge University Press, 2009), 62–63.

10. George Fox encouraged the creation of this testimonial genre of Quaker sufferings in the 1650s, urging his followers to document and circulate examples of the punishments inflicted upon them. A. Marjon Ames, " 'Prisoners for the Truth's Sake': Early Quaker Sufferings and the Establishment of Orthodoxy" (Ph.D. diss., University of Mississippi, 2008), 92–99.

11. My interpretation of embodied religious experience and gendered suffering has been informed by Janet Moore Lindman, *Bodies of Belief: Baptist Community in Early America* (Philadelphia: University of Pennsylvania Press, 2008); Janet Moore Lindman and Michele Lise Tarter, *A Centre of Wonders: The Body in Early America* (Ithaca: Cornell University Press, 2001); Michele Lise Tarter, "Nursing the New Wor(l)d: The Writings of Quaker Women in Early America, *Women and Language* 16, no. 1 (1993), 22–26; David Hillman and Carla Mazzio, eds., *The Body in Parts: Fantasies of Corporeality in Early Modern Europe* (New York: Routledge, 1997), xii; Laura Gowing, *Common Bodies: Women, Touch and Power in Seventeenth-Century England* (New Haven: Yale University Press, 2003). See also Gill, *Women in the Seventeenth-Century Quaker Community*, 42; Brad Gregory, *Salvation at Stake: Christian Martyrdom in Early Modern Europe* (Cambridge: Harvard University Press, 1999).

12. Helen Plant, " 'Subjective Testimonies': Women Quaker Ministers and Spiritual Authority in England: 1750–1825," *Gender and History* 15, no. 2 (2003), 296–318; Rebecca Larson, *Daughters of Light: Quaker Women Preaching and Prophesying in the Colonies and Abroad, 1700–1775* (New York: Knopf, 1999), 26, 14–42; Mack, *Visionary Women*, 278–79.

13. Quakers gained only limited freedoms under the Act of Toleration of 1689. Those Quakers who did not publicly oppose the Doctrine of the Trinity technically were tolerated in their worship. But most Quakers refused to take oaths,

which prohibited them from enjoying the full measure of protection accorded to other Dissenters by the act. Further laws were designed in the mid-1690s to make allowance for this, but Quakers continued to face legal and financial persecution until the removal of the requirement to pay tithes in the 1730s. John Marshall, *John Locke, Toleration and Early Enlightenment Culture: Religious Intolerance and Arguments for Religious Toleration in Early Modern and 'Early Enlightenment' Europe* (Cambridge: Cambridge University Press, 2006). See also Mack, *Visionary Women*, 343, 411.

14. I explore some of the intersections between Quaker quietism and radical preaching in more detail in an article published in *Early American Studies* in 2011. Amanda E. Herbert, "Companions in Preaching and Suffering: Itinerant Female Quakers in the Seventeenth- and Eighteenth-Century British Atlantic World," *Early American Studies* 9, no. 1 (Winter 2011), 73–113.

15. Larson, *Daughters of Light*, 255.

16. Gill, *Women in the Seventeenth-Century Quaker Community*, 48.

17. Bacon, *Mothers of Feminism*, 34.

18. *An Account of the Travels, Sufferings & Persecutions of Barbara Blaugdone, Given forth as a Testimony to the Lord's Power, and for the Encouragement of Friends* (London, 1691), Jenks Collection, BX 7730.B645 A1, HCQC.

19. *This is a short relation of some of the cruel sufferings (for the truth's sake) of Katharine Evans and Sarah Chevers, in the Inquisition in the Isle of Malta . . .* (London, 1662).

20. Phyllis Mack notes that Burden had gone to New England in order to "prophesy and to collect her late husband's debts." Mack, *Visionary Women*, 215.

21. Sewel, *History of the . . . Quakers*, 290–291.

22. Bacon, *Wilt Thou Go on My Errand?*, 68.

23. Rosemary Anne Moore, *The Light in Their Consciences: Faith, Practices, and Personalities in Early British Quakerism, 1646–1666* (State College: Pennsylvania State University Press, 2000), 28; tales told against Howgill are from Peters, *Print Culture and the Early Quakers*, 148.

24. Criticisms of Susanna Aldridge and Elizabeth Redford are found in Mack, *Visionary Women*, 365.

25. Ibid., 362.

26. Elizabeth Hudson Morris, *Diary of minister's travels*, 1721–83, 975A, HCQC.

27. Letter from Robert "King" Carter to William Dawkins, 20 February 1727/8, Carter Family Papers, Mss1 C2468a3–4, Virginia Historical Society (hereafter cited as VHS).

28. Hudson Morris, *Diary of minister's travels*, 1721–83, 975A, HCQC.

29. *An Account of the Travels, Sufferings & Persecutions of Barbara Blaugdone . . .*

30. *Some Account of the Life and Religious Exercises of Mary Neale, formerly Mary Peisley, Principally Compiled from her own Writings* (Dublin, 1795), HCQC.

31. *Strength in Weakness Manifest: in the Life, Various Trials, and Christian Testimony of that faithful Servant and Handmaid of the Lord, Elizabeth Stirredge . . .* (London, 1746).

32. Cristine Levenduski, *Peculiar Power: A Quaker Woman Preacher in Eighteenth-Century America* (Washington: Smithsonian Institution Press, 1996), 31.

33. Letter from Elizabeth Lloyd Pemberton to her cousin Deborah Moore, 16 January 1707/8, 955/Edward Wanton Smith Collection, box 11, HCQC.

34. David Booy, *Autobiographical Writings by Early Quaker Women* (Burlington, Vt.: Ashgate, 2004), 183–88.

35. Elizabeth Webb, A Short Account of my Viage into America with Mary Rogers my Companion, c. 1697–99, 975B, HCQC.

36. Margaret Ellis, *Diary of minister's travels*, 1739–52, 975B, HCQC.

37. *God's Mighty Power Magnified: as manifested and revealed in his faithful handmaid Joan Vokins . . .* (London, 1691), Jenks Collection, BX 7742 V89 G5, HCQC.

38. The relative danger of transatlantic sea travel is a matter of debate among scholars; although some historians have shown that sea travel was frequently undertaken and relatively safe, it is nonetheless true that Quaker women and men expressed particular fears about piracy and illness and frustrations about the cramped quarters, limited diet, and bad hygienic conditions common to life at sea. Alison Games, *Migration and the Origins of the English Atlantic World* (Cambridge: Harvard University Press, 1999), 60; Raymond L. Cohn, "Maritime Mortality in the Eighteenth and Nineteenth Centuries: A Survey," *International Journal of Maritime History* 1 (1989), 159–91. Contrasting opinions are found in Ian K. Steele, *The English Atlantic, 1675–1740: An Exploration of Communication and Community* (Oxford: Oxford University Press, 1986), 5.

39. James Bowden, *The History of the Society of Friends in America* (London, 1850), 1:52–68, 126–29.

40. Sewel, *History of the . . . Quakers*, 316.

41. Susanna Morris, Travel Diary, c. 1682–1755, 1000/Gulielma M. Howland Collection, HCQC. See also Carla Gerona, *Night Journeys: The Power of Dreams in Transatlantic Quaker Culture* (Charlottesville: University of Virginia Press, 2004).

42. The sailors' fears were probably informed by the idea that witches could cause destructive storms; Quakers and singlewomen were often accused of witchcraft. Lyndal Roper, *Witch Craze: Terror and Fantasy in Baroque Germany* (New Haven: Yale University Press, 2004), 55, 223.

43. Sewel, *History of the . . . Quakers*, 188–93.

44. Hudson Morris, *Diary of minister's travels*, 1721–83, 975A, HCQC.

45. Bacon, *Wilt Thou Go on My Errand?*, 65.

46. Ibid., 51.

47. Ellis, *Diary of minister's travels*, 1739–52, 975B, HCQC.

48. David Booy states that Curwen was "probably from the middling sort," as her son was a glover. Booy, *Autobiographical Writings*, 108–13.

49. *God's Mighty Power Magnified: as manifested and revealed in his faithful handmaid Joan Vokins . . .* (London, 1691), Jenks Collection, BX 7742 V89 G5, HCQC.

50. William Rawlin, *The Laws of Barbados, Collected In One Volume* (London, 1699), 120.

51. As early as 1672 George Fox printed a pamphlet which decried the "so called, and so stileing" Anglican priests in Barbados. Furious that slaves were not allowed to attend church services, Fox asked Barbados's non-Quaker religious leaders, "If you be Ministers of Christ, are you not Teachers of Blacks and Taunies (to wit, Indians) as well as of the Whites? For is not the Gospel to be preached to all Creatures? And are not they Creatures?" Fox was especially incensed that Quakers were forbidden to associate with the slaves, raging, "Why do you find fault with the Quakers (so called) for teaching of their Families, and instructing . . . the Blacks, and Taunies, and Whites?" George Fox, *To the Ministers, Teachers, and Priests, (So called, and so Stileing your Selves) in Barbadoes* (1672).

52. Oscar Williams, *African Americans and Colonial Legislation in the Middle Colonies* (New York: Garland, 1998), 33.

53. Gary B. Nash and Jean R. Soderlund, *Freedom by Degrees: Emancipation in Pennsylvania and Its Aftermath* (New York: Oxford University Press, 1991), 10, 29.

54. Gary B. Nash, *Forging Freedom: The Formation of Philadelphia's Black Community, 1720–1840* (Cambridge: Harvard University Press, 1988), 13–14.

55. Ellis, *Diary of minister's travels*, 1739–52, 975B, HCQC.

56. Thomas Weld, *The perfect pharisee under monkish holinesse opposing the fundamentall principles of the doctrine of the gospel, and scripture-practices of gospel-worship manifesting himselfe in the generation of men called Quakers* (London, 1653).

57. Laura Gowing, *Domestic Dangers: Women, Words and Sex in Early Modern London* (Oxford: Clarendon, 1996).

58. *This is a short relation of some of the cruel sufferings (for the truth's sake) . . .* (London, 1691). I have also drawn on an edition printed in London one year later.

59. Sewel, *History of the . . . Quakers*, 567–70.
60. Ibid., 419–21. For a more detailed examination of the imagery in Sewel's text, see Herbert, "Companions in Preaching and Suffering."
61. William Edmundson, *Journal of the Life, Travels, Sufferings, and Labour of Love in the Work of the Ministry* . . . (London 1715); this is quoted in Mack, *Visionary Women*, 358.
62. *Some Account of the Early Part of the Life of Elizabeth Ashbridge . . .* (Philadelphia, 1807).
63. Susanna Morris, Travel Diary, b1682–d1755, 1000/Gulielma M. Howland Collection, HCQC.
64. Elizabeth Webb, "A Short Account of my Viage into America with Mary Rogers my Companion," c. 1697–99, 975B, HCQC.
65. Ellis, *Diary of minister's travels*, 1739–52, 975B, HCQC.
66. Alan Bray, *The Friend* (Chicago: University of Chicago Press, 2003), 217.
67. Booy, *Autobiographical Writings*, 183–88.
68. Phyllis Mack argues that women insisted on homosocial companionship mainly out of a "concern to avoid giving cause for slander." Mack, *Visionary Women*, 228.
69. *God's Mighty Power Magnified: as manifested and revealed in his faithful hand-maid Joan Vokins* . . . (London, 1691).
70. *A short journal of the labours and travels in the work of the ministry of that faithful servant of Christ, Deborah Bell* (London, 1762). "Pill," (n. 1), *Oxford English Dictionary Online*, 3d ed. (March 2006).
71. Susanna Morris, Travel Diary, b1682–d1755 1000/Gulielma M. Howland Collection, HCQC.
72. Mary Peisley, letter to her friend Elizabeth Fuller Shackleton, November 16, 1754, 859/Shackleton Family Papers, HCQC.
73. Hudson Morris, *Diary of minister's travels*, 1721–83, 975A, HCQC.
74. Ibid.
75. As David Harris Sacks has shown for seventeenth-century Bristol, residents of port towns voiced fears that their children would be stolen and forced into transatlantic servitude by evil spirits who "like the devil . . . cozened, enticed, or tempted his, or sometimes her, victims into base servitude by taking advantage of their idleness. With false demeanor and engaging words, he appealed to their lust for fleshly pleasures and convinced them that 'they shall goe into a place where food shall drop into their mouthes: and being thus deluded, they take courage, and are transported.' " The fact that Ashbridge was offered the lure of a female friend rather than food is additionally revealing of the importance of Quaker female companionship. David Harris Sacks, *The Widening Gate: Bristol*

and the Atlantic Economy, 1450–1700 (Berkeley: University of California Press, 1991), 304–5.

76. *Some Account of the Early Part of the Life of Elizabeth Ashbridge . . .* (Philadelphia, 1807). Christine Levenduski agrees that "finding agreeable companionship seemed to concern [Ashbridge] as much as did the predicament of her captivity." Levenduski, *Peculiar Power*, 76.

77. Laurel Thatcher Ulrich, *Goodwives: Image and Reality in the Lives of Women in Northern New England 1650–1750* (New York: Vintage, 1982), 202. See also Linda Colley, *Captives: Britain, Empire, and the World, 1600–1850* (London: Anchor, 2002).

78. *An Account of the Travels, Sufferings & Persecutions of Barbara Blaugdone . . .* Blaugdone's insistence that the man's knife had gone "through all of my clothes" mirrors language used by women in rape accusations, in which female victims spoke of damage to their clothing and the breaches of their personal space and bodies. Gowing, *Common Bodies*, 90–100.

79. *An Account of the Travels, Sufferings & Persecutions of Barbara Blaugdone . . .*

80. The story was false, as both Evans and her partner survived their imprisonment. *This is a short relation of some of the cruel sufferings (for the truth's sake) . . .*

81. *God's Mighty Power Magnified: as manifested and revealed in his faithful handmaid Joan Vokins . . .* (London, 1691).

82. *This is a short relation of some of the cruel sufferings (for the truth's sake) . . .*

83. *The Life and Spiritual Sufferings of That Faithful Servant of Christ Jane Hoskins, A Public Preacher among the People called Quakers* (Philadelphia, 1771).

84. Rachel Warburton, " 'The Lord hath joined us together, and wo be to them that should part us': Katharine Evans and Sarah Cheevers as Traveling Friends," *Texas Studies in Literature and Language* 47, no. 4 (Winter 2005), 402–24.

85. Bacon, *Wilt Thou Go on My Errand?*, 125.

86. Hudson Morris, *Diary of minister's travels*, 1721–83, 975A, HCQC.

87. Christine Trevett, writing of Quaker female prophets in the late seventeenth century, claims no knowledge of women ever using the term *yokemate* or *yokefellow* to describe their travel companions. Phyllis Mack, although she identifies male use of *yokemate*, also notes that she is "not aware of any testimonials to women traveling companions or 'yokefellows.' " Recent scholarship has begun to explore these relationships, although none pursue the historical definitions of the term *yokemate* in detail. Myles, "Border Crossings," 23; Warburton, *Traveling Friends*, 417; Stevie Davies, *Unbridled Spirits: Women of the English Revolution: 1640–1660* (London: Women's Press, 1998), 8.

88. William Whittingham, *The Bible and Holy Scriptures conteyned in the Olde and Newe Testament* (Geneva, 1561), II Corinthians 6:14.

89. Thomas Becon (as Theodore Basille), *The golde[n] boke of christen matrimonye moost necessary [and] profitable for all the[m], that entend to live quietly and godlye in the Christen state of holy wedlock . . .* (London, 1543).

90. William Gouge, *A learned and very useful commentary on the whole epistle to the Hebrews . . .* (London, 1655). Chapter 58 is titled, "Of the mutual good that a believing Husband and Wife may do each other."

91. Richard Allestree, *The practice of Christian graces, or, The whole duty of man laid down in a plaine and familiar way for the use of all, but especially the meanest reader* (London, 1658).

92. Letter from John Camm to Margaret Fell, possibly 5 March 1654. As quoted in Mack, *Visionary Women*, 229.

93. Richard Adams Day, *Told in Letters: Epistolary Fiction Before Richardson* (Ann Arbor: University of Michigan Press, 1966), 54–55. Ruth Bloch argues that the associated term used by the *Academy of Complements*, *help-meet*, had particular and meaningful connotations in colonial British America, where it frequently "appeared in the literature written and read in America." Bloch finds that this term was part of "the earliest and most indigenous American literary ideal, associated above all with New England Puritanism." Ruth H. Bloch, *Gender and Morality in Anglo-American Culture, 1650–1800* (Berkeley: University of California Press, 2003).

94. Leo Damrosch, *The Sorrows of the Quaker Jesus: James Nayler and the Puritan Crackdown on the Free Spirit* (Cambridge: Harvard University Press, 1999), 124; Gill, *Women in the Seventeenth-Century Quaker Community*, 14–15.

95. Mack, *Visionary Women*, 224.

96. *The Life and Spiritual Sufferings of That Faithful Servant of Christ, Jane Hoskins . . .*, 25.

97. *This is a short relation of some of the cruel sufferings . . .*

98. Sewel, *The History of the . . . Quakers*, 535–37.

99. Mack, *Visionary Women*, 9.

100. Rachel Warburton's literary study of the Quaker companions Katherine Evans and Sarah Cheevers suggests that the two women "elevate[d] their relationship above marriage." Warburton compares the friendship of Evans and Cheevers to the classically inspired, elite masculine ideals of friendship proposed by Montaigne. In her literary interpretation of Evans's and Cheevers's works, Bernadette Andrea draws on the seventeenth-century Oxford scholar Robert Burton as a contradictory model for the women. Warburton, " 'The Lord hath joined us together," 402–24; Andrea, *Women and Islam*, 61; see also Su Fang Ng, *Literature and the Politics of the Family in Seventeenth-Century England* (Cambridge: Cambridge University Press, 2007), 195–221.

101. Brad Gregory, "The Other Confessional History: On Secular Bias in the Study of Religion," *History and Theory*, Theme Issue 45 (December 2006), 133.

102. Susanna Morris, Travel Diary, c. 1682–1755, 1000/Gulielma M. Howland Collection, HCQC.

103. *A short journal of the labours and travels in the work of the ministry of that faithful servant of Christ, Deborah Bell* (London, 1762).

104. *Some Account of the Life and Religious Exercises of Mary Neale, formerly Mary Peisley, Principally Compiled from her own Writings* (Dublin, 1795), 23.

105. "Mary Penington, 1616–1682, 'Some Account of the Circumstances in the Life of Mary Penington' . . . ," in *Hidden in Plain Sight: Quaker Women's Writings 1650–1700*, ed. Mary Garman, Judith Applegate, Margaret Benefiel, and Dortha Meredith, 224 (Wallingford, Penn.: Pendle Hill Publications, 1996).

Chapter 6. Reconciling Friendship and Dissent

1. Sarah Savage, Diary, 1686–88, Z-D/Basten/8, Cheshire and Chester Archives and Local Studies (hereafter cited as CCAL). The Cheshire and Chester Archives manuscript is not paginated.

2. Patricia Crawford, *Women and Religion in England, 1500–1720* (New York: Routledge, 1996), 191.

3. Ibid., 189.

4. Ibid., 190–91.

5. Michael R. Watts, *The Dissenters: From the Reformation to the French Revolution* (Oxford: Oxford University Press, 1978), 1:265.

6. Crawford, *Women and Religion*, 187.

7. I follow Savage, therefore, in making no firm distinctions between these categories. I use the terms *Nonconformist, Puritan, Presbyterian*, and *Dissenter* interchangeably, although *Puritan* was used sometimes as a derogatory term, and furthermore there were some doctrinal distinctions between these groups in the seventeenth and eighteenth centuries. Patrick Collinson, *Godly People: Essays on English Protestantism and Puritanism* (London: Hambledon, 1983), 1.

8. Watts, *The Dissenters*, 248, 160, 313.

9. Between 1650 and 1800 over half of all Dissenting Academies were located either within Wales itself or in the counties bordering it; Philip Henry's own Broad Oak Academy was therefore located within an active, committed association of Welsh and borderlands Nonconformist ministers, scholars, and families. Of the sixty-two Dissenting Academies identified by Irene Parker six were listed in Wales and thirty in counties bordering Wales; nineteen were

listed outside of Wales. Of these nineteen, just over half (ten) were located in London, an acknowledged center of Puritan worship. Four Academies gave no evidence of location. Michael Watts also finds that there was an especially "heavy concentration of Presbyterians" in Lancashire, Cheshire, Devon, and Bristol; further, Dissenters made up a significant 5.74 percent of the population in early eighteenth-century Wales, which compares closely with the 6.21 percent found in the whole of England. Irene Parker, *Dissenting Academies in England: Their Rise and Progress and Their Place among the Educational Systems of the Country* (New York: Octagon, 1969), appendix 1, "The Chief Dissenting Academies," 137; Watts, *The Dissenters*, 269–71.

10. Parker, *Dissenting Academies*, 55; J. B. Williams, *Memoirs of the life and character of Mrs. Sarah Savage, to which are added memoirs of her sister, Mrs. Hulton* (London, 1828), 2.

11. Patricia Crawford and Laura Gowing, eds. *Women's Worlds in Seventeenth-Century England* (New York: Routledge, 2000), 170.

12. Williams, *Memoirs*, 18, 116. The first child, born in 1688, was a boy named Thomas, who died in infancy. The Savage children surviving to adulthood were Sarah Savage Lawrance, Molly Savage Holland, Katherine Savage Savage (she married her cousin, keeping her maiden name), Hannah Savage Witton, and Philip Savage. In the diary Savage typically referred to her female children (and her sisters) by their first names or first initials until they were married; thereafter they were referred to by their last names. Therefore "Daughter M" (Molly Savage) became "Daughter Holland."

13. Williams, *Memoirs*, 45–46.

14. Patricia Crawford, "Katherine and Philip Henry and Their Children: A Case Study in Family Ideology," *Transactions of the Historic Society of Lancashire and Cheshire* 134 (Liverpool, UK: 1984), 41.

15. Sarah Savage, Diary, 1686–88, Z-D/Basten/8, CCAL.

16. Mrs. S. Savage, Diary, entitled "Mrs. S. Savage's diary from May 31st 1714 to Decem 25th 1723," MS Engl.misc.e.331, Bodleian Library (hereafter cited as BOD). As this diary is paginated, hereafter the Bodleian manuscript will be designated "Savage, Diary" along with appropriate page number. Savage, Diary, 123.

17. The date of Savage's death is uncertain. Patricia Crawford and Laura Gowing record it as 1745; J. B. Williams, her nineteenth-century biographer, recorded it as 1752. Crawford and Gowing, *Women's Worlds*, 170; Williams, *Memoirs*, 139.

18. Savage, Diary; Sarah Savage, Diary, 1724–45, MS Savage 4, Harris Manchester College Library.

19. Sarah Savage, Devotional Journal, 1714–38, Henry Papers, Add. 42849, ff. 109r–169v, British Library. This diary appears in *The History of Old Age in England, 1600–1800*, ed. Lynn Botelho and Susannah R. Ottaway, 159–205 (London: Pickering and Chatto, 2009).

20. Sarah Savage, Diary, 1727–30 and 1739–43, Osborn c506, James Marshall and Marie-Louise Osborn Collection, Beinecke Rare Book and Manuscript Library, Yale University; Sarah Savage, Diary, 1724–51, SC 313, Special Collections Research Center, Syracuse University Library.

21. Sarah Savage, Journal Volume 13, 1743–48, Henry MSS 90 (2), Dr. Williams's Library.

22. The piece studied most by scholars has been the first volume of Savage's diary. This manuscript has been analyzed to great effect by the two scholars who have examined Savage in any detail, Patricia Crawford and Effie Botonaki. Crawford's and Botonaki's analyses of Volume One center around Sarah Henry Savage's account of her courtship and eventual marriage with John Savage; this revealing story, combined with the fact that Volume One is reliably written in Savage's own hand, have undoubtedly drawn most scholars to the manuscript. Crawford and Gowing, *Women's Worlds*; Effie Botonaki, "Seventeenth-Century Englishwomen's Spiritual Diaries: Self-Examination, Covenanting, and Account Keeping," *Sixteenth Century Journal* 30, no. 1 (1999), 3–21; Crawford, *Women and Religion*; Crawford, "Katherine and Philip Henry"; and Patricia Crawford, "Attitudes to Pregnancy from a Woman's Spiritual Diary, 1687–8," *Local Population Studies* 21 (1978), 43–45; Sara Mendelson and Patricia Crawford, *Women in Early Modern England, 1550–1720* (Oxford: Clarendon, 1998), 228.

23. In a few places in this chapter I will draw briefly on other Sarah Savage papers (found in Harris Manchester College Library and Dr. Williams's Library) for context.

24. Paul Seaver, *Wallington's World: A Puritan Artisan in Seventeenth-Century London* (Stanford: Stanford University Press, 1985), viii–ix.

25. Andrew Cambers, "Reading, the Godly, and Self-Writing in England, circa 1580–1720," *Journal of British Studies* 46 (October 2007), 796–825. See also Henk Dagstra, Sheila Ottway, and Helen Wilcox, eds., *Betraying Our Selves: Forms of Self-Representation in Early Modern English Texts* (New York: Macmillan, 2000); Botonaki, "Seventeenth-Century Englishwomen's Spiritual Diaries," 3–21; Hilary Hinds, *God's Englishwomen: Seventeenth-Century Radical Sectarian Writing and Feminist Criticism* (New York: St. Martin's, 1996); Shari Benstock, "The Female Self Engendered: Autobiographical Writing and Theories of Selfhood," *Women's Studies* 20 (1991), 5–14.

26. For evidence of Savage reading the diaries and papers of her female friends, see Savage, Diary, 87–208. For an example of women passing personal papers to female relatives in the seventeenth century, see Alice Thornton, *The Autobiography of Mrs. Alice Thornton, of East Newton, Co. York* (Durham, UK, 1875), 337–38; and Amy Louise Erikson, *Women and Property in Early Modern England* (New York: Routledge, 1993), 190–91, 222, 225.

27. This manuscript is also kept at the Cheshire and Chester Records Office. Sarah Savage, Diary, 1774, CR 147/5, CCAL. In this chapter I have noted Savage's use of the heart symbol by placing the word *heart* within brackets: [heart].

28. Savage, Diary, 68.

29. Williams, *Memoirs*, 125.

30. Sarah Savage, Diary, 1686–88, Z-D/Basten/8, CCAL.

31. Crawford and Gowing, *Women's Worlds*, 189.

32. Savage, Diary, 47.

33. Ilana Krausman Ben-Amos, *The Culture of Giving: Informal Support and Gift-Exchange in Early Modern England* (New York: Cambridge University Press, 2008); Williams, *Memoirs*, 123.

34. Savage, Diary, 25; Williams, *Memoirs*, 35.

35. Savage, Diary, 3.

36. Ibid., 21.

37. Ibid., 154.

38. Linda Pollock, *With Faith and Physic: The Life of a Tudor Gentlewoman, Lady Grace Mildmay 1552–1620* (London, 1993).

39. Savage, Diary, 24.

40. Ibid., 159.

41. Ibid., 78, 97.

42. Sarah Savage, Diary, 1686–88, Z-D/Basten/8, CCAL.

43. Savage, Diary, 19.

44. Marilyn Yalom, *A History of the Breast* (New York: Alfred A. Knopf, 1997), 61; Kathryn Schwarz, "Missing the Breast: Desire, Disease and the Singular Effect of the Amazons," in *The Body in Parts: Fantasies of Corporeality in Early Modern Europe*, ed. David Hillman and Carla Mazzio, 146–69 (New York: Routledge, 1997); Caroline Walker Bynum, *Holy Feast and Holy Fast: The Religious Significance of Food to Medieval Women* (Berkeley: University of California Press, 1987), especially "Woman's Body as Food," 269–76, and figs. 24–27.

45. Rosemary Moore, *The Light in Their Consciences: Early Quakers in Britain, 1646–1666* (University Park: Pennsylvania State University Press, 2000), 126;

Michele Lise Tarter, "Nursing the Wor(l)d: The Writings of Quaker Women in Early America, *Women and Language* 16, no. 1 (1993), 22–26; Phyllis Mack, *Visionary Women: Ecstatic Prophecy in Seventeenth-Century England* (Berkeley: University of California Press, 1992), 40; and Anne Myles, "Border Crossings: The Queer Erotics of Quakerism in Seventeenth-Century New England," in *Long Before Stonewall: Histories of Same-Sex Sexuality in Early America*, ed. Thomas A. Foster, 118 (New York: New York University Press, 2007).

46. Savage, Diary, 169.
47. Ibid., 17.
48. Ibid., 127.
49. Ibid., 159. The passage is underlined in Savage's text.
50. *Geneva Bible* (1587); Savage, Diary, 159.
51. Williams, *Memoirs*, 153.
52. Ibid., 122.
53. Savage, Diary, 18.
54. Ibid., 94.
55. David Cressy, *Birth, Marriage and Death: Ritual, Religion and the Life-Cycle in Tudor and Stuart England* (Oxford: Oxford University Press, 1997), 97–194; Caroline Bicks, *Midwiving Subjects in Shakespeare's England* (Burlington, Vt.: Ashgate, 2003), 160.
56. Savage, Diary, 191.
57. Williams, *Memoirs*, 211–12.
58. Savage, Diary, 2.
59. Ibid., 40.
60. Ibid., 34.
61. Ibid., 67.
62. Williams, *Memoirs*, 167.
63. Alan Bray, *The Friend* (Chicago: University of Chicago Press, 2003), 217–18. Williams, *Memoirs*, 164.
64. Watts, *The Dissenters*, 228–29.
65. Savage, Diary, 65.
66. Cambers, *Reading, the Godly and Self-Writing*; Botonaki, *Seventeenth-Century Englishwomen's Spiritual Diaries*.
67. Williams, *Memoirs*, 117.
68. Crawford, *Women and Religion*, 185–208; Mendelson and Crawford, *Women in Early Modern England*, 225–31, 235–36.
69. Williams, *Memoirs*, 115.
70. Ibid., 119–20.
71. Sarah Savage, Diary, 1686–88, Z-D/Basten/8, CCAL.

72. It is possible that Savage misreported her friend Mary's name as Martha: this is the only time a Martha Robinson was mentioned in the diary, although Mary Robinson made regular appearances. Or it could be that Martha Robinson was related to Mary Robinson. Savage, Diary, 100.

73. Ibid., 133–34.

74. Ibid., 3.

75. Ibid., 103.

76. Ibid., 130. The underlining is present in Savage's text.

77. Ibid., 102.

78. Ibid., 117.

79. Crawford, "Katherine and Philip Henry," 43.

80. Savage, Diary, 97–98.

81. Sarah Savage, Diary, 1686–88, Z-D/Basten/8, CCAL.

82. Savage, Diary, 134.

83. Ibid., 173.

84. Ibid., 191.

85. The first infamous Sacheverell riot took place in 1710, with further riots occurring in Henry Sacheverell's name in 1714 and 1715. Abbie Turner Scudi, *The Sacheverell Affair* (New York: Columbia University Press, 1939); Geoffrey Holmes, *The Trial of Dr. Sacheverell* (London: Methuen, 1973); F. F. Madan, *A Critical Bibliography of Dr. Henry Sacheverell*, ed. W. Speck (Lawrence: University of Kansas Libraries, 1978).

86. Savage, Diary, 48.

87. Ibid. 56.

88. Ibid., 55.

89. Ibid., 55–56.

90. Ibid., 56–57.

91. Ibid., 58–59.

92. "Wrenbury Wakes" was probably a local festival or carnival; this type of holiday, sometimes called a wake or revel, was retained in rural areas past the Reformation. "Feast," (n. 2c) *Oxford English Dictionary Online*, 2d. ed. (1989).

93. Savage, Diary, 57.

94. Ibid., 60.

95. Ibid., 66.

96. Ibid., 68.

97. Ibid., 221.

98. Ibid., 35.

99. Sarah Savage, Diary, 1686–88, Z-D/Basten/8, CCAL.

100. Savage, Diary, 10.

101. Ibid., 27.

102. Ibid., 68. This is probably a reference to works written by Bishop Joseph Hall (1574–1656), either his *Contemplations on the Historical Passages of the Old and New Testaments* (c. 1626) or his *Contemplations Upon the Principall Passages of the Holy Storie* (1612).

103. Leonard D. Tourney, *Joseph Hall*, Twayne's English Authors Series (New York: Twayne, 1979), 250:19.

Epilogue

1. Sarah Jennings is better known by her married name, Sarah Churchill, Duchess of Marlborough, later confidante of Queen Anne. At the time these letters were written Jennings had not yet made her very famous and intimate acquaintance with Anne Stuart. Rachel Weil, *Political Passions: Gender, the Family and Political Argument in England 1680–1714* (New York: Manchester University Press, 1999), 187–272.

2. The building Parker referenced was the Château de Chambord at Chambord, Loir-et-Cher, France; the building is known for its intricate roofline and many terraces and towers. Parker particularly mentioned her frolicking on the château's famous double-helix staircase: "[There were] 2 vast pare of stairs that turnes double about one another but after a maner so intrycate for mee to describe or you to comprehend, wee devided companies & they told mee that the farther wee went from one another the sooner wee shold meet . . . it fell out just as they had told mee, wee mett all on a large trerrase & as I fancy'd without any inchangment." Mary Parker (nee Fortrey), Lady Fitzharding, Letters to Sarah Churchill, Lady Marlborough (nee Jennings), 1677–89, Blenheim Papers, Add. 61474, ff. 1–5b, 10, British Library (hereafter cited as BL). I would like to thank Rei Kanemura for her excellent transcription of these letters.

3. H. W. Parke, *Sibyls and Sibylline Prophecy in Classical Antiquity* (New York: Routledge, 1988), 1–22; and David Potter, "Sibyl," in the *Oxford Classical Dictionary*, ed. S. Hornblower and A. Spawforth, 3d ed. (New York: Oxford University Press, 1996), 1400–1401. I thank John Hyland for his help with these references.

4. Some of the letters were written in Paris and some in Rouen. Mary Parker (nee Fortrey), Lady Fitzharding, Letters to Sarah Churchill, Lady Marlborough (nee Jennings), 1677–89, Blenheim Papers, Add. 61474, ff. 1–5b, 10, BL.

Index